HERMAN HERTZBERGER

LESSONS
FOR STUDENTS
IN ARCHITECTURE

UITGEVERIJ 010 PUBLISHERS, ROTTERDAM

This book reflects the material discussed in Hertzberger's lectures on architecture at Delft Technical University from 1973 on, and contains elaborated versions of the lecture notes previously published as 'Het openbare rijk' (Public Domain) 1982, 'Ruimte maken, ruimte laten' (Making Space, Leaving Space) 1984, and 'Uitnodigende vorm' (Inviting Form) 1988.

Compilation by Laila Ghaït, Marieke van Vlijmen
Translation from the Dutch by Ina Rike
Book design by Reinout Meltzer, Rotterdam
Printed by G.J. Thieme bv, Nijmegen

© 1991
Herman Hertzberger / Uitgeverij 010 Publishers
1993 Second revised edition

CIP
Hertzberger, Herman
Lessons for Students in Architecture/Herman Hertzberger;
[transl. from the Dutch by Ina Rike].- Rotterdam: Uitgeverij 010.-III.
Met lit. opg.
ISBN 90-6450-100-9
SISO 710 UDC 72 NUGI 923
Trefw.: bouwkunst

FOREWORD

'Les choses ne sont pas difficiles à faire, ce qui est
difficile, c'est de nous mettre en état de les faire.'
(Brancusi)

It is inevitable that the work you do as an architect should
serve as the point of departure for your teaching, and
obviously the best way to explain what you have to say is
to do so on the basis of practical experience: that,
indeed, is the common thread of this book. Instead of
presenting each individual work separately and
explaining all their distinctive features in turn, the different
textual components have been organized in such a way
that, as a whole, they offer something in the way of a
theory; it is the way the elements are organized that
transforms practice itself into theory.

When you discuss your own work you have to ask yourself
what you acquired from whom. Because everything you
find comes from somewhere. The source was not your own
mind, but was supplied by the culture you belong to. And
that is why the work of others is so manifestly present here
by way of a context. You could say that in so far as this
book contains lessons, they are the lessons of Bramante,
Cerdá, Chareau, Le Corbusier, Duiker & Bijvoet, Van
Eyck, Gaudí & Jujol, Horta, Labrouste, Palladio, Peruzzi,
Rietveld, Van der Vlugt & Brinkman, and of all the others
who lent me their eyes so that I could see and select
precisely what I needed to carry my own work a step
further. Architects (and not only they) are in the habit of
concealing their sources of inspiration and even of trying
to sublimate them - as if that would ever be possible. But
in so doing the design-process gets clouded, while by
disclosing what moved and stimulated you in the first
place you may well succeed in explaining yourself and
motivating your decisions.
The examples and influences which abound in this book
constitute the cultural context within which an architect
works, and an impression is given of the range of
concepts and mental images that must serve as his tools
(can a person's output of ideas ever be greater than the
input?).
Everything that is absorbed and registered in your mind
adds to the collection of ideas stored in the memory: a
sort of library you can consult whenever a problem arises.
So, essentially, the more you have seen, experienced and
absorbed, the more points of reference you will have to
help you decide which direction to take: your frame of
reference expands.

The capacity to find a fundamentally different solution to a
problem, i.e. to create a different 'mechanism', depends
entirely on the wealth of your experience, just as a
person's expressive potential in terms of language cannot
transcend that which is expressible with his vocabulary.
Recipes for design are impossible to give, as everyone
knows. I have not attempted to do so, and the question
whether it is possible at all to learn how to design is not
really at issue here.
The aim of my 'lessons' has always been to stimulate
students, to evoke in them an architectural frame of mind
that will enable them to do their own work; my aim in this
book is the same.

Herman Hertzberger

CONTENTS

A PUBLIC DOMAIN

1 PUBLIC AND PRIVATE

The concepts 'public' and 'private' can be interpreted as the translation into spatial terms of 'collective' and 'individual'.
In a more absolute sense you could say:
public: an area that is accessible to everyone at all times; responsibility for upkeep is held collectively.
private: an area whose accessibility is determined by a small group or one person, with responsibility for upkeep.

This extreme opposition between private and public - like the opposition between collective and individual - has resulted in a cliché, and is as unsubtle and false as the supposed opposition between general and specific, objective and subjective. Such oppositions are symptoms of the disintegration of primary human relations.
Everyone wants to be accepted, wants to belong, wants to have a place of his or her own. All behaviour in society at large is indeed role-induced, in which the personality of each individual is affirmed by what others see in him. In our world we experience a polarization between exaggerated individuality on the one hand and exaggerated collectivity on the other. Too much emphasis is placed on these two poles, while there is not a single human relationship with which we as architects are concerned that focuses exclusively on one individual or on one group, nor indeed exclusively on everyone else, or 'the outside world'. It is always a question of people and groups in their interrelationship and mutual commitment, i.e. it is always a question of collective and individual vis à vis each other.

'Wenn aber der Individualismus nur einen Teil des Menschen erfasst so erfasst der Kollektivismus nur den Menschen als Teil: zur Ganzheit des Menschen, zum Menschen als Ganzes dringen beide nicht vor. Der Individualismus sieht den Menschen nur in der Bezogenheit auf sich selbst, aber der Kollektivismus sieht den Menschen überhaupt nicht, er sieht nur die "Gesellschaft", Beide Lebensanschauungen sind Ergebnisse oder Aeusserungen des gleichen menschlichen Zustands.
Dieser Zustand ist durch das Zusammenströmen von kosmischer und sozialer Heimlosigkeit, von Weltangst und Lebensangst, zu einer Daseinsverfassung der Einsamkeit gekennzeichnet, wie es sie in diesem Ausmass vermutlich noch nie zuvor gegeben hat. Um sich vor der Verzweiflung zu retten, mit der ihn siene Vereinsamung bedroht, ergreift der Mensch den Ausweg, diese zu glorifizieren. Der moderne Individualismus hat im wesentlichen eine imaginäre Grundlage. An diesem Charakter scheitert er, denn die Imagination reicht nicht zu, die gegebene Situation faktisch zu bewältigen.
Der moderne Kollektivismus ist die letzte Schranke, die der Mensch vor der Begegnung mit sich selbst aufgerichtet hat ...; im Kollektivismus gibt sie, mit dem Verzicht auf die Unmittelbarkeit persönlicher Entscheidung und Verantwortung, sich selber auf. In beiden Fällen ist sie unfähig, den Durchbruch zum Anderen zu vollziehen: nur zwischen echten Personen gibt es echte Beziehung.
Hier gibt es keinen anderen Ausweg als den Aufstand der Person um der Befreiung der Beziehung willen. Ich sehe am Horizont, mit der Langsamkeit alller Vorgänge der wahren Menschengeschichte, eine grosse Unzufriedenheit heraufkommen.
Man wird sich nicht mehr bloss wie bisher gegen eine bestimmte herrschende Tendenz um anderer Tendenz willen empören, sondern gegen die falsche Realisierung eines grossen Strebens, des Strebens zur Gemeinschaft, um der echten Realisierung willen.
Man wird gegen die Verzerrung und für die reine Gestalt kämpfen. Ihr erster Schritt muss die Zerschlagung einer falschen Alternative sein, der Alternative "Individualismus oder Kollektivismus".'
(Martin Buber, *Das Problem des Menschen*, Heidelberg 1948, also published in Forum 7-1959, pp 249)

'If however individualism comprehends only part of mankind, so collectivism only comprehends mankind as a whole of man, or man as a whole. Individualism perceives man only in his self-orientation, but collectivism does not perceive man at all, it relates only to 'society'. Both life-views are the products or expressions of the same human conditions.

This state of affairs is characterized by the confluence of cosmic and social homelessness, of a world-anxiety and a life-anxiety which have probably never existed to this degree before. In an attempt to escape from the insecurity brought on by his feelings of isolation, man seeks refuge in their glorification of individualism. Modern individualism has an imaginary basis. This is why it is doomed, for the imagination is unable to deal factually with a given situation.

Modern collectivism is the last barrier that man has erected to protect him from his encounter with himself... in collectivism it surrenders because it waives the claim to immediacy of personal decision and responsibility. In neither case is it capable of effecting a breakthrough to the other; only between real people can a real relationship exist.

There is no other alternative here than the rebellion of the individual for the sake of the liberation of the relationship. I can see looming on the horizon, slowly like all processes of the true human history, a great discontent.

People will no longer rise up as they did in the past against a certain prevailing trend in favour of a different trend, but against the false realization of a great striving, the striving after communality, for the sake of the true realization.

People will fight against distortion and for purity. The first step must be the destruction of a false alternative, of the alternative: 'individualism or collectivism'.'

The concepts 'public' and 'private' may be seen and understood in relative terms as a series of spatial qualities which, differing gradually, refer to accessibility, responsibility, the relation between private property and supervision of specific spatial units.

2 TERRITORIAL CLAIMS

An open area, room or space may be conceived either as a more or less private place or as a public area, depending on the degree of accessibility, the form of supervision, who uses it, who takes care of it, and their respective responsibilities.

Your own room is private vis à vis the living room and e.g. the kitchen of the house you live in. You have a key to your own room, which you look after yourself. Care and maintenance of the living room and kitchen is basically a responsibility shared by those living in the house, all of whom have a key to the front door.

In a school each class-room is private vis à vis the communal hall. This hall is in turn like the school as a whole, private vis à vis the street outside.

STREETS AND DWELLINGS, BALI (1-4)

The rooms of many dwellings on Bali are often separately constructed little houses, grouped around a sort of inner court or yard which may be entered through a gate. Once you have passed this gate you do not have the feeling that you are entering the actual dwelling, although this is in fact the case. The separate dwelling units: kitchen area, sleeping quarters, and sometimes a death-house and birth-house, have a far greater intimacy and they are less easily accessible, certainly to a stranger. In this way the actual home comprises a sequence of distinct gradations of accessibility.

Many streets on Bali constitute the territory of one extended family. On this street are situated the homes of

1
2
3   4

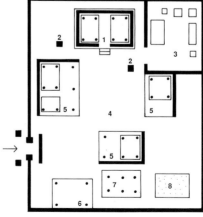

1	SLEEPING QUARTERS FOR PARENTS	5	BEDROOM
2	ALTAR	6	KITCHEN
3	FAMILY TEMPLE	7	STORAGE FOR RICE
4	LIVING AREA / GUESTS	8	THRESHING FLOOR

the different family units which together make up the extended family. These streets have an entrance gate, which is often fitted with a low bamboo fence to keep small children and animals inside, and although they are basically accessible to everyone you still tend to feel like an intruder or at best a visitor.

Apart from the different nuances in territorial claims, the Balinese distinguish within the public space, temple grounds comprising a series of successive enclosures with clearly marked entrances, fence-openings or the divided stone gateways (known as tjandi bentar). This temple area serves as both street and playground for the children. Also for the visitor it is accessible as a street - at least when there are no active religious manifestations going on - but even then the visitor feels some reluctance. As a stranger to the place you feel honoured to be allowed to enter.

All over the world you encounter gradations of territorial claims with the attendant feeling of accessibility. Sometimes the degree of accessibility is a matter of legislation, but often it is exclusively a question of convention, which is respected by all.

PUBLIC BUILDINGS

So-called public buildings such as the hall of the central post office or railway station may (at least during the hours that they are open) be regarded as street-space in the territorial sense. Other examples of differentiated degrees of access to the general public are given below, but the list can of course be extended to include other personal experiences:

• college quadrangles in England, as in Oxford and Cambridge; the way they are accessible for everyone through the porches, forming a sort of sub-system of pedestrian routes traversing the entire city centre.
• public buildings, e.g. the hall of a post office, railway station, etc.
• the courtyards of housing blocks in Paris, where a concierge usually reigns supreme.
• 'closed' streets, to be found in great variety all over the world, sometimes patrolled by private security guards.

Central Station
Haarlem, Holland

5

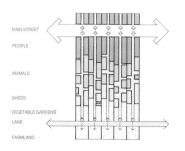

MAIN STREET

PEOPLE

ANIMALS

SHEDS

VEGETABLE GARDENS
LANE

FARMLAND

VILLAGE OF MÖRBISCH, AUSTRIA (6-8)

The streets in the Austrian village of Mörbisch near the
Hungarian border (published in Forum 9-1959) contain large
doors such as those giving access to farms - but here they
give access to side-streets along which dwellings, stables,
barns and gardens are situated.

**These examples show how inadequate the terms public
and private are, while the so-called semi-private or
semi-public areas which are often tucked away
inbetween are too equivocal to accommodate the
subtleties that must be taken into account in designing
for every space and every area.**

6   7   8
        9
  10 11

**■ Wherever individuals or groups are given the oppor-
tunity to use parts of the public space in their own
interests, and only indirectly in the interest of others,
the public nature of the space is temporarily or permanently put into perspective through that use. Examples
of this too are to be found everywhere in the world.**

*Dutch street,
nineteenth century*

On Bali -once again used as an example- the rice is
spread out to dry on large parts of the public roads and

even on the curbs of the macadamized highway, where it
is left undisturbed by traffic and pedestrians alike, since
everyone is aware of the importance of the contribution of
each member of the community to the rice harvest. (9)
Another instance of public merging with private is the
laundry hanging to dry in the narrow streets of the towns
of Southern Europe: a collective expression of
appreciation for the clean washing of each family
hanging from a network of cables spanning the street from
one family home to its neighbours across the way.

Naples

Other examples are the nets and ships being repaired on the quays in fishing villages and ports, and the Dogon: wool stretched across a village square.

The use of public space by residents as if it were 'private' strengthens the user's claim to that area in the eyes of others. The extra dimension given to the public space by this claim in the form of use for private purposes will be discussed in more detail below, but first we will look at what the consequences of this are for the architect.

BIBLIOTHÈQUE NATIONALE, PARIS 1862-68 / H. LABROUSTE (12)
In the main reading room of the Bibliothèque Nationale in Paris the individual work-surfaces facing each other are separated by a raised middle 'zone'; the lamps in the centre of this ledge provide light for the four directly adjoining work-surfaces. This central zone is obviously more accessible than the lower, individual work-surfaces, and is clearly intended for shared use by those seated on both sides.

CENTRAAL BEHEER OFFICE BUILDING (13-19)
In the early years, before the modern 'clean-desk' trend had set in, the desks in the offices were fitted with ledges which, when the desks were placed back to back, provided a raised central zone similar to that dividing the reading tables in the Bibliothèque Nationale in Paris. By this articulation a place is reserved for those objects shared by several users, such as telephones and potted plants. The space under the ledges provides more private storage space for each individual user. Articulation in terms of greater or lesser (public) accessibility can also prove to be useful in the smallest details.

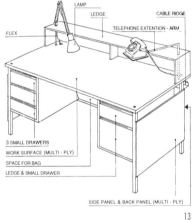

13

12 14

Glass doors between two equally public and therefore equally accessible spaces, for instance, provide ample visibility on both sides, so that collisions can easily be avoided on a strictly equal basis. Doors without transparent panels will then have to give access to more private, less accessible spaces. When such a code is consistently adopted throughout a building it will be understood rationally or intuitively by all the users of the premises and can thus contribute to clarifying the concepts underlying the organization of accessibility.

Further classification can be obtained by the shape of glass panes, the type of glass: semi-transparent or opaque, and half-doors.

When, in designing each space and each segment, you are aware of the relevant degree of territorial claim and the concomitant forms of 'accessibility' with respect to the adjoining spaces, then you can express these differences in the articulation of form, material, light and colour, and thereby introduce a certain ordering in the design as a whole. This can in turn heighten the awareness of inhabitants and visitors of how the building is composed of different ambiances as far as accessibility is concerned. The degree in which places and spaces are accessible offers standards for the design. The choice of architectonic motifs, their articulation, form and material are determined, in part, by the degree of accessibility required for a space.

3 TERRITORIAL DIFFERENTIATION

Montessori School, Delft

Hotel Solvay, Brussels 1896/V.Horta
(see also page 84)

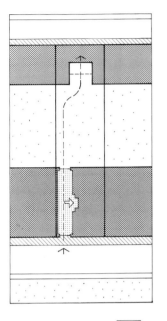

25 26
27 28
29

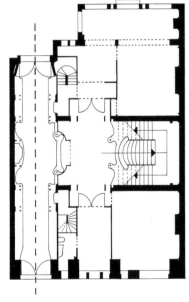

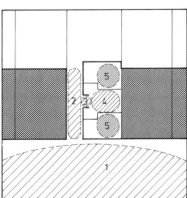

By marking the gradations of public accessibility of the different areas and parts of a building on a groundplan a sort of map showing the 'territorial differentiation' will be obtained. This map will show clearly which aspects of accessibility exist in the architecture as such, which claims are laid on specific areas and by whom, and what kind of division of responsibilities for care and maintenance of the different spaces may be expected, so that these forces may be intensified (or attenuated) in the further elaboration of the plan.

4 TERRITORIAL ZONING

The character of each area will depend to a large extent on who determines the furnishing and arrangement of the space, who is in charge, who takes care of it and who is or feels responsible for it.

30

CENTRAAL BEHEER OFFICE BUILDING (30,31)

The surprising effects obtained by the people who work at Centraal Beheer in the way they had arranged and personalized their office spaces with colours of their own choice, potted plants and objects they are fond of, is not merely the logical consequence of the fact that the interior finishing was deliberately left to the users of the building. Although the bareness of the stark, grey interior is an obvious invitation to the users to put the finishing touches to their space according to their personal tastes, this in

31

itself is no guarantee that they will do so.

More is needed for this to happen: to start with, the form of the space itself must offer the opportunities, including basic fittings and attachments etc., for the users to fill in the spaces according to their personal needs and desires. But beyond that, it is essential that the liberty to take personal initiatives should be embedded in the organizational structure of the institution concerned, and this has much more far-reaching consequences than you might think at first sight. For the fundamental question, then, is how much responsibility the top is prepared to delegate, i.e. how much responsibility will be given to the individual users at the lower echelons.

It is important to bear in mind that in this case it was only because the responsibility for the arrangement and finishing of the spaces had been so explicitly left to the users that such an exceptional commitment to invest love and care on their working environment could come about. It was thanks to this that the opportunities offered by the architect were in fact seized, with such surprisingly successful results.

While this building was originally erected as a spatial expression of the need for a more human environment (although many people suspected that this might be motivated by staff recruitment considerations), there is at present a tendency to dehumanize, largely owing to cuts in expenditure affecting staff in particular. But at least the building can be said to offer some welcome resistance to this trend, and with any luck it will succeed in holding its own. What is disappointing is that what we thought was a step towards a greater responsibility for the users has turned out to be just about the last step that can be taken, for the time being at least.

Now, in 1990, there is not much left of the imaginative and colourful decoration of the work spaces. The heyday of personal expressiveness in the 1970s has given way to neatness and orderlines. It seems as if the urge to make a personal statement has faded, and that people are more inclined to conform, nowadays. Perhaps due to the scare of rising unemployment in the 1980s it is now apparently considered wiser to take a less extraverted stand in general, and the effects of this are already to be seen in the cool impersonal atmosphere which pervades most offices today.

Faculty of Architecture MIT, Cambridge USA Workshop 1967 (32,33)

How much influence users can, in extreme cases, exert on their living or working environment is clearly demonstrated by the adjustments to the existing architecture that were made by students of architecture at the M.I.T. The student objected to having to work at drawing-boards arranged in long, stiff rows, all facing the same way. Using discarded construction materials that were regarded as left-overs, they constructed the kind of spaces they wanted - in which they could work, eat, sleep, and receive their tutors on their own ground.

One would expect each new group of students to want to make their own adjustments, but the situation turned out otherwise. The outcome of the fierce dispute with the local fire prevention authorities that ensued was that all the structures would have to be dismantled unless a full sprinkler system was installed throughout the area. Once this had been done, the situation in fact became permanent,

32
33

and the environment, if it still stands today, may be seen as a monument to the enthusiasm of a group of students of architecture. But we should not be surprised if everything is (or will soon be) cleared away - the bureaucracy of centralistic management is firmly back in control.

The influence of users can be stimulated, at least if this is done in the right places, i.e. where sufficient involvement may be expected; and because that depends on accessibility, territorial claims, organization of maintenance and division of responsibilities, it is essential for the designer to be fully aware of these factors in their proper gradations. In cases where the organizational structure precludes the users from exerting any personal kind of influence on their surroundings, or when the nature of a particular space is so public that no one will feel inclined to exert any influence on it, there is no point in the architect trying to make provisions of this kind. However, the architect can still take advantage of the reorganization that moving into a new building always necessitates anyway, to try to exert some influence on the reappraisal of the division of responsibilities, at least in so far as they concern the physical environment. One thing can lead to another. Simply by putting forward arguments which can reassure the top management that delegating responsibilities for the environment to the users need not necessarily result in chaos, the architect is in a position where he can contribute to improving matters, and it is certainly his duty to at least make an attempt in this direction.

MONTESSORI SCHOOL, DELFT (34,35)
A ledge above the door, given extra width so that objects can be placed on it - as in this case between class-room

and hall - is more likely to be put to use if it is accessible from the appropriate side, i.e. from inside the class-room. The shelf above it may create an aesthetically pleasing effect by setting back the glass pane, but it is not likely to be put to use.

CENTRAAL BEHEER OFFICE BUILDING (36-39)
Whereas the office spaces in the Centraal Beheer building, in which each worker has his own private island to work in, are taken care of by the users, no member of the office staff feels directly responsible for the central space of the building. The greenery in this central space is looked after by a special team (cf. Public Works), and the pictures on the walls are hung there by the art-provision service.
These employees too do their job with great dedication and care, but there is a striking difference in atmosphere

34 35
36 37

undergoing thorough renovation and cleaning, during which process a large number of adjustments are being made to comply with contemporary workplace requirements.

VREDENBURG MUSIC CENTRE (40)
The underlying idea which proved so successful in Centraal Beheer does not apply to the refreshment counters in the Music Centre in Utrecht.
The situation there varies considerably from one concert to the next, with different counters being used and different attendants serving the public. Since no special affinity between individual employees and specific work spaces was to be expected here, there was every reason for the refreshment areas to be completed and wholly furnished by the architect.
In both buildings - Centraal Beheer as well as the Music Centre - the rear walls are fitted with mirrors.
In the former, however, they were installed by the staff, and in the latter they were designed by the architect according to the same overall principles throughout the building. The mirrors on the rear wall enable you to see who is in front of you, behind you and next to you.
They recall the theatre paintings of Manet (41), who used mirrors to draw the space into the flat picture-plane, thus defining the space by showing the people in it and how they are grouped.
The Music Centre has a competent and dedicated housekeeping staff to look after the place.

between that communal area and the individual work spaces in all their diversity.
At the refreshment counters in this central space you were served by the same girl every day; the refreshments department was organized in such a way that each attendant was allocated to a specific counter.
She felt responsible for that counter and in due course she regarded it as her own domain, and gave it a personal touch. These coffee counters have since been removed, and tidy seats and coffee dispensers have been installed in their place. The entire building is currently

38
39   40

This cannot be said of, say, the refreshment cars of the Dutch railways: the attendants constantly switch trains. The only commitment that these attendants ever have with respect to the car in which they work is that they are under orders to leave the place clean and tidy for the next shift. Imagine how different things would be if the same attendant always worked on the same train. While the restaurant-car has disappeared - from Dutch trains at any rate - a new form of catering has emerged in air travel. But the meals served on planes are more like an imposition on the traveller than a service; they are served at times that suit the airline rather than the passenger (as well as being much too expensive, since they are included in the already high price of the airline ticket).

41
42
43

From Lufthansa Bordbuch, 6/88

5 FROM USER TO DWELLER

The translation of the concepts 'public' and 'private' in terms of differentiated responsibilities thus makes it easier for the architect to decide in which areas provisions should be made for users/inhabitants to make their own contributions to the design of the environment and where this is less relevant.

In the organization of a plan, as you design it in terms of groundplans and sections and also in the principle of the installations, you can create the conditions for a greater sense of responsibility, and consequently also greater involvement in the arrangement and furnishing of an area. Thus users become inhabitants.

MONTESSORI SCHOOL, DELFT (44-47)

The classrooms of this school are conceived as autonomous units, little homes as it were, all situated along the school hall, as a communal street. The teacher, 'mother', of each house decides, together with the children, what the place will look like, and therefore what kind of atmosphere it will have.

Each classroom also has its own small cloakroom, instead of the usual communal space for the whole school, which usually means that all the wall-space is taken up by rows

of pegs so that it cannot be used for anything else. And if each classroom would have its own toilet this too would contribute to improving the children's sense of responsibility (this proposal was turned down by the educational authorities on the grounds that separate toilets were needed for boys and girls - as if they have them at home too - which would require installing twice as many). It is quite conceivable for the children in each class to keep their 'home' clean, like birds their nest, thereby giving expression to the emotional bond with their daily environment.

The Montessori idea, indeed, comprises so-called housekeeping duties for all children as part of the daily programme. Thus much emphasis is placed on looking after the environment, whereby the children's emotional affinity with their surroundings is strengthened.

Each child, too, can bring along his own plant to the classroom, which he or she has to care for. (The awareness of the environment and the need to look after it figures prominently in the Montessori concept. Typical examples are the tradition of working on the floor on special rugs - small temporary work areas which are respected by the others - and the importance that is attached to tidying things away in open cupboards). A further step towards a more personal approach to the children's daily surroundings would be to make it possible to regulate the central heating per classroom. This would heighten the children's awareness of the phenomenon of warmth and the care that goes into keeping warm, as well as making them more aware of the uses of energy.

A 'safe nest' - familiar surroundings where you know that your things are safe and where you can concentrate without being disturbed by others - is something that each individual needs as much as each group. Without this there can be no collaboration with others. *If you don't have a place that you can call your own you don't know where you stand!* There can be no adventure without a home-base to return to: everyone needs some kind of nest to fall back on.

The domain of a particular group of people should be respected as much as possible by 'outsiders'. That is why there are certain risks attached to so-called multifunctional usage. Take a schoolroom: if it is used for other purposes outside school hours, e.g. for neighbourhood activities, all the furniture has to be pushed aside temporarily, and it is evidently not always put back into its proper place. Under such circumstances figures modelled in clay which are left out to dry, for instance, can easily be 'accidentally' broken or someone's pencil sharpener turns out to have vanished into thin air.

44

45

It is important for children to be able to display the things they have made in, say, the handwork lesson without fear of their things being destroyed, and they should be able to leave unfinished work exposed without there being the danger of it being moved or 'tidied away' by 'strangers'.

After all, even a thorough cleaning job done by someone else can leave you feeling quite lost in your own space the next morning.

A schoolroom, conceived as the domain of a group, can show its own identity to the rest of the school if it is given the opportunity to make a display of the things (that the children have made or work they have done in class) that the group is especially involved in. This can be done informally by using the partition between hall and classroom as display space, and by making plenty of windows with generous sills in the partition.

A small showcase (in this case even illuminated) is a challenge to the group to present itself in a more formal way. The exterior of the classroom can then function as a sort of 'shop window' which shows what the group has to 'offer'.

In this way each class can present a picture which the others can relate to, and which marks the transition between each classroom and the communal hall space.

Apollo Schools (48-50)

If the space between classrooms has been used to create porchlike areas, as in the Amsterdam Montessori school, these areas can serve as proper workplaces where you can study on your own, i.e. not in the classroom but not shut out either. These places consist of a work-surface with its own lighting and a bench enclosed by a low wall. In order to regulate the contact between classroom and hall as subtly as possible half-doors have been installed here, whose ambiguity can generate the right degree of openness towards the hall while offering the required seclusion from it, both at the same time, in each situation. Here again we find (as in the Delft school) the glass showcase containing the classroom's own miniature museum and display.

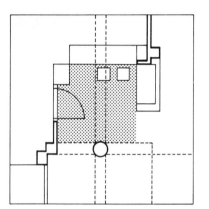

6 THE 'IN-BETWEEN'

The value of this concept is most explicit in the threshold 'par excellence', the entrance to a home. We are concerned here with the encounter and reconciliation between the street on the one hand and a private domain on the other.

The wider significance of the concept of in-between was introduced in Forum 7,1959 (La plus grande réalité du seuil) and Forum 8,1959 (Das Gestalt gewordene Zwischen: the concretization of the in-between).

The threshold provides the key to the transition and connection between areas with divergent territorial claims and, as a place in its own right, it constitutes, essentially, the spatial condition for the meeting and dialogue between areas of different orders.

The child sitting on the step in front of his house is sufficiently far away from his mother to feel independent, to sense the excitement and adventure of the great unknown.

Yet at the same time, sitting there on the step which is part of the street as well as of the home, he feels secure in the knowledge that his mother is nearby. The child feels at home and at the same time in the outside world. This duality exists thanks to the spatial quality of the threshold as a platform in its own right, a place where two worlds overlap, rather than a sharp demarcation.

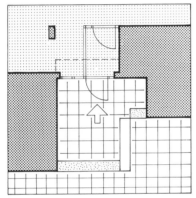

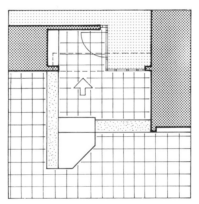

52 54
53 55
56

MONTESSORI SCHOOL, DELFT (52-56)

The entrance to a primary school should be more than a mere opening through which the children are swallowed up when the lessons begin and spat out again when they end. It should be a place that offers some kind of welcome to the children who came early and to pupils who don't want to go straight home after school. Children, too, have their meetings and appointments. Low walls that can be sat on are the least you can offer, a sheltered corner is better, and the best of all would be a roofed area for when it rains.

The entrance to a kindergarten is frequented by parents - they say goodbye to their children there, and wait for them when school is over for the day. Parents waiting for their children thus have a fine opportunity to get to know each other, and to arrange for the children to play at each others' homes, in short this public space, as a meeting ground for people with common interests, serves an important social function. As a result of the most recent conversion in 1981(56), this entrance no longer exists.

the door to be opened, while the welcoming gesture of the place gives you the feeling that you have almost been let in already.

You could say that the bench by the front door is a typically Dutch motif - it can be seen on many old paintings, but in our own century Rietveld, for instance, created the same arrangement, complete with a half-door, in his famous Schröder house. Utrecht 1924 (59).

DE OVERLOOP, HOME FOR THE ELDERLY (57,58)

A sheltered area at the front door, the beginning of the 'threshold', is the place where you say hello or goodbye to your visitors, where you stamp the snow off your boots or put up your umbrella.

The sheltered entrances to the apartments that belong to the nursing home De Overloop in Almere are fitted with benches next to the front doors. The front doors are located two by two to form a combined porch which, however, is still divided into separate entrances by a vertical partition projecting from the façade. The half-doors enable whoever is sitting outside to keep contact with the interior of the apartment, so that you can at least hear the phone ring. This entrance zone is evidently regarded as an extension of the home, as is shown by the mats that have been laid outside. Thanks to the overhang you do not have to wait in the rain for

57

59

58

DE DRIE HOVEN, HOME FOR THE ELDERLY (60)

In situations where there might be a need for contact between inside and out, for instance in a home for the elderly where some of the residents spend a lot of their time in the solitude of their own rooms due to diminished mobility, waiting for someone to visit them, while other residents outside would also welcome some contact, it is a good idea to install doors with two sections, so that the upper part can be kept open while the lower half is closed. Such 'half' doors constitute a distinctly inviting gesture: when half open the door is both open and closed, i.e. it is closed enough to avoid making the intentions of those inside all too explicit, yet open enough to facilitate casual conversations with passers-by, which may lead to closer contact.

Concretization of the threshold as an in-between means, first and foremost, creating a setting for welcomes and farewells, and is therefore the translation into architectonic terms of hospitality. Besides, the threshold as a built facility is just as important for social contacts as thick walls are for privacy.
Conditions for privacy and conditions for maintaining social contacts with others are equally necessary. Entrance, porches, and many other forms of in-between spaces provide an opportunity for 'accommodation' between adjoining worlds. This kind of provision gives rise to a certain articulation of the building concerned, which requires both space and money, without its function being easily demonstrable - let alone quantifiable - and which is therefore often very difficult to accomplish, and requires constant effort and persuasion during the planning phase.

DOCUMENTA URBANA DWELLINGS (61-70)

The meander-shaped housing block which was termed 'snake' consists of segments, each designed by different architects. The communal staircases were placed in a fully-lit situation rather than in the more usual residual, generally dimly-lit space.

In a multi-family house the emphasis should not lie exclusively on the architectural provisions to prevent excess noise and inconvenience from neighbours; special attention must be paid in particular to the spatial disposition, which may be conducive to the social contacts that may be expected to exist between the various occupants of a building. Therefore we have given the staircases more prominence than usual. Communal staircases should not only be a source of aggravation where accumulation of dirt and cleaning are concerned - they should also serve, for instance, as a playground for the small children of neighbouring families. They have therefore been designed with a maximum of light and openness in mind, like glass-roofed streets, and can be overlooked from the kitchens. The open entrance porches with two front doors, one after the other, show to the communal territory a little more of their inhabitants than traditional closed doors usually do.

Although care has naturally been taken to ensure adequate privacy on the terraces, neighbouring families are not fully isolated from one another. We have aimed at designing the exterior spaces in such a way that the

60
61

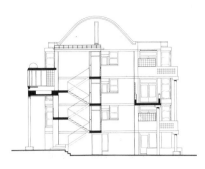

62   63
     64   65
     66   67

necessary screening detracts as little as possible from the spatial conditions for contact between neighbours. Incidentally, such expansion of the minimum space required for 'circulation purposes' proves to attract not only children - it also serves as a place for neighbours to

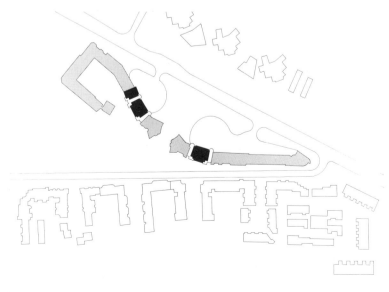

Building at right: O. Steidle, architect

sit and talk. Indeed, in this case the residents also provided the furnishings.

In addition to an ordinary front door the dwellings have a second glass door which can also be locked and which leads to the actual staircase, so that an open entrance-space is obtained. Since this intermediary space between staircase and front door is interpreted differently by different people - i.e. not exclusively as part of the stairs but equally as an extension of the dwelling - it is used by some as an open hallway, into which the atmosphere of the home is allowed to

penetrate. In this way, depending on which of the two doors is regarded as the real front door, the residents can display their individuality which normally remains concealed in the privacy of the home, while at the same time the staircase loses some of the usual no-man's-land feeling and may even acquire a truly communal atmosphere. The principle of the vertical pedestrian walkway as applied in the Kassel housing project was further elaborated in the LiMa housing estate in Berlin. The staircases of this complex lead up to communal roof-terraces. It was eventually decided that it would not be necessary to incorporate the play-balconies that were featured in the Kassel project, as the secluded courtyard in itself offers adequate play-space for the youngest children in particular.

CITÉ NAPOLÉON, PARIS 1849 / M.H. VEUGNY (71-74)

Cité Napoléon in Paris, one of the first attempts, and certainly the most remarkable, to arrive at a reasonable solution to the problem of distance between the street and front door in a multi-storey residential building. This interior space, with all its stairs and overpasses, reminds one of the multi-storeyed buildings in a mountain village. A reasonable amount of light reaches the top floors through the glass roof. The residents of the upper floors do actually open their windows onto this interior space, and the presence of potted plants at least shows that the people care. Even while it did not prove possible - in spite of the builders' best intentions - to make this interior space (closed off as it is from the street outside) into a truly functional interior street by our standards, when you think of all those gloomy useless stairways that have been built since 1849 this is indeed a shining example.

71 72
73
74

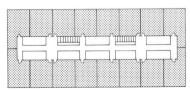

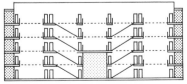

0   5   10

7 PRIVATE CLAIMS ON PUBLIC SPACE

The in-between concept is the key to eliminating the sharp division between areas with different territorial claims. The point is therefore to create intermediary spaces which, although on the administrative level belonging to either the private or the public domain, are equally accessible to both sides, that is to say that it is wholly acceptable to both that the 'other' makes use of them.

DE DRIE HOVEN, HOME FOR THE ELDERLY (75-77)
The hallways serve as streets in a building which must function as a city for its severely disabled inhabitants, because they are mostly incapable of leaving the premises without assistance. The dwelling units situated along this 'street' all have, in pairs, porch-like areas which on the one hand belong to the dwellings, but on the other hand are still part of the 'street area'. The residents put their own things there, they look after that space and often grow plants and flowers there as if it were part of their own home, as a sort of veranda at street level. Yet the porch-like area remains completely accessible to passers-by, it remains part of the street.

It is extremely difficult to reserve the few square metres that are needed for such a purpose within the endless network of regulations and norms concerning minimum and maximum dimensions which govern every conceivable aspect of architectural design.

In the case of social housing it is regarded on the administrative level as an impermissible reduction of the size of the dwelling unit, or as an unnecessary expansion of the corridor: the functionality of each square metre is, after all, measured according to quantifiable utility. The love and care that the residents invest in this space, which is not, strictly speaking, part of their apartment, hinges on an apparently minor detail, namely the window which allows them to keep an eye on the objects that have been placed outside, not only as a precaution against theft but also simply because it's nice to be able to see your own things or to see how your plants are doing. The architect needs an inordinate amount of ingenuity to get this idea past the watchful eye of the fire prevention authority.

The lighting fixtures in 'De Drie Hoven' next to the front doors were installed in small projecting walls, in such a way that a mat can easily be placed underneath. Using their leftover bits of carpet, the residents appropriate and furnish the little space thus created, thereby extending the limits of their home ground beyond the front door.

75

76 77

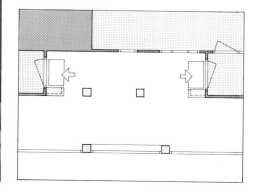

Provided we incorporate the proper spatial suggestions into our design, the inhabitants will be more inclined to expand their sphere of influence outwards to the public area. Even a minor adjustment by way of spatial articulation of the entrance can be enough to encourage expansion of the personal sphere of influence, and thus the quality of public space will be considerably increased in the common interest.

DIAGOON DWELLINGS (78-83)

What could be done with the pavements in 'living-streets' if the inhabitants were to be given responsibility for the space, may be imagined on the basis of the experiment with the pavement in front of the Diagoon dwellings in Delft. The area in front of the dwellings has not been laid out as a front garden; it has simply been paved like an ordinary sidewalk, and hence as part of the public domain although, strictly speaking, it is not.

The areas belonging to the different houses have not been marked, nor does the layout contain any suggestion of private claims. The paving material consists of the usual concrete tiles, which automatically evoke associations with a public road because sidewalks are usually paved with

resolved in mutual agreement. It is here that every inhabitant plays the roles that express what sort of person he wants to be, and therefore how he wants others to see him. Here, too, it is decided what individual and collective have to offer each other.

	79	80
	81	82
78		
	83	

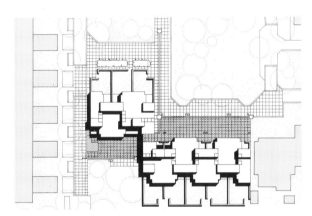

exactly the same tiles. The inhabitants then start removing some of the tiles to put plants there instead. 'Dessous les pavés la plage'. The rest of the tiles are left in place wherever a path to the front door is wanted, or a space to park the family car close to the house. Each resident uses the area in front of his house according to his own needs and wishes, taking up as much of the area as he requires and leaving the rest as publicly accessible.

If the layout had started out from the idea of separate, private areas, then no doubt everyone would have made the best of it for his own benefit, but then there would have been an irreversibly abrupt division between private and public space, instead of the intermediary zone that has now evolved: a merging of the strictly private territory of the houses and the public area of the street. In this area in-between public and private, individual and collective claims can overlap, and resulting conflicts must be

LiMa Housing (84-89)

The LiMa housing estate is located at one end of a triangular area, the corner of which is marked by a church. The volumes of this church are very loosely related to the general architectural alignment. The completion of

building on this triangular island entails leaving the church to stand apart as a detached self-contained structure. The courtyard itself is quite unlike the often depressing traditional Berlin courtyard, and is conceived as a public space with six pedestrian access routes, including connections with both the street and the neighbouring courtyard. These pedestrian routes constitute part of the communal open staircases. The centre of the courtyard is marked by the large segmented sand-pit, which was decorated with mosaics along the curved sides by the resident families themselves.

It was not difficult to rouse the enthusiasm of the residents for this project - who were keenly interested in the design of the courtyard as it was - especially after they had seen photographs of Gaudí's park and the Watts Towers. Technical and organizational assistance was provided by Akelei Hertzberger, who has undertaken various similar projects in the past with equally successful results.

At first it was especially the children who contributed their 'tiles', but soon also the adults joined in bringing

along every piece of crockery they could lay their hands on.

No architect nowadays would be able to lavish so much attention on a sand-pit, nor would that be necessary, because it can just as well be left to the inhabitants themselves. A better way of responding to the offered incentive is hard to imagine. But more important still is that it has become their own sand-pit and their own concern: if a fragment of the mosaic falls off or proves to be too sharp, for instance, something will be done about it without if being necessary to hold special meetings, write official letters, or to sue the architect.

A street area with which the inhabitants themselves are involved and where individual marks are put down for themselves and for each other is appropriated jointly, and is thus turned into a communal space.

8 PUBLIC WORKS CONCEPT

*Bijlmermeer
Housing Estate,
Amsterdam*

Familistère Housing Project, Guise, France

90 91
92

Photo-montage

The point is to give public spaces form in such a way that the local community will feel personally responsible for them, so that each member of the community will contribute in his or her own way to an environment that he or she can relate to and can identify with.

It is the great paradox of the collective welfare concept, as it has developed hand in hand with the ideals of socialism, that actually makes people subordinate to the very system that has been set up to liberate them.

The services rendered by the Municipal Public Works departments are felt, by those for whose benefit those departments were created, as an overwhelming abstraction; it is as if the activities of Public Works are an imposition from above, the man in the street feels that they 'have nothing to do with *him*', and so the system produces a widespread feeling of alienation.

The public gardens and green belts around the blocks of flats in the new urban neighbourhoods are the responsibility of the Public Works departments, which do

all they can to make these areas as attractive as possible - within the limits of the allocated budgets - on behalf of the community.

But the results that are achieved in this way cannot help being stark, impersonal and uneconomical, compared with what could have been achieved if all the flat-dwellers had been offered the opportunity of using a small plot of land (even if no bigger than a parking space) for their own purposes.

What has now been collectively denied them could have become the contribution of each inhabitant to the community, while the space itself could have been used far more intensively if all that personal love and care had been lavished on it.

An example of this is to be seen at the Familistère in Guise, France: a housing project which was set up on behalf of the Godin stove factory: a working and dwelling community modelled after the ideas of Fourier. Although it dates from the nineteenth century, as an example of what can be done it is still of topical interest today.

VROESENLAAN HOUSING, ROTTERDAM 1931-34 /
J.H. VAN DEN BROEK (93,94)
Communal amenities can blossom only through the communal effort on the part of the users. That must have been the idea underlying the communal interior spaces - without fences and partitions - that were designed in the twenties and thirties.

93
94

DE DRIE HOVEN, HOME FOR THE ELDERLY (95)

The fenced-in field with animals, which owes its existence to the initiative of a staff member of 'De Drie Hoven', has gradually developed into a miniature zoo, with a pheasant, a peacock, chickens, goats, plenty of ducks in a pond teeming with fish. For the elderly residents of the home the animals are a pleasant and interesting sight, and the rooms with a view of the 'menagerie' are the most sought-after.

Home-made sheds for the animals to spend the night in had been provided by enthusiasts, but by the time this popular scheme had proved a success and expansion became necessary, the Department of Housing Inspection decided that things could not go on like this: they stipulated that a professional construction plan would have to be submitted, and would have to be approved by all the proper authorities and committees.

For the local population the 'menagerie' represents a standing invitation to get involved in taking care of the animals or simply to stroll over and see how they are doing. When do city children get to see animals? The only animals most of them ever see in their home environment are privately owned pets, dogs kept on leashes, because forms of shared ownership and responsibility for animals appear to be impossible to organize. The idea of doing so doesn't even arise - local inhabitants, after all, do not normally have any influence on how their communal spaces are laid out and used. But then Public Works can hardly be expected to look

after animals all over town. For that a whole new department with a specialized staff would be needed, not to mention thousands of notices saying 'Do Not Feed the Animals'.

The allotments and the animals at 'De Drie Hoven' are a natural inducement for social contact between the elderly residents and the local population - both groups being deprived in a different way. The residents of the home are forced by circumstance to be outsiders in the city, but thanks to 'their' garden they can offer some compensation for what the others lack - outsiders as they, too, are in the grounds of 'De Drie Hoven'.

These examples serve to illustrate how the best intentions can lead to disillusionment and indifference. Things start to go wrong when the scale becomes too big, when the upkeep and management of a communal area can no longer be left to those directly involved, and a special organization becomes necessary, with its own specialized staff, with its own interests and concerns regarding continuity and, possibly, expansion. When the point has been reached that an organization's prime concern becomes to ensure its own continued existence - regardless of the aims for which it was established, i.e. to do for others what they can no longer be expected to do for themselves - at that point bureaucracy rears its head. Rules become a straitjacket of regulations. The sense of personal

responsibility is lost in a stifling hierarchy of answerability to one's superiors. While there is nothing wrong with the intentions of the individual link in this interminable chain of interdependencies, they are rendered virtually irrelevant because they are too far removed from those for whose benefit the whole system was invented in the first place.

The reason why city dwellers become outsiders in their own living environment is either that the potential of collective initiative has been grossly overestimated, or that participation and involvement have been underestimated. The occupants of a house are not really concerned with the space outside their homes, but nor can they really ignore it. This opposition leads to alienation from your environment and - in so far as your relations with others are influenced by the environment - also to alienation from your fellow residents.

The mounting degree of control imposed from above is making the world around us increasingly inexorable: and this elicits agression, which in turn leads to further tightening of the web of regulations. A vicious circle is the result, the lack of commitment and the exaggerated fear of chaos have a mutually escalating effect.

The incredible destruction of public property - which is on the rise in the world's major cities - can probably particularly be blamed on alienation from the living environment. The fact that public transport shelters and public telephones are completely destroyed week in week out is a truly alarming indictment of our society as a whole.

What is almost as alarming, however, is that this trend - and its escalation - is dealt with as if it were a mere problem of organization: by undertaking periodical repairs as if they were a question of routine maintenance, and by applying extra reinforcements ('vandal-proofing'), the situation appears to be accepted as 'just one of those things'. The whole suppressive system of the established order is geared to avoiding conflicts; to protecting the individual members of the community from incursions by other members of the same community, without the direct involvement of the individuals concerned. This explains why there is such a deep fear of disorder, chaos and the unexpected, and why impersonal, 'objective' regulations are always preferred to personal involvement. It seems as if everything must be regulated and quantifiable, so as to permit total control; to create the conditions in which the suppressive system of order can make us all into lessees instead of co-owners, into subordinates instead of participants. Thus the system itself creates the alienation and, by claiming to represent the people, obstructs the development of conditions that could lead to a more hospitable environment.

■ The architect can contribute to creating an environment which offers far more opportunities for people to make their personal markings and identifications, in such a way that it can be appropriated and annexed by all as a place that truly 'belongs' to them. The world that is controlled and managed by everyone as well as for everyone will have to be built up of small-scale, workable entities, no larger than what one person can cope with and look after on his own terms.

Each spatial component will thus be more intensively used (whereby the space is enhanced), while it is also more fair to the users to demonstrate their intentions. More emancipation generates more motivation, and in this way energy can be released which is otherwise suppressed by centralized decision-making. This amounts to a plea for decentralization, for devolution wherever at all possible, and for the handing over of responsibilities to where they belong - in order to take effective measures to solve the problems of the inevitable alienation from the 'urban desert'.

96

9 THE STREET

Beyond our front door or garden gate begins a world we have little to do with, a world upon which we can exert hardly any influence. There is a growing feeling that the world beyond the front door is a hostile world of vandalism and agression, where we feel threatened rather than at home. Yet to take this widespread feeling as the point of departure for urban planning would be fatal.

Surely it is far better to go back to the optimistic and utopian concept of the 'reconquered street', which we could see so clearly before us less than two decades ago. In this view, inspired by the post-war existentialistic zest for life (especially Provo as far as Holland is concerned) the street is again conceived as what it must have been originally, namely as the place where social contact between local residents can be established: as a communal living-room, as it were. And the concept that social relations can even be stimulated by an efficacious application of the architectonic means is already to be found in Team X and especially in 'Forum', where, as a central theme, this issue was repeatedly raised.

The devaluation of this street concept may be due to

Amsterdam, workers district, streetlife in the 19th century: quite different from today, but remember how cramped and inadequate housing was in those days.

Gioggia, Italy. Traffic-free living street. Looking for a place in the shade.

the following factors:
• the increase in motorized traffic and the priority that it is given;
• the inconsiderate organization of the access areas to the dwellings, in particular that of the front doors vis à vis each other owing to indirect and impersonal access routes such as galleries, elevators, covered passages (the inevitable by-products of high-rise constructions) which diminish contact with the street level;
• the effacement of the street as communal space owing to block siting;
• decreased densities of housing, while also the number of inhabitants per dwelling has greatly decreased. So the decrease in the population density is accompanied by an increase in dwelling space per inhabitant and in the width of the streets. The consequence is inevitably that today's streets are far emptier than those of the past; besides, the improvement in size and quality of housing means that people spend more time indoors and less in the street;
• the better the economic circumstances of people the less they need each other as neighbours and the less they tend to do things together.

The increased prosperity seems on the one hand to have encouraged individualism while on the other allowing collectivism to assume proportions quite beyond anyone's grasp.
We must try to deal with these factors - even if the architect is unable to do more than exert an incidental influence on the aforementioned rather fundamental aspects of social change - by creating the conditions for a more viable street area wherever possible. And this means that it must be done on the level of spatial organization, i.e. by architectonic means.

■ Situations where the street serves as a communal extension of the dwellings are familiar to us all. Depending on the climate, either the sunny parts or the shaded areas are the most popular, but motorized traffic is always absent or at least far away enough as not to prevent the residents from seeing each other and making themselves heard.
Living-streets which no longer serve exclusively as a traffic route and which are organized in such a way that there is also room for children to play are becoming an increasingly familiar sight both in new

Spangen Housing, Rotterdam 1919/ M. Brinkman. Traffic-free living street. Looking for a place in the sun.

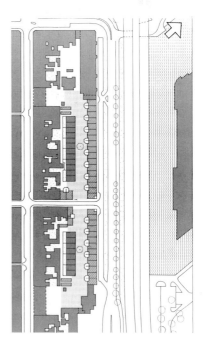

housing estates and in renovation projects - at least in Holland. The interests of the pedestrian are being taken into consideration at last, and with the 'woonerf' (residential area with severe traffic restrictions and priority at all times for pedestrians) designation as a legal basis he is slowly regaining his rightful place - or at least he is no longer treated as an outlaw. However once the motorists have been tamed to behave in a more disciplined fashion, their vehicles are still so cumbersome, so large, and especially so numerous, that they take up more and more of the public space.

HAARLEMMER HOUTTUINEN HOUSING (100-109)
The central theme in the Haarlemmer Houttuinen is the street as living space, as elaborated in association with Van Herk and Nagelkerke, the architects of the other side of the street. The decision - which had more to do with politics than with town-planning - to reserve an area of 27 metres up to the railway for 'traffic purposes' obliged us to build at least up to this imposed limit of alignment; as a result there was no room there for back gardens (which would in fact have been permanently in the shade anyway).

101
100 102

In sum these unfavourable circumstances - i.e. undesirable orientation and traffic noise - meant that this north side should definitely accommodate the rear wall, and so automatically all emphasis came to lie on the living-street facing south. This 'living-street' is accessible only to the residents' own motorcars and delivery vehicles; due to the fact that it is therefore closed to general motorized traffic and to its width of 7 metres - an unusually narrow profile by modern standards - a situation reminiscent of the old city is created. The necessary street fittings such as lights, bicycle racks, low

fencing and public benches are dispersed in such a way that only a few parked cars are enough to obstruct the passage of further traffic. Trees are to be planted to form a centre halfway between the two street sections. The structures projecting from the façades - the exterior staircases and living-room balconies - articulate the profile of the street, making it seem less wide than the 7 metres it measures from house-front to house-front. The consequence is a zone that provides space for the street-level terraces of the ground-floor dwellings. These pavement gardens with their low surrounding walls are

no bigger than the first-floor balconies; they could certainly not be any smaller, but the question rises whether they would have been better if larger. As they offer far less privacy than the living-room balconies, one could ask oneself whether the ground-level residents are at a disadvantage, but on the other hand the immediate contact with passers-by and general street activity seems to be attractive to many people, especially when the street regains some of its former communal quality. Strips have been left open adjoining the private outdoor spaces; the organization of these strips has deliberately been left undecided. The public works department could not resist laying down paving stones in these spaces. The inhabitants for their part are now already putting plants there, thus successively appropriating this basically public area.Dutch housing construction has traditionally devoted much attention to the problems of access to upper storeys, and a great variety of solutions have been developed in the Netherlands - all aimed at giving each dwelling its own individual front door with maximum accessibility from the street wherever possible. Indeed the solution we have adopted is simply another variation on this essentially ancient theme: the iron

103

104

*Reijnier Vinkeleskade,
Amsterdam 1924/
J.C. van Epen*

exterior staircases lead to a first-floor landing with the front door of the upper-storey dwelling; from there the staircase continues inside the building, leading through the sleeping quarters of the ground-floor dwelling to the dwelling above.

The entrances to the upper dwellings, located on 'public balconies' overlooking the street, do not constitute an obstruction to the ground-floor dwellings, but provide the latter with some degree of shelter for their own entrances. Because the stairs themselves are light and transparent the space underneath is fully utilizable for mailboxes, bicycles and children's play. Considerable effort went into separating the access areas to the upper dwellings from the garden spaces in front of the ground-floor dwellings. This is reflected in the clear definition of residents' responsibilities as far as keeping their own access areas clean. The absence of such distinct definition would undoubtedly result in far less intensive utilization of the available space by the respective inhabitants.

105 106
    107a
    107b
108 107c 109

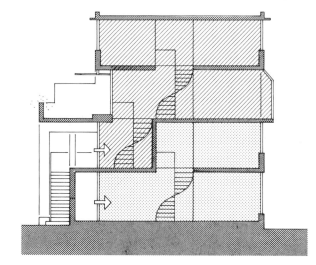

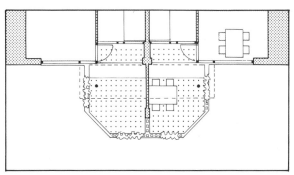

Second floor

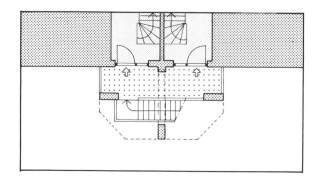

First floor

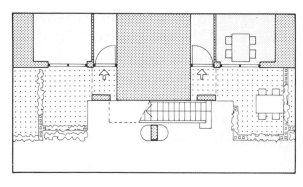

Ground floor

The concept of the living-street is based on the idea that its inhabitants have something in common, that they expect something of each other even if only because they are aware that they need each other. This feeling, however, seems to be disappearing rapidly from our lives. The affinity between inhabitants seems to diminish as the independence that comes with greater prosperity increases. This anonymity is even praised by believers in collectivism/centralization: if people have too much to do with each other, there is the danger of too much 'social control', they argue.

Indeed, the more isolated and alienated people become in their everyday environment, the easier it is to control them by decisions taken over their heads. Even though 'social control' need not by definition be negative, it does of course exist and its negative effects are indeed felt when one cannot do anything without being judged and spied upon by others, as in an all too close-knit village community.

We must grasp every opportunity of avoiding too rigid separation between dwellings, and of stimulating what is left of the feeling of belonging together.

In the first place this feeling of belonging together revolves around everyday social interaction, such as children playing together out in the street, baby-sitting for each other, keeping in touch concerning each other's health, in short all those cares and joys

that perhaps seem so self-evident that one tends to underestimate their importance.

■ Dwelling units function better if the streets on which they are sited function well as a living-street, and that in turn depends especially on how receptive they are, i.e. upon whether the atmosphere inside the homes can blend with the communal atmosphere of the street outside. This is largely determined by the planning and detailing of the layout of the neighbourhood.

SPANGEN HOUSING, ROTTERDAM 1919 / M. BRINKMAN
(110,111)

The access galleries in the Rotterdam Spangen housing scheme (1919!) are still unequalled in what they offer the residents. Since there are only front doors on one side of this type of 'living-street' the residents have only their next-door neighbours for company. This is a disadvantage compared with a normal street, where there are of course neighbours across the way, too. Nonetheless, here in Spangen social contact between neighbours is exceptionally intense, which goes to show how important the absence of traffic is. Yet the social interaction that takes place on the access gallery is inevitably shut off from the street below, to which the dwellings in fact turn their backs. You cannot be in two places at once.

110 111

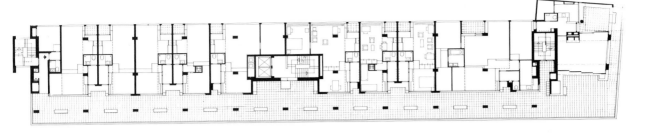

WEESPERSTRAAT STUDENT ACCOMMODATION (112-115)
The dwelling units for married students on the fourth floor were an inducement to build a gallery-street, which could be seen as a prototype for a living-street, free from traffic and with a view of the rooftops of the old city. It is safe there for even the youngest toddlers to play out of doors, while their parents can also sit in front of their homes. The example this design was based on was in fact the Spangen complex of 45 years ago.

One of the problems in gallery-streets is the placement of bedroom windows: if they open onto the gallery there is the disadvantage of insufficient privacy. This situation can be improved by raising the floor of the bedroom, so that those inside can look out of the window over the heads of the people outside, while the window is too high for those outside to be able to look into the room.

The building as a whole has since become much less open; and consequently the gallery street is no longer publicly accessible.

112
113
114 115

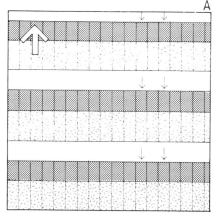
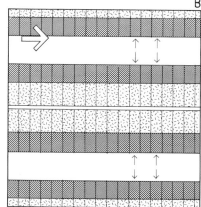
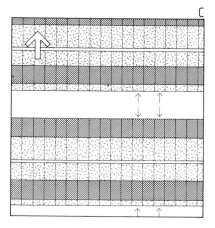

SITING PRINCIPLES (116)

How this works is to be seen, in an elementary form, in the siting principles adopted in some form or other in all newly constructed housing projects.

The demand for more openness and better sunlight conditions for all dwelling units led, in twentieth-century urban planning, to the abandonment of the hitherto customary perimeter block siting.

That resulted in the loss of the contrast between the quiet seclusion of the enclosed courtyards and the bustle and traffic noise of the street outside. The façades giving onto the streets were the fronts (and so the architects concentrated their efforts on them) while the more informal rear façades with their balconies and clothes-lines - some favoured by their orientation, others quite the opposite - was the so-called living side. This arrangement was superseded by strip siting, with two-fronted dwellings, which created the possibility of positioning all the gardens on the side (diagram a). It is important to realize, though, that with this type of layout all the front doors of one row of houses look out onto the gardens of the next row. So everyone lives on a half-street, as it were, with the spaces between the blocks all essentially the same instead of alternating between garden space and street space. Incidentally, the strip siting principle allows for the same form of allotment so long as the orientation is suitable (diagram b) but even if that is not the case it is worth making every effort to ensure that the fronts of the blocks (i.e. where the front doors are located) face each other (diagram c). If the entrances of the dwellings face each other everyone looks onto the same communal space - you can see the neighbours' children hurrying off to school in the morning (is our clock slow again?).

But having a full view of your neighbours also encourages inquisitiveness, and so with this type of siting it is even more important than with type c to position windows and front doors vis à vis each other carefully, in such a way that some privacy at least is offered at each entrance to protect against too much prying. In the case of the traditional so-called closed housing block scheme, all the gardens and all the entrances face each other. The garden areas are therefore different in nature from the street areas.

ROYAL CRESCENTS, BATH, ENGLAND 1767 / J.WOOD, J.NASH (117-119)

Although certainly not designed with a view to neighbourly interaction, the curved street-walls of the 'crescents' in Bath are particularly interesting in this respect.
Due to the concavity of the curve the houses have a view of one another. It is the same effect as when you are

116 abc

117 118 119

sitting in a train and the tracks describe a curve: you can suddenly see a string other carriages full of fellow-passengers, whose presence you had not been aware of. A curved street-wall with the houses in the row overlooking the same area thus contributes to the communal nature of that area.

While the concave side of a curved wall can encourage the feeling of belonging together, the convex side at the back sees to it that the houses turn away from each other as it were, and this can contribute to the privacy of the gardens. The crescent solution therefore works both ways.

RÖMERSTADT, FRANKFURT, GERMANY 1927-28 / E. MAY (120-123)

Ernst May, like his more famous fellow architect Bruno Taut, was among the leading pioneers of German housing construction. The numerous housing schemes he built in Frankfurt in the period 1926-1930 show how keen May's eye was for the urban details that can improve living conditions. The lesson he teaches is that the rather dull allotment plans that usually result from the limited budgets for social housing can actually be transformed into an excellent living environment in spite of the restricted means, so long as the plans are worked out with the proper sense of orientation and proportion. Of course it is important to realize that the architecture of the dwellings and the design of the surroundings were the responsibility of the same man, who moreover did not make a distinction between architecture and urban planning and therefore succeeded in attuning dwellings and environment to each other is such a way that they become complementary parts of a single whole.

The Römerstadt housing scheme is situated on a gentle slope by the river Nidda. The parallel streets follow the direction of the valley, and although it might have been especially obvious here, with the terraced streets, to plan the garden consistently on the valley side, it was decided to make the front doors of the row-houses on either side of the road face each other. The inequality of the two entrance sides, resulting from the orientation and the (slight) difference in level, was compensated for by organizing the street space in such a way that the houses on the side with less favourably sited gardens would have a green zone at the front.

A characteristic detail is that the pavement stops short of the façade, leaving a narrow strip bare directly adjoining the north wall. This is an obvious place for plants, and creepers grown up all over the façade, thus softening its starkness.

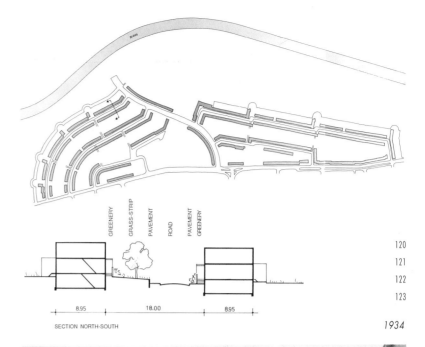

120
121
122
123

SECTION NORTH-SOUTH

1934

1985

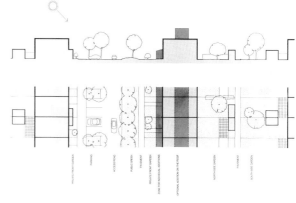

HET GEIN, HOUSING (124-128)

The layout of the housing estate 'Het Gein' in Amersfoort is such that the emphasis came to lie especially on the quality of the living-streets. The terrain was divided as much as possible into long straight blocks and parallel streets. At first sight this yields less rather than more variety than the conventional layout, but the idea is that quiet straight streets provide a better starting-point for variations within the allotments. It is like a sytem of warp and weft, as the warp (streets) in a woven piece of cloth constitute a strong (even colourless if necessary) structure, while the weft gives the weave its colour. An important requirement, though, is that the living-streets be kept as traffic-free as possible. Much attention has also been paid to the street profiles; they are not only essential for the quality of each individual dwelling, but also for the way they interrelate. The fronts, and hence also the front doors of the dwellings, face each other two by two on either side of the street. The streets have a south-east to north-west orientation, which means that one side catches more

sunlight than the other. That is why the streets are asymmetrically organized: the parking spaces have been moved to one side of the street - the shady side. The other, sunnier side, is largely filled with greenery. The dwellings with front doors on the sunny side and consequently with gardens on the shadier side have been compensated for this with an extra space (1.80 m wide) along the front, which can be used to install covered porches, conservatories, awnings, or other individual conveniences. These additions were already supplied by us from the outset in the case of a number of dwellings, which might well serve to stimulate occupants of similar dwellings to follow these examples if they can afford to do so. How this zone is eventually used by everyone concerned will constitute the main source of diversity - not as a product of design but rather as an expression of individual choices. Some of the dwellings, too, have roof extensions, and assurances have also been given that more additions will be permitted in a specially appointed zone in the future. The garden sheds are located either close to the house or in the garden,

124 125
127
126 128

depending on sunlight conditions. In the partially shaded gardens, this still made it possible to create a sunny spot with some shelter. The allotments with a more favourable orientation have their shed close to the house so that it becomes attractive to construct some kind of connection in the space between the two.

ACCESSIBILITY OF FLATS

Dwellings should be as accessible as possible directly from the street, and preferably not too far removed from it, as is often the case in multi-storey buildings. Whenever, as in the case of flats, you can only reach your own home indirectly by way of communal halls, elevators, staircases, galleries or arcades, there is the risk of these communal spaces being so anonymous that they discourage informal contacts between residents, and degenerate into a vast no-man's-land. Even if the need for a certain amount of privacy for each unit in multi-story buildings has been taken into account, people who live nextdoor, above, or under each other, do have lot to do which each other, while the spatial conditions for this are lacking. Also in a block of flats it is difficult to know where to welcome friends and where to say goodbye. Do you accompany them to your front door and leave them to go down the stairs alone, or do you walk them all the way down to where their car is parked in the parking lot? And what a lot of dragging around with luggage you have to do to pack the car when you go on holiday! If your children are still too small to play outside on their own, the situation is really problematical.

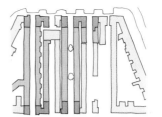

Living-street, Hamburg between Löwenstraße and Falkenried, Germany

'The fun begins, getting the car and trailer ready.' From ANWB Tourist Guide.

In residential neighbourhoods we must give the street a living-room quality not only for day-to-day inter-action but also for more special occasions, so that both communal activities and activities of importance to the local community can take place there.

The street can also be the setting for community activities, such as the celebration of special occasions that concern all the local inhabitants. It is impossible to design the street area in such a way that people suddenly take to having their meals out of doors together.

Living-street, Saxmundham, England 1887. 'Celebrating Queen Victoria's Jubilee. By the late 1880s the Queen's popularity had surmounted the earlier waves of Republicanism, and came to a climax in the Jubilees of 1887 and 1897, by which time she was as much loved and revered as any monarch in Britain before and since. Notice that a policeman, in the centre of the picture, with the jug in his right hand, is among the official persons who are helping to serve the populace. The day is warm enough for many of the ladies at the table on the right to have opened their parasols to protect them against the sun. A sunburnt face in a woman was, of course, a thing to be avoided at all costs if she would maintain any sort of social position.' (Gordon Winter, A country camera 1844 - 1914, Penguin London)

130
131
129 132

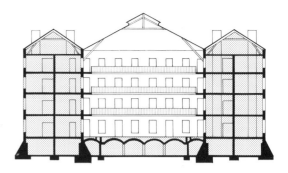

Yet it would be a good idea to keep this kind of image at the back of your mind as a sort of standard that your design must in principle be capable of meeting. Although people in northern countries are not in the habit of taking their meals out of doors, it does happen every now and again, and so we should see to it that this is not rendered impossible a priori by the spatial organization of the place. Perhaps people will even be more inclined to put the public space to new uses if the opportunities for doing so are explicitly offered to them.

Just as important as the disposition of the residential units vis à vis each other is the fenestration, the placement of bay windows, balconies, terraces, landings, doorsteps, porches - whether they have the correct dimensions and how they are spatially organized, i.e. adequately separated but certainly not too much so. It is always a question of finding the right balance to enable the residents to withdraw into privacy when they want to but also to seek contact with others. Of crucial importance in this respect is the space around the front door, the place where the house ends and the living-street begins. It is what the dwelling and the living-street have to offer each other that determines how well or how badly they will both be able to function.

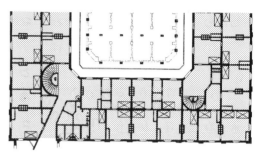

133
134
135
136

FAMILISTÈRE, GUISE, FRANCE 1859-83 (133-136)

The Familistère in Guise in the north of France constitutes a dwelling community established by the Godin stove factory after the utopian ideas of Fourier. The complex comprises 475 dwelling units, divided into three adjoining blocks with inner courtyards, as well as extensive facilities such as a crèche, school and laundry. In the large covered courtyards of the Familistère in Guise the surrounding dwellings literally constitute the walls. Although the shape of the courtyard and the prison-like manner in which the front doors are situated along the galleries strikes us today as somewhat primitive, this early 'block of flats' is still a pre-eminent example of how street and dwellings can be complemen-tary. The fact, moreover, that these courtyards are roofed makes them extra inviting for communal activities such as those which were apparently held there in the old days, when the housing complex still functioned as a truly collective form of habitation.

'Every attempt to reform work relations is doomed to failure unless it is accompanied by the reform of building for the purpose of creating a comfortable environment for the workers, which is fully attuned to their practical needs as well as to providing access to the pleasures of community living which every human being deserves to enjoy.'

(A. Godin, *Solutions Sociales*, Paris 1894)

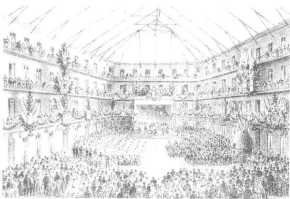

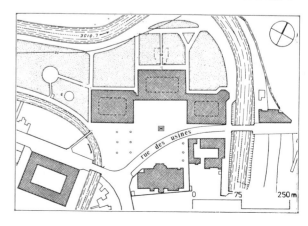

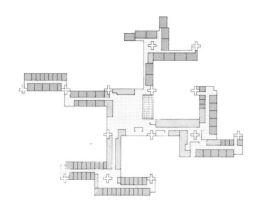

De Drie Hoven, Home for the Elderly (137-140)

In hospitals, homes for the elderly and similar large living-communities the restricted mobility of the residents makes it imperative to conceive the plan almost literally as a small-scale city. In the case of De Drie Hoven everything had to be accessible within a relatively short distance under the same roof, because hardly anyone is capable of leaving the premises without assistance. And thanks to the large size of the home it was possible to realize such a comprehensive programme of amenities that the institution could indeed approximate the nature of a city in that sense, too. The residents accommodate themselves to their environment as if it were a village community.

Strongly influenced by the notion of devolution in the organization, the complex has been divided up into a number of 'wings', each with its own 'centre'. The different departments come together in the central 'common room'. This disposition of the spaces has resulted in a sequence of open areas which, from a spatial point of view, reflect the sequence: neighbourhood centre, community centre, city centre - a composite whole within which each 'clearing' or open area serves a specific function. Yet this pattern is dominated as it were by the central 'courtyard', which the residents themselves call the 'village square'.

This 'village square' is not, strictly speaking, bordered by dwelling units, as is literally the case with the roofed courtyards of the Familistère in Guise, but as far as usage and social relations are con-cerned it does constitute the focus of the complex. This is where all activities that are organized for and by the resident community take place: parties, concerts, theatre and dance performances, fashion shows, markets, choir performances, card-game evenings, exhibitions and festive meals for special occasions! Something special goes on there almost every day. This 'village square' is a very free interpretation of the usual auditorium for special events, which would be unused half the time if it were a separate, less centrally located hall.

137 138

139 140

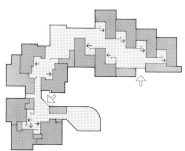

MONTESSORI SCHOOL, DELFT (141,142)

In the Montessori School the communal hall has been conceived in such a way that the hall relates to the classrooms as a street relates to the houses. The spatial relation between class-rooms and hall and the shape of the hall were conceived as the 'communal living-room' of the school. The experience of how this functions in the school can, in turn, serve as a model for what could be realized in a street.

141 142

143 144

KASBAH, HENGELO 1973 / P. BLOM (143,144)

No one has been more actively engaged in researching the reciprocity of dwelling and street-space than Piet Blom. Whereas the Kasbah scheme (see Forum 7, 1959 and Forum 5, 1960-61) was concerned especially with what the disposition of the dwellings themselves could generate, in the 'urban area' created in Hengelo the dwellings do not constitute the walls of the street but rather the 'roof of the

city', leaving the large ground-level space underneath for all communal activities and events. However, only incidental use is made of the exceptional opportunities in terms of space that are offered here.

There is quite a lesson to be learnt here. The dwellings are too isolated from the street below - they are, so to speak, turned away from it, they face upwards, and not much of the street can be seen from the windows, while even the entrances are indirectly positioned vis à vis the street. In that respect the form of the street space, as counterform to the dwellings, does not create the conditions for everyday usage. Besides, this space is probably too large to be filled, because there are not enough amenities - amenities which would have existed as a matter of course in a self-contained village of the same size.

But just try to imagine this scheme in the heart of Amsterdam, with a busy market in the street below!

That must have been the kind of situation that Piet Blom envisaged when he conceived his design.

Having departed from the traditional block siting principle, architects have endeavoured, inspired especially by Team X and Forum, to invent a stream of new dwelling forms. This often gave rise to spectacular results, but whether they function properly is only partially dependent on the quality of the dwellings themselves. What is at least as important is whether the architect can find a way, using the dwellings as his construction material, to form a street that functions adequately. The quality of each is dependent on that of the other: *houses and streets are complementary!*

That the constructed result is so often disappointing is because architects all too often have a mistaken idea of the way in which the actual street-space will be experienced and used in their scheme. Apart from the fact that they tend to rely too heavily on the effectiveness of specific provisions (which all too often turn out to be far less viable than envisaged) the most common error lies in the miscalculation of the ratio between the size of the public space and the number of people that may be expected to use it.
If the street area is too large, too little happens in too few places, and in spite of all the good intentions to the contrary, the consequence is vast spaces which assume the nature of a 'desert' simply because they are too empty. Too many projects - however well-designed - would function satisfactorily if only a market were to be held on a sunny Saturday: the kind of market you can easily conjure up in your imagination, but of which in reality there is only one per 100,000 dwellings.
You should really have to test your plan continually for 'population density' by roughly indicating the number of people on your blue-print that may be expected to make use of the different areas in varying situations. By doing that you will at least get some idea about whether there is perhaps a surfeit of space for recreation, for instance. While vast spaces often appeal to the architect's imagination as having a certain air of serenity, it is often doubtful whether the local population will feel the same way. For dwellings and buildings in general a wide variety of forms can be devised, so long as the street-space is formed in such a way that it can serve as a catalyzing agent between the local inhabitants in everyday situations, so that at least the distance between the individual inhabitants of the all too often hermetically sealed dwellings is not increased, but rather that the spatial organization may serve to stimulate social interaction and cohesion.

145
146

Via Mazzanti
Verona, Italy

10 THE PUBLIC DOMAIN

Student march in Galeria Vittorio Emanuele, Milan. 'With the student revolt, education has returned to the city and to the streets and has thus found a field of rich and diversified experience which is much more formative than that offered by the old school system.
Perhaps we are headed toward an era in which education and total experience will again coincide, in which the school as an established and codified institution no longer has any reason for existence.'
(from an article 'Architecture and education' by Giancarlo de Carlo in 'Harvard Education Review' 1969)

147

148 149

If the houses are private domains, then the street is the public domain. Paying equal attention to housing and street alike means treating the street not merely as the residual space between housing blocks, but rather as a fundamentally complementary element, spatially

organized with just as much care so that a situation is created in which the street can serve more purposes besides motorized traffic. If the street as a collection of building blocks is basically the expression of the plurality of individual, mostly private, components, the sequence of streets and squares as a whole potentially constitutes the space where it should be possible for a dialogue between inhabitants to take place.
The street was, originally, the space for actions, revolutions, cele-brations, and throughout history you can follow from one period to the next how architects designed the public space on behalf of the community which they in fact served.
So this is a plea for more emphasis on the enhancement of the public domain in order that it might better serve both to nurture and to reflect social interaction.With respect to every urban space we should ask ourselves how it functions: for whom, by whom and for what purpose.
Are we merely impressed by its sound proportions or does it perhaps also serve to stimulate improved relations between people?
When a street or square strikes us as beautiful it is not just because the dimensions and proportions are pleasing but also because of the way it functions within the city as a whole. This need not depend exclusively on the spatial conditions, although they often help, and obviously these cases are interesting as examples for the architect and urban planner.

PALAIS ROYAL, PARIS 1780/ J.V.LOUIS (148, 149,150)
In 1780 rows of houses with shopping arcades under-neath were erected on three sides of what was originally the garden of the Palais Royal in Paris.Today it is one of the most 'sheltered' public spaces in the city, while at the

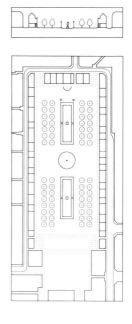

same time serving as an important short-cut from the Louvre area to the Bibliothèque Nationale. The small oblong park derives its spatial quality and its pleasant atmosphere not only from the sound proportions of the regularly articulated surrounding buildings, but also from the variegated layout with areas of grass, chairs, benches, sand-pits and an open-air café for the city-dwellers to choose from.

PUBLIC SQUARE, VENCE, FRANCE (151)

In countries with a warm climate the street naturally figures much more prominently in the lives of the people than in countries with a cold climate. Public squares like those in Vence are to be found in every village and every town in the countries bordering on the Mediterranean. In many places tourism has severely eroded the traditional way of life, and hence the original function of public spaces, but nevertheless these spaces are still eminently suited to communal activities - and perhaps even more so in these changed times, as for instance open-air concerts organized for tourists prove.

ROCKEFELLER PLAZA, NEW YORK (152)

Rockefeller Plaza in the heart of New York functions even in winter as a sort of urban living-room, when people from all over go there to skate on the temporary ice-rink. The skaters show off their prowess to the onlookers, and although there is not all that much going on, it can happen that the passers-by experience a certain feeling of togetherness, the kind of feeling which you might expect in a theatre, a church, or in some other place where people gather together, and which arises here spontaneously thanks partly to the spatial conditions that have been created.

151
152

150

153 154
155

PIAZZA DEL CAMPO, SIENA, ITALY (153-155)

If there is any public space whose enclosed form and exceptional location evokes the impression of an urban living-room it is the Piazza del Campo in Siena. Although it is rather inward-looking, with its somewhat stern buildings dominated by the Palazzo Communale, its saucer-like hollow with steep alleys radiating from it still unmistakably creates an atmosphere of openness and light. The sunny side of the piazza is lined with open-air cafes which are full all year round, especially with tourists.

The situation changes completely when the Palio dell Contrade is held, and all the different neighbourhoods compete with each other in horse races. This annual event, which is both a ceremony and a proper contest, casts a spell on the entire town and its population, and the lovely shell-shaped space overflows with crowds of people who, standing along the raised edges, all have a good view of the race taking place in the centre. At such times the open-air cafes make way for grandstands, and the windows of every single house with a view of the piazza are filled to capacity, either with paying spectators or with friends of the families. And of the eve of the contest 15,000 people dine out in the streets of all the neighbourhoods.

PLAZA MAYOR, CHINCHON, SPAIN (156,157)

In Chinchon, a small town south of Madrid, the central market square is transformed into an arena when the annual corrida is held. This plaza, shaped like a Greek amphitheatre situated in a hollow on the hillside, is entirely surrounded by buildings, with shops and cafés under the arcades below and dwellings above. All these dwellings have wooden balconies running from one end of the façade to the other, joining up to form a continuous tiered circle facing the square. Whenever a corrida is held the balconies become grandstands, with rows of seats which the residents sell to make some extra money. In this way private dwellings, located in such prominent and strategic places in the life of the community, temporarily take on a public status.

156 157
158

The way these balconies are all constructed along the
same principles as an open additional wooden zone
cantilevered from the relatively closed façades -
obviously with this extra public function in mind - they
draw the space together to form a large unified whole
resembling the classical Italian theatre with its vertically
tiered rows of boxes.

DIONNE SPRING, TONNERRE, FRANCE (158)

Communal wash-places (or the centrally located water
pumps or taps in small rural communities) have always
been a popular meeting-ground for local inhabitants,
where the latest news and gossip is exchanged. Running
water and washing-machines have put an end to
this.'Women have more time for themselves now', is an
argument often heard in defense of modernization. At
the famous spring of Tonnerre the place where the water
wells up from deep down in the earth was enclosed by a
simple circular dam. This solution intensifies the
grandeur of this natural phenomenon, while at the same
time creating the simple conditions for a communal
wash-place for the people who happen to live in the
vicinity.

We don't make wash-places anymore (car-washing
installations don't count). Are there in fact still places
where everyday activities give rise to the need to create
communal facilities in the public area, such as those that
are still to be found in less prosperous parts of the
world?

11 PUBLIC SPACE AS CONSTRUCTED ENVIRONMENT

Until the nineteenth century few buildings were public, and even then not completely so. The public accessibility of such buildings as churches, temples, mosques, spas, bazaars (amphi-)theatres, universities, etc. is subject to certain restrictions imposed by those in charge or by the owners. Truly public spaces were nearly always out of doors. The nineteenth century was the golden age of the public building, constructed in principle with funds provided by the community. The types of buildings that were developed in that period constituted the building-blocks for the city, and we can still learn from those examples which architectural and spatial means can best be used to make a building more inviting and hospitable.
The industrial (r)evolution opened up a new mass market. The acceleration and massification of production and distribution systems led to the creation of department stores, (world) exhibitions, covered market-places and of course to the construction of public transport networks, with railway stations and metro, and consequently to the rise of tourism.

VICHY, FRANCE (159,160)

A particularly interesting example is the 'watering-place' with natural springs, such as Vichy in France. The hopes and expectations concerning the health-giving properties of the water are a welcome subject of conversation for all visitors. The cures that have been prescribed for them take some time, which means that their paths cross regularly in the park in the centre of the town where the springs are located. The main walks through the park are roofed with lightweight metal structures, which gives the stroller the feeling of being both inside and out of doors at the same time.
The general atmosphere is that of an endless open-air café, with countless benches and chairs where those seeking to be cured of their ailments can sit and take the local health-giving water. The permanent stream of visitors is a determining factor of the urban life as a whole: there are many shops, restaurants, a casino and all manner of facilities for the visitors, which provide the local inhabitants with an important source of income. Thus an early form of tourist industry developed here.

The most basic reason for social intercourse has always been trade, which in all forms of community life takes place to a certain extent in the streets. Town and country meet when the individual farmer goes to town to sell his wares, and to spend the proceeds on other goods. Meanwhile news is exchanged.

LES HALLES, PARIS 1854-66 / V. BALTARD (162-164)
The market halls in Paris constituted an indispensable link in the chain of distribution of goods in the city - a relay-station as it were in a mammoth system, where producer and consumer no longer maintain direct contact with one another. The market halls consisted of vast areas with span-roofs and a sheltered area for loading and unloading. This hub of activity did not fail to leave its mark on the surrounding neighbourhood: there were, for instance, many all-night restaurants, some of which still exist, as a reminder of the old days.

The continuing expansion of scale, especially in transportation of food-stuffs, made it necessary to move the entire centre elsewhere (to Rungis). The vast steel-framed pavilions, once vacated, were demolished in 1971, in spite of intensive campaigns to prevent this from happening. It is always difficult to find premises to accommodate theatre performances, sports manifestations and other events that attract large audiences, and these halls would have served very well for this purpose. The demolition of these halls and what they have been replaced by can indeed be seen as a symbol of the destruction of the public (street-) space as an 'arena' of urban life.

161 163
162 164

COMMUNITY CENTRES / F. VAN KLINGEREN (165)

The community centres designed by Van Klingeren (he called them agoras) such as those in Dronten and Eindhoven were attempts to assemble under one roof all the activities that take place in a city centre. It is this kind of setting that generates new social roles and new exchanges - which cannot evolve in the new urban areas and neighbourhoods because no one has thought of making the necessary provisions.

Due to planning in terms of separately situated boxes with separate entrances, rather than in terms of an integrated urban fabric, the 'boxes' tend to have an adverse effect on the viability of the environment as a whole and, paradoxically, the better they function, the more they detract from the quality of life in the street. Thus they are, really, no more than 'artificial' urban centres which owe their existence to the inadequacy of urban provisions and the lack of an all-encompassing view of the necessary correlation between newly-built residential neighbourhoods and the existing urban core.

However interesting these community centres may have been as a social experiment in the 1960's, it is not surprising that, under the present social conditions with so much less tolerance and community spirit, they are no longer in use today. Especially the noise of the activities going on in adjoining spaces was felt to be disturbing, and soon people started to erect walls and other kinds of partitions, thereby undermining the spatial unity that was fundamental to the design.

THE EIFFEL TOWER, PARIS 1889 / G. EIFFEL (166)

The Eiffel Tower, which was erected for the World Exhibition. is not only the tourists' symbol of Paris, but also, as originally intended, a monument to the new ideas that had emerged in the course of the nineteenth century. Here we see, in a more suggestive form than ever before, the concrete expression of social change as manifested in the expansion of scale and the centralization of power. A construction such as the Eiffel Tower demonstrates that which becomes possible when innumerable small components, each with its specially assigned function and place, are combined in such a way as to form a centrally conceived entity, of which the whole far exceeds the sum of the parts. The subtlety of this feat of engineering becomes comprehensible when you realize that a scale model of the structure 30 cm. high would weigh a mere 7 grams (Guide Michelin). The greater the control of the active forces the greater the expansion that could be achieved. The Eiffel Tower is an embodiment of the principle of centralization - which can produce such an awe-inspiring force out of so many tiny subordinate forces. It is a demonstration of the proud accomplishment of an audacious plan undertaken in all innocence with no thought of the monstrous and all-engulfing forces that would ultimately be unleashed. The 'tour de force' of the distribution system, whereby the goods produced by a mass of individuals are distributed through a maze of intermediary channels among a mass of consumers, is based on a sophisticated structure of division of labour, specialization, and efficacious contracts. And it is undoubtedly this kind of organizational technique that feeds the self-propagating Moloch of scale-expansion and the diminution of the individual's influence on the process as a whole.

EXHIBITION PAVILIONS

The world exhibitions - those international showcases of
mass production, for which new markets had to be found
or created - necessitated the construction of enormous
exhibition halls such as the Crystal Palace in London
(1851) (167, 168), and the Grand Palais (1900) (169) and Petit
Palais in Paris, both of which are still standing. These vast
halls of steel and glass were the first palaces for the
consumer, who rules and is ruled by the consumer society
(consumers both consume and are themselves consumed in
a consumer society).

This age of new production methods and systems also
gave birth to new construction methods: the introduction
of steel as a building material made it possible to erect
roof structures with an enormous span within a very short
time. Besides, glass panes could now be inserted in the
steel roof-frames, and the resulting transparency gave the
vast hall an airy, light atmosphere. Indeed, the new
structures were more like bell-jars enclosing a space
offering basic shelter from the exterior weather conditions,
and therefore resembled gigantic glass-houses (such as
those still standing in Laken near Brussels and in London's
Kew Gardens) rather than the usual solid buildings.
(Incidentally, the Crystal Palace itself was a direct product
of traditional glass-house construction). The large spans,
too, undoubtedly, contribute to the feeling of not being
inside a building in the conventional sense. While the use
of steel structures made such wide spans possible, and the
new possibilities offered by the new construction methods
were eagerly exploited, the question rises whether they
were truly functional. Perhaps not, because even though
the vast glass roofs undeniably provided excellent
illumination for huge spaces, a few columns more would
not have made that much difference from a functional
point of view. Once again, the sheer feasibility seems to
have created the need as much as the need called for new
techniques and possibilities. Just as the Eiffel Tower
clearly demonstrated a way of thinking, so that way of
thinking was undoubtedly inspired by the new possibilities
of construction: thus demand generates supply and vice
versa (which came first: the chicken or the egg?). It is in
fact very difficult not to associate the vast span-roofs and
the way in which they evolved as well as the minimal
spatial articulation that they entailed with the emergence
of a way of thinking which has led to the vast expansion
of scale and the attendant centralization of today.

167 168
169

Magasin du Printemps, Paris 1881-1889/ P. Sedille

Au Bon Marché, Paris 1876/L.C. Boileau

170 172
171

DEPARTMENT STORES, PARIS

The expansion of the scale of consumption and market which found expression in the steel-and-glass exhibition halls of the last century also manifested itself, on a local level, in the large department stores.

Unlike the bazaars and other kinds of covered street markets where large numbers of individual vendors came together under the same roof to sell their wares, the department store is a single, centrally managed enterprise that claims to run a shop that is so large that everything can be bought there. It is actually a sort of general store, but blown up to gigantic proportions, and with an exceptionally variegated stock.

Whereas the merchandise in the general store is kept behind the counter on shelves reaching from floor to ceiling, accessible only to the salesman, in the department store it is the many storeys that are visible on all sides of a large central hall - like the shelves in the general store, with the important difference that they are wholly accessible to the buying public.

The glass roof which is to be found in nearly all the traditional department stores (e.g. les Grands Magasins in Paris) produces the same spatial effect, basically, as a single, large shop, even though the surrounding spaces are divided into separate departments for different goods.

The central hall of Galerie Lafayette offers the public a royal welcome, the majestic free-standing staircase being especially inviting (the staircase was eventually dismantled to obtain a few extra square metres of sales-space).+

Galerie Lafayette, Paris 1900

RAILWAY STATIONS

The construction of an expanding railway network opened up the world to travel and to the interchange of products, thereby making the world both smaller and larger. The stations that were erected in the towns and villages, like so many gate-buildings, constituted the cornerstones of the system. Not only did the railway stations introduce a new type of building into the towns, usually situated in a prominent place in the centre, they also brought with them a whole new range of related urban facilities and activities, such as hotels, places to eat and drink, and invariably shops. And quite often they developed quite independently into businesses in their own right, depending only partly on the custom of train passengers. The halls of many railway stations have gradually developed into public spaces, roofed parts of the city, where you can still buy articles when all the other shops are closed, where you can change money, use the telephone, buy magazines, go to the toilet, have your photograph taken in a booth, get information, find a taxi, or have a quick meal (or an elaborate one - quite a number of railway stations are renowned for their restaurants). This concentration continues in the direct vicinity, with cafés, restaurants and hotels. In Great Britain the hotels are often actually part of the station. In short, the bustle and activity surrounding the arrival and departure of the trains leads to a greater concentration of facilities in the area around a railway station than anywhere else in the city.

UNDERGROUND RAILWAY STATIONS

The entrances and exits of underground urban transport networks like the Paris metro and the London underground have the same impact, on a smaller scale and in many different locations in the city, as the main railway stations. Especially the Paris metro, with its distinctive forms is, as it were, one vast construction which emerges above ground in all the different neighbourhoods all over the city, as a familiar and instantly recognizable landmark. What the railway station is to the city, the metro entrance is to a neighbourhood: a place which attracts local amenities and business. The labyrinthine halls and passages of the main intersections are a favourite haunt of street musicians, especially in winter, when they seek shelter in this subterranean part of the city.

Central Station, Glasgow, Great Britain

173
174

Paris metro station Place Dauphine 1898-1901/H. Guimard

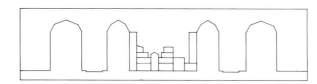

12 PUBLIC ACCESSIBILITY OF PRIVATE SPACE

Although the large buildings which are intended to be accessible to as many people as possible are not permanently open and although the opening hours are in fact imposed from above, such buildings do imply a fundamental and considerable expansion of the public world.

The most characteristic examples of this shift of emphasis are undoubtedly the arcades: glass-roofed shopping streets such as those that were constructed in the nineteenth century, and of which many impressive examples still survive all over the world. The arcades served in the first place to exploit the open interior spaces, and they were therefore commercial undertakings entirely in keeping with the trend towards opening up sales areas for a new buying public. In this way pedestrian circuits emerged in the nucleus of shopping areas. The absence of traffic permits the route to be narrow enough as to afford the potential buyer a good view of the shop-windows on either side.

175
176
177 178

PASSAGE DU CAIRE, PARIS 1779 (175-178)
An interesting example of the arcade concept is to be seen, in an elementary form, in the Passage du Caire in Paris. The complete building-up of the exceptionally shaped interior space was conceived together with the

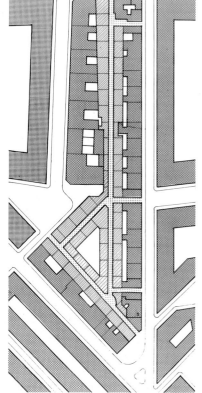

outer shell according to a rational principle of ordering which, to a certain extent and subject to certain rules, permitted a free disposition of the architectonic elements. Many of the businesses located here are connected with the premises situated on the periphery, so that an informal network of passages could develop in and between the sales points in addition to the official entrances.

SHOPPING ARCADES

In Paris, where the shopping arcade was invented and where it flourished (many arcades still exist, especially in the first and second 'Arrondissements') there are three consecutive blocks with connecting interior passages: Passage Verdeau, Passage Jouffroy, and Passage des Panoramas. Together they form a brief chain crossing the Boulevard Montmartre, and, if continued, it is easy to imagine how a network of covered pedestrian routes could have developed quite independently of the surrounding street pattern.

Shopping arcades exist all over the world, in diverse forms and dimensions depending on the local conditions - often they have lost their original glamour as expensive shopping districts although in many places they still

Galerie Vivienne, Paris

Paris, 2nd arrondissement

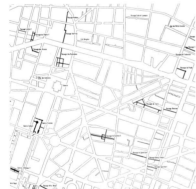

Passage des Panoramas, Paris

179 181
180 182

Strand Arcade,
Sydney

accommodate the more luxurious stores, such as the
Galerie St. Hubert in Brussels and the Galeria Vittorio
Emanuele in Milan, which are felt by everyone to be the
heart of the city.

(For a survey, analysis and history of the arcade see: J.F. Geist,
Passagen, ein Bautyp des 19.Jahrhunderts, München 1969)

183 184
    185
    186

The principle of the arcade regained topical relevance
when the traffic burden in the streets of city centres
became so heavy that the need arose for areas exclusively
for pedestrians, i.e. a separate 'system' for pedestrians
alongside the existing street pattern. The nineteenth-
century types of arcade ran *through* the blocks, like short-
circuits, and their primary purpose was to put the interior
areas to use.

But although the buildings were traversed by these
passages, their outward appearance was not affected: the
exterior, the periphery, continued to function separately
and independently as a façade in its own right. In the
case of many covered pedestrian routes of contemporary
design the exterior of the complex within which the
activity is concentrated resembles the unhospitable rear
walls of a building. This reversal - turning the building
mass inside-out, as it were - is no less than the sheer
perversion of the principle underlying the arcade.

The high, long passages, illuminated from above
thanks to glass roofing, give you the feeling of an
interior: thus they are 'inside' and 'outside' at the same

Galleria dell'Industria
Subalpina, Turin

time. Inside and outside are so strongly relativized vis à vis each other that you cannot tell whether you are inside one building or in the space connecting two separate buildings. In so far as the opposition between building masses and street space serves to distinguish - broadly, at any rate - between the private world and the public, the enclosed private domain is transcended by the inclusion of arcades. The inner space is made more accessible, while the fabric of streets becomes more close-knit. The city is turned inside out, both spatially and also as far as the principle of its accessibility is concerned.

The concept of the arcade contains the principle of a new system of accessibility with which the borderline between public and private is shifted and hence partially erased, whereby spatially at any rate the private domain becomes more publicly accessible.

The break away from the closed perimeter block siting in twentieth-century urbanism, meant the disintegration of the clear-cut spatial definition given by the street pattern. As the autonomy of the buildings grew, their interrelationship diminished, so that they now stand devoid of alignment as it were, like an irregular scattering of megaliths far away from each other in an excessively large open space. The 'rue corridor' has degenerated into an 'espace corridor'.

This new open type of siting, so innovative for the 'physical' conditions of housing construction in particular, has had a disastrous effect on the cohesion of the whole - a fate that has befallen most cities. The more buildings stand apart as autonomous volumes with individualized façades and private entrances the less cohesion there is, but also and especially the

189 190

187 188

184-188:
Galleria Vittorio
Emmanuele, Milan

Eaton Center,
Toronto

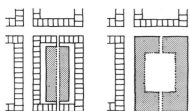

must not be allowed to lead to an architecture of street walls with the actual dwellings as mere punctuation marks or props to support the décor. We must not forget that the Modern Movement aimed specifically at the improvement of buildings, and notably at the improvement of the dwellings by means of better siting to ensure more sunlight, wider views, more satisfactory exterior spaces etc.

The face of a city is half the truth - satisfactory housing is the other, complementary half.

The many examples of open urbanism, as designed in the 1920s and 1930s, are indeed still of great relevance, at least if each is judged according to its own specific qualities.

191 192
193

greater the opposition between public and private space, even though the housing blocks may be designed with access galleries or interior covered streets or indeed with surrounding private space. Urbanism with buildings as autonomous freely dispersed monuments has given rise to a huge exterior environment - at best a pleasant park landscape where you always feel 'outside'.

While modern architects and town planners already started breaking open the city before the Second World War, the demolition work was continued by the war; later on the traffic mania dealt this fragmentation the 'coup de grâce' wherever it could. So all of us are by now convinced of the need for reconstruction of the interior of the city and for a revival of interest and concern for the street area, and hence for the exterior of the buildings. But that

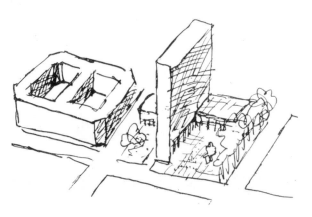

Le Corbusier's most important statement in this context is, that a large space which would in the normal run of things have been inaccessible as part of the private domain, by virtue of its accessibility is a contribution to the city as a whole.

It is important to bear in mind, however, that this solution would have lost much of its quality if the surrounding blocks had been designed according to the same principle. In that case the area as a whole would have presented the usual picture of an average modern city. It is precisely the surprise of the contrast that makes the principle so clear in this case.

We must consider the quality of street-space and of buildings in relation to each other. A mosaic of interrelationships - as we imagine urban life to be - calls for a spatial organization in which built form and exterior space (which we call street) are not only complementary in the spatial sense and therefore reciprocate in forming each other, but also and especially - for that is what we are primarily concerned with here - in which built form and exterior space offer maximal accessibility to penetrate each other in such a way that not only the borderlines between outside and inside become less explicit, but also that the sharp division between private and public domain is softened.If you enter a place gradually, the front door is divested of its significance as a single and abrupt moment; it is extended, as it were, to form a step-by-step sequence of areas which are not yet explicitly inside but also less explicitly public. The most obvious expression of such a mechanism of accessibility was to be seen in the arcades, and it is indeed not surprising therefore that the arcade idea still serves as an example today.

MINISTRY OF EDUCATION AND HEALTH,
RIO DE JANEIRO 1936-37 / LE CORBUSIER (193-196)

In his concept Le Corbusier did not adapt himself to the order of traditional building blocks, as envisaged in the urban plan. Instead of a solid mass with majestic façades surrounding the site on all sides, Le Corbusier designed his building in a free form, as a high-rise construction on columns, so that you don't have to walk around the block but that you can, instead, cross the distance diagonally underneath.

The height of the columns and the distance between them were selected in such a way that the resulting space has a liberating effect.The feeling of liberation is all the more striking because one doesn't expect a situation like this in the surroundings, and it is therefore a special and stimulating sensation to find oneself there.

194

195 196

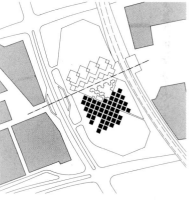

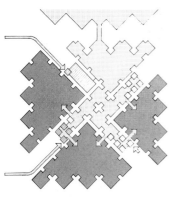

CENTRAAL BEHEER OFFICE BUILDING (197-200)
The urban plan, wholly in keeping with the 'traditional' open construction of the first half of this century, i.e. without a strict alignment of the buildings and without street walls within which the building had to be

197 198
199
200

situated, therefore called for a self-contained architectural design with no references to the buildings in the direct vicinity. Instead of a single, colossal constructed volume, a more transparent conglomerate of numerous smaller components was achieved, thanks to the differentiation into more or less independent small blocks separated by arcade-like passages (i.e. essentially publicly accessible space).
And since there are exits and entrances throughout the complex it looks more like a piece of a city than like a single building - most of all it resembles a kind of settlement.
Not only is the design conceived in such a way that members of the staff leave their work-spaces to take a break, talk and have coffee at one of the many counters in the central space of the complex - as if they were taking a stroll in the city-centre - this area can moreover be literally public.
This opportunity for public accessibility would have been fully exploited if the original plan had been carried out: namely to situate the new railway station of Apeldoorn directly adjoining the complex, so that you could reach the platforms by way of Centraal Beheer (plans were even worked out in consultation with the Dutch railways to install sales points for train tickets inside the complex). While the building, as an autonomous entity, is put into perspective on the formal level by its articulation in terms of a large number of smaller architecturalcomponents, on the practical level a similar articulation is achieved

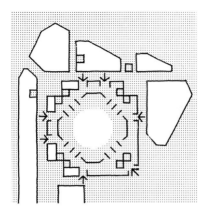

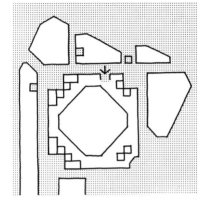

by the adopted principle of accessibility - that is, that you can enter the building from all directions, gradually and in stages.

Under the influence of the growing security risk in public spaces, Centraal Beheer, too, has imposed certain restrictions on public accessibility. All entrances are nowadays guarded with tv cameras, and the need is being felt more and more strongly for a single central entrance to the complex as a whole, which moreover has become less straight forwardly legible since the contraction of two of the buildings into one volume.

VREDENBURG MUSIC CENTRE (201-203)

An attempt was made to avoid the traditional form of a concert hall in the sense of a 'temple of music' and instead to arrive at a less formal, less awe-inspiring and therefore hopefully an atmosphere that is more inviting to the uninitiated. Besides revolutionizing the overall 'image', also the 'mechanism' of accessibility has been drastically altered. You do not enter by way of an imposing main entrance, you enter step by step. First you are in a covered passage, which leads to the many entrances (as if you were going into a department store), then you find yourself in the foyers of the Music Centre, from where you proceed to the actual auditorium. The large number of entrances along the passage (or arcade) and also directly on the square - when they are all open - make the building as a whole temporarily part of the street. And indeed, that is how

the building functions during the weekly free concerts in the lunch-hour. On those days you see shoppers strolling into the building, often surprised, often listening attentively although they have not come to hear the concert, and sometimes just taking a short cut to the next street.

CINEAC CINEMA, AMSTERDAM 1933 / J. DUIKER (204,205)
Duiker not only succeeded wonderfully in fitting the entire architectural programme diagonally into the tiny building site (each centimetre of which had to be put to use), he also managed to leave the corner where the entrance is located open, so that the street-corner can continue to function a public space. In this way one cuts the corner behind the tall column, and, being guided by the curved glass awning, might be tempted to buy a ticket to the non-stop film-show.(This awning was faced with wood in 1980; also the illuminated sign was removed, thus disfiguring this, the last of Duiker's major works.)The space that was restored to the street is an integral part of the architecture, partly because of the specific location on a corner, and partly because of the materials that were employed (the same kind of tiles on the floor as in the rest of the building, and the glass awning). It is therefore equivocal: private yet public.

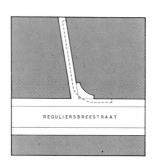

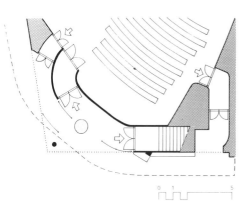

While the expression of the relativity of the concepts of interior and exterior is first and foremost a question of spatial organization, whether an area tends more towards a street-like atmosphere or more towards an interior depends especially on the spatial quality.

And besides, whether people will recognize the area concerned as interior or as exterior, or as some intermediary form, depends to a large extent on the dimensions, the form and the choice of materials.

In the case of both Centraal Beheer (206) and Vredenburg Music Centre (207) the spaces in the parts which are intended as semi-street areas are extra high and narrow, with illumination from above as in the traditional shopping arcade. This type of cross-section evokes the alleys of old cities, and this evocation is further intensified by the application of the kind of materials for floors and walls that we are accustomed to seeing out of doors. As you penetrate further into the Music Centre this feeling is underscored by the use of wood for the floors and walls. The adjoining shopping precinct Hoog Catharijne is paved with marble, the spaces there are much wider and only incidentally illuminated from above. The horizontal character, with predominantly artificial lighting, and the shiny, glamorous-looking marble makes Hoog Catharijne resemble a vast department store rather than the public space that it essentially is.

206
207

HOTEL SOLVAY, BRUSSELS 1896 / V. HORTA (208-211)

Although the doors in the façade are unmistakably the main entrance of the building, when you enter them you find that they do not give onto a conventional hall but that they give access to a passage leading straight through the house to another pair of doors opening onto a courtyard at the back.

This passage was intended to allow carriages to enter so that people could alight in front of the real door to the house without getting wet.

The real front door is therefore situated at right angles to the façade, and in itself marks the beginning of a spatial sequence comprising entrance hall and staircase leading to the first floor with the main rooms located along the entire front and rear walls, with Horta's characteristic use of glass partitions to create an open connection with the stairwell.

208

209 210

211

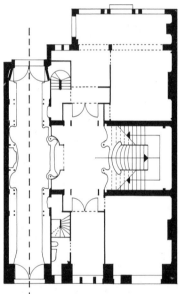

The passage traversing the building gives the impression of being part of the street, even though it is in fact a strictly private and space and part of the house. This impression is strengthened by the street-like materials that have been applied in this space, especially the paving stones and the raised stone border.

A characteristic Horta detail is the fluent transition between façade and pavement, so that the borderline between building and street and likewise between private property and public space fades, indeed does not seem to exist at all anymore since the materials of façade and pavement are the same. It is almost impossible to imagine how this could have been arranged with the local authorities, because they always adhere to a strict separation of private and public space.

PASSAGE POMMERAYE, NANTES, FRANCE, 1840-43 (212-214)
Although the construction materials and the forms that
are applied in most arcades are of the type that 'belong'
outside, sometimes the opposite is the case, as in the
Passage Pommeraye in Nantes. This connection cutting
across a block between two streets on different levels is
one of the most beautiful arcades still in existence,
especially because of its different levels which are both
visible from the central space and connected by a large
wooden staircase.
The use of wood, which you would not expect to find in
such a situation, emphasizes the feeling of being indoors
- not only visually, but also audibly. Inside and outside
are thus doubly relativized here, which makes this
arcade the example par excellence of how the
opposition between interior and exterior can be
eliminated.

214

'THE LETTER' / PIETER DE HOOGH (1629-1684) (215)

Pieter de Hoogh's painting demonstrates the relativity of the notions of outside and inside, in the way it is evoked not only by means of the spatial distinctions but also and especially by the expression of the materials and their temperatures in the varying degrees of light.

The interior, with its cool shiny tiles and the severe windows in the background, has an outside temperature in which contrasts with the warm glow of the exterior façade in the sunlight. The open front door without a doorstep makes a smooth transition between the living quarters and the street with its carpet-like surface. The roles of the inside and outside appear to be reversed, creating a spatially cohesive ensemble which expresses, above all, accessibility.

Just as the application indoors of the kind of spatial organization and material that refer to the outdoor world make the inside seem less intimate, so spatial references to the indoor world make the outside seem more intimate; it is therefore the bringing into perspective of inside and outside and the ambiguity that this gives rise to that intensifies both the sense of spatial accessibility and the sense of intimacy.

A step-by-step sequence of indications by architectonic means ensures a gradual entrance and exit. The entire complex of experiences elicited by the architectonic means contributes to this process: gradations of height, width, degree of illumination (natural and artificial), materials, different floor-levels. The different sensations within this sequence evoke a variety of associations, each corresponding with a different gradation of 'inside-ness and outside-ness' on the basis of recognition of previous, similar experiences.

Not only does each sensation refer to a specific gradation of inside-ness and outside-ness, by extension it also refers to corresponding usage.

In the foregoing I have posited that the use made of an area, the sense of responsibility for that area, and the care lavished on it, are all connected with the territorial claims and management, but architecture has by virtue of the evocative qualities of all explicitly spatial images, forms and materials, the capacity to stimulate a certain kind of usage.

Concepts such as public and private thus shrink to mere administrative entities.

By selecting the appropriate architectonic means the private domain can thus become less fortress-like and more accessible, while the public domain can, once it becomes more responsive to personal responsibilities and the personal care of those directly concerned, be far more intensively used and thus be enriched.

While the trend at the end of the sixties seemed to be towards a greater openness of society in general and of buildings in particular, as well as the revival of the street - the public domain par excellence- there is currently a growing movement towards restricting that accessibility, and towards retreating into one's own 'fortress' out of fear of aggression and the wish to feel secure on one's own ground. But in so far as the balance between open-ness and closed-ness is a reflection of our fairly open society, we in the Netherlands, with our solid tradition, may have the most favourable conditions imaginable for the realization of buildings that are fundamentally more accessible and streets that are fundamentally more inviting.

215

B MAKING SPACE, LEAVING SPACE

'Der Gegenpad von Zwang ist nicht Freiheit, sondern Verbundenheit. Zwang ist eine negative Wirklichkeit, und Verbundenheit ist die positive; Freiheit ist eine Möglichkeit, die wiedergewonnene Möglichkeit. Vom Schicksal, von der Natur, von den Menschen gezwungen werden: der Gegenpol is nicht, vom Schicksal, von der Natur, von den Menschen frei, sondern mit ihm, mit ihr, mit ihnen verbunden und verbündet sein; um dies zu werden, muss man freilich erst unabhängig geworden sein, aber die Unabhängigkeit ist ein Steg und kein Wohnraum.'

'The antipode of compulsion is not liberty, but alliance. Compulsion is a negative reality, and alliance a positive one; liberty is an option, a regained option. Compulsion at the hands of fate, of nature, of people: its antipode is not liberation from fate, from nature and from people, but alliance with them. To achieve this bond, however, people must first become independent, but independence signifies a narrow path, not living-space.'
(Martin Buber, *Reden über Erziehung*, Heidelberg 1953)

1 STRUCTURE AND INTERPRETATION

Part A of this study dealt with the reciprocity of public and private spheres of influence, and what the architect can do to contribute to that balance - at least if he is aware in each situation of which specific responsibilities apply and how they can be interpreted. Part two will deal with the reciprocity of form and usage, in the sense that form not only determines both usage and experience, but that it is itself equally determined by them in so far as it is interpretable and can therefore be influenced. In so far as something is designed for everyone, that is as a collective starting-point, we must concern ourselves with all conceivable individual interpretations thereof - and not only at a specific moment in time, but also as they change in time.

The relation between a collective given and individual interpretation as it exists between form and usage as well as the experience thereof may be compared to the relation between language and speech.
Language is a collective instrument, the common property of a group of people capable of using that instrument to shape their thoughts and to convey them to each other, so long as they observe the conventions of grammar and syntax, and so long as they use recognizable words - i.e. words that mean something to the listener. The remarkable thing is that each individual can be understood by another, even when he or she expresses very personal feelings and concerns in a highly personal way.
Moreover, speech is not only consistently an interpretation of language, but language is in turn also influenced by what is often spoken, and in due course the language changes under that steady influence. So you might say that language not only determines speech, but that language itself is at the same time determined by speech. Language and speech relate to one another dialectically.

The concept of structure tends to obscure rather than clarify. Anything that has been put together, however shoddily, soon tends to be described as a structure. (And then there are the negative associations with so-called structural thinking in institutions and business organizations, and of course in politics.) Here 'structure' refers to new forms of oppression by new wielders of power. Everything in architecture, good or bad, in which the constructive aspect occupies a visually prominent position, and which has to do with repetition of prefabricated components (whether of concrete or of some other material), with grids or frames, rigid or shaky or both - it is all labelled structuralism. The original and by no means empty meaning of structure and structuralism indeed appears to have been submerged by loads of architectural jargon. Structuralism denoted, initially, a way of thinking originating from cultural anthropology, which rose to prominence in Paris during the sixties and which, especially in the form developed by Claude Lévi Strauss, exerted a strong influence on the various social sciences. The term is closely bound up with Lévi Strauss: his ideas - especially where they dealt with the afore-mentioned relationship between the collective pattern and individual interpretations - were particularly inspiring for architecture.
Lévi Strauss, for his part, was inspired by the linguist Ferdinand de Saussure (1857-1913), who was the first to study the distinction between 'langue' and 'parole', between language and speech. Language is structure par excellence, a structure that, in principle, contains the possibilities to express everything that can be communicated verbally. It is indeed a prerequisite for the ability to think. For an idea can only be said to exist in so far as it permits formulation in words; we use language not only to convey our ideas, language actually shapes those ideas as we express them. Formulating and thinking go hand in hand: we formulate as we think, but we also think as we formulate.
Within this system - a coherent expanse of values - the different interrelationships are laid down in rules, but there is still a lot of freedom of action within the same system thanks, paradoxically, to the very same fixed rules that delimit this freedom.

In the philosophy of structuralism this idea is extended to encompass an image of man whose possibilities are constant and fixed, like a pack of cards with which you can play different games depending on the way they have been dealt.
Different cultures, whether so-called primitive or so-called civilized, play a transformation of the same game, as it were; the main directions are fixed while the interpretation differs continually
(Lévi Strauss, La Pensée Sauvage 1962)

Having studied and compared the myths and legends of diverse cultures Lévi Strauss observed that the same themes recur, and thus came to the conclusion that, through application of transformation-rules, there was a high degree of correspondence in structure. All patterns of behaviour within different cultures, he maintained, were transformations of each other; however different, the relation vis à vis their own system within which they perform a function would, in principle, be constant.

'In the same way, if you compare a photograph and its negative - even though the two images are different - you will find that the relationships between the component parts remain the same' (M. Foucault).

'To put it in more popular terms, when you get down to the essentials, different people under different circumstances do the same things in different ways and different things in the same way.

'Man is the way he is made, but the point is what does he make of the way he is made' (J.P. Sartre), meaning the degree of freedom he succeeds in creating within the restriction of his own possibilities.

The most simplified summary of the structure-idea can be given on the basis of, say, the game of chess. Within an essentially childishly simple set of rules governing the freedom of movement of each piece in the game, good players succeed in creating an infinite range of possibilities. The better the player is the richer the game, and within the official set of rules other, unofficial sub-rules arise on the basis of experience, which develop into official rules in the hands of experienced players whose experience in their application in turn influences the original given, and who thus, by extension, contribute to regulating the system. Moreover, chess is an outstanding example of how a fixed set of rules does not restrict freedom but rather creates freedom. Noam Chomsky, the American linguist (who happens to be remembered especially for his opposition to the United States intervention in Vietnam), compared languages in a way similar to how Lévi Strauss compared myths - and concluded that there had to be a linguistic ability analogous in all men. He took as his starting-point a 'generative grammar', a sort of underlying pattern to which all languages can be traced fundamentally and for which an innate ability exists. So in this sense different languages, like different forms of behaviour, could be seen as transformations of each other. Generally speaking all this does not seem to be far removed from Jung's 'archetypes'. This leads to the feeling that also the creation of form and spatial organization on analogous grounds could be traced back to an innate ability of all men in the most diverse cultures to arrive at ever different interpretations of essentially the same 'arch-forms'. Moreover Chomsky introduced the concepts 'competence' and 'performance'. Competence is the knowledge that a person has of his or her language, while performance refers to the use he makes of that knowledge in concrete situations. And it is with this more general re-formulation of the terms 'langue' and 'parole' that a link can indeed be established with architecture. In architectural terms you could say that 'competence' is form's capacity to be interpreted, and 'performance' is the way in which form is/was interpreted in a specific situation.

2 FORM AND INTERPRETATION

Broadly speaking, 'structure' stands for the collective, general, (more) objective, and permits interpretation in terms of what is expected and demanded of it in a specific situation. One could also speak of structure in connection with a building or an urban plan: a large form which, changing little or not at all, is suitable and adequate for accommodating different situations because it offers fresh opportunities time and again for new uses.

CANALS, AMSTERDAM (216-220)

The pattern of the canal belts in Amsterdam gives the city-centre its distinctive layout and makes it easy to find one's way. Not only do the successive concentric semi-circles enable one to find one's bearings throughout the centre, they also indicate the passage of time - much like the year-rings of a tree. It is obvious that their original function as

216
217
218

Herengracht,
Amsterdam 1672/
G. van Berkheyde

defensive structures can now be seen merely as the motive underlying their specific layout, which had and still has, potentially, so much more to offer. Besides serving purposes of defence, the canals were used mainly for the transport of the incoming and outgoing goods to which the city owed much of its wealth; and in the days before public sewage systems they served as open drains for the city's waste. Today the canals constitute the principal green belts of the centre, and the boat-tours offer masses of tourists an opportunity of appreciating the beauty of its architecture from an exclusive viewpoint. But they also represented a possibility of gaining quite a lot of extra space - a possibility that had an especially strong appeal in the days when urban expansion was a top priority, for they were seen as providing a solution to the traffic problems which assumed such gigantic proportions in the 1950s and 1960s. Many canals in Holland were filled in at that time, which meant that irreparable damage was done to many Dutch towns and cities. In Amsterdam the damage was restricted to a number of radial canals - fortunately the unique semi-circular layout of the main canals was not tampered with. House-boats are still tolerated in some of the canals because the authorities are aware of their importance as substitute dwellings in a time of severe housing shortage. But they would like to get rid of them altogether as soon as possible, because they have no conception of how this informal and constantly changing variety contributes to the liveliness of the city - especially where the general appearance of the city is dominated by formal, dignified architecture, as along Amsterdam's canals.

However, when we look at old photographs, we see that the canals presented a much busier and untidier picture in the last century due to the trading business that took place there: the city centre was not only shaped by beautiful architecture, but equally by the lively and colourful bustle of activity around the many boats carrying their cargoes right into the heart of the city.

The cityscape changes fastest of all with the seasons, especially along the canals where the trees create a completely different spatial effect in summer than in winter, when they are bare. Then the different façades are sharply silhouetted against the sky, forming an almost graphic delimitation of the urban space. And finally there is of course the dramatic change of appearance when the canals freeze and the emphasis shifts from the streets lining the canals to the icy centre dotted with skaters. On those relatively rare occasions both the atmosphere and the sense of space changes completely for a while.

219 220
221

MEXCALTITÀN, MEXICO (221-223)

'The desire to create an environment that can be put to various uses can sometimes be stimulated by specific local circumstances. In Mexcaltitàn, a village situated in the San Pedro river, Mexico, the periodical changes in the water level due to the heavy rainfall in late summer transform the street temporarily into canals, so that the whole place undergoes a veritable metamorphosis.

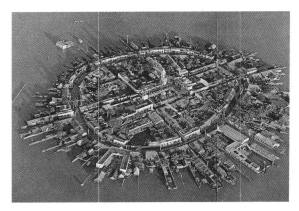

Life in the village is wholly determined by these natural conditions. The streets continue to serve for traffic and transportation equally efficiently, albeit in different 'aggregate' states, with each fully exploiting the specific usage potential'.[4]

222 223
224 225

ESTAGEL, FRANCE (224,225)

'Many rivers flowing into the Mediterranean change considerably in volume over the year, depending on the season. In Estagel near Perpignan it is the Agly river that appears and vanishes depending on the season: either it is non-existent or it rushes past along the age-old river-bed. But even when it is dry the river dominates the small town. During dry periods the river-bed in the town - a cement trench - becomes part of the public space and offers the local children a special playground of their own. A gutter running in the centre of the river-bed

collects the rainwater from the streets: this drain is to the river what the river is to the town, it is a miniature version, both in terms of size and in terms of time, with periods of dryness alternating with the flow of water. To the children it is an enhancement of their playground - to them it is a river in its own right, with all the excitement and sometimes problems that a river brings with it.'[4]

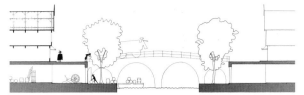

OUDE GRACHT, UTRECHT (226-233)

In Utrecht the natural difference in level between street and canal has yielded an extraordinary and very effective profile. Already in the fourteenth century goods used to be transported in barges over the canals; they were loaded and unloaded on the quay-sides in front of the storage spaces below street level. These storage spaces, or warehouses, continue under the street to form the basement of the shops situated on the street above. The merchandise could thus quite easily be raised or lowered via a simple vertical connection with the quay-side. At one

spot there was a sloping tunnel through which horse-drawn carts could get from the street to the quay and vice versa, for transportation to locations elsewhere in the town.

When the old practice of transportations over water was discontinued, these quays lost their original function, until in recent years they started to serve as terraces for cafes and restaurants located in the former warehouses, the latter having been for the most part sectioned off from the shops above when the transportation of merchandise ceased to go over water, leaving the quay-sides largely unused.

So nowadays the old quays have been put to use again, albeit differently, and when the weather is fine they are once again crowded with people. They are indeed exceptionally well situated, along the canals where shelter from wind and traffic noise is provided by the storey-high quay walls. Also the distance between these walls on either side of the canal, with the quay-sides below street level along the water, is very favourable for a pleasantly proportioned location. The bend in the canal at this point only enhances the space, giving it a pleasing enclosedness without obstructing the view.

Finally (and who could have designed this) there are lovely trees growing on this lower level, which naturally contribute more than anything else to the unique and pleasant atmosphere of this part of the old city centre. Although this profile was thus created for specifically urban purposes, it has now, a century later, been transformed, without any fundamental changes being necessary, into an entirely different kind of place. It is easy to imagine the scene when the water in the canals freezes over, providing a natural skating rink. The quay-sides then become the perfect place to tie on one's skates, while the street above becomes the domain of spectators. This transformation provides yet more proof of just how much this type of urban form can accommodate, in such a way as to be appropriate to each situation as it arises. And although the scale is much larger, the banks of the Seine in Paris offer comparable conditions. The clochards

226ab   227

228

229   230   231

have had to give up their traditional haunts under the bridges: a traffic artery has now claimed this marginal zone by the waterside.

232 233
234
235a
236 237 238

VIADUCT PLACE DE LA BASTILLE - RUE RAMBOUILLET, PARIS (234-243)
The viaduct was built for the railway, as in so many cities where traffic arteries enter an urban agglomeration. The 72 arches were filled with whatever came in handy. The viaduct served as a sort of framework, a string of clearly defined compartments, that could be filled in at will.
The viaduct itself remains largely unchanged, much as it always was and as it can remain - a permanent structure always ready to accommodate new purposes which in their turn add new meanings to the surroundings. It is quite remarkable how little notice the fillings seem to take

of the semi-circular shape of the frame - hardly a convenient shape for buildings and apparently offering no incentive to create a specific counter-form. As if it were the most obvious thing in the world, all the arches were filled in with buildings which were constructed on the same principles as a free-standing house. The viaduct itself did not serve as a starting-point or source of inspiration, but nor was it apparently felt as a hindrance; even the narrow side-streets were able to pursue their course straight through the long stone obstacle, which itself both penetrates and is penetrated by the urban fabric. Now that it is no longer used for trains it has been designated as a promenade, leading to the new opera building on the site of the former Gare de Vincennes. There is a plan to fill in the arches with identical frontages, according to today's civilized and entirely conventional ideas about order. In that case a unique urban monument would have to make way for a standard solution.

239

240 241

235b

242 243

View of viaduct on the rue Rambouillet with former Gare de la Bastille (1859); the new opera now stands here.

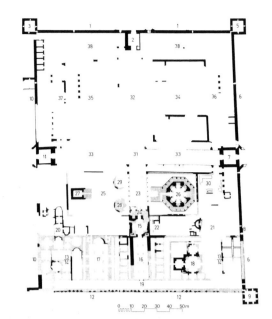

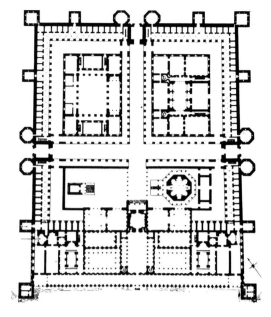

244 245
246
247 248

PALACE OF DIOCLETIAN, SPLIT, YUGOSLAVIA, 4TH CENTURY A.D.
(244-251)

Under the heading 'An emperor's home becomes a town
for 3000 people in Split' the architect Bakema wrote
about the ruins of this Roman palace, which still
constitutes the nucleus of Split today (Forum, 2-1962).
What were once parts of the palace structure now serve
as walls for dwellings. What were once niches are now
rooms, and what were once halls of the palace are now
dwellings, and everywhere you can still see fragments that
recall the original function of the structures. This enormous
building, being wholly absorbed by the surrounding city,
was capable of serving a new and different purpose, with
the city being able to accommodate itself fully to the given
form. What we see here is a metamorphosis - the original
structure is still present inside, but the way the old has
been swallowed up by the new makes one wonder what

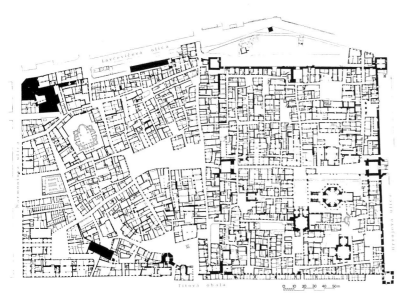

would be left, structurally speaking, if one were to subtract the later fillings. The process is irreversible - the palace is there all right, inside, but it cannot be recalled! Nor is it conceivable that, under different circumstances, a completely different way of adapting to what is left of the original structure will ever be realized; at any rate what is left of the structure does not offer the slightest suggestion of that ever happening.

The example of Split is especially interesting in that it demonstrates the divorcement of form and function so clearly, and it is worth mentioning here because, already in 1962, it was a source of inspiration for our way of thinking about architectural forms such as amphitheatres - although the latter, unlike the palace in Split, not only *permitted* new forms of usage but even *evoked* such new applications by virtue of their specific shape and structure.

249 250
251

THE AMPHITHEATRES OF ARLES AND LUCCA (252-254)

'The amphitheatre of Arles was used as a fortress in the Middle Ages; then it was filled in with buildings and was inhabited as a town until the nineteenth century.
The amphitheatre of Lucca was absorbed by the town and at the same time kept open as a public square. Within the nameless urban fabric the oval space is a landmark, it lends its name and identification to the surroundings.
The two amphitheatres, constructed for the same purpose, assumed different roles under changed circumstances. Each took on the colour of the new environment which

circumstances, without the structure itself essentially changing. Besides, the Arles example - now that this arena has been restored to its original state - shows that this kind of process of transformation is basically reversible. A more convincing instance of 'competence' and 'performance' in architecture is hard to imagine. And the fact that these two amphitheatres are not identical only underscores the polemic quality of the situation: for just as the autonomy of the oval form is emphasized by the process of transformation, so the form as 'archetype' imposes itself almost inescapably.

252

'The arenas of Nîmes and Arles, transformed into secluded little, hamlets, while the remains of the two Gallo-Roman towns were abandoned to the lizards and the snakes- that gives us a good idea of urban deterioration after the fall of Rome. At Nîmes the Wisigoths transformed the arena into a mini-town of two thousand inhabitants, which one entered through four gates situated at the four cardinal points. Churches were constructed inside the arena. The same was true of Arles, the arenas became fortresses.'
(Michel Ragon quoting from Pierre Lavedan, 'Histoire de l'urbanisme, antiquité- moyen Age', Paris 1926)

absorbed it and which was absorbed by it, the environment in its turn also being coloured by the ancient structure in its centre. Not only were they thus taken for granted in their new form as an integral part of the urban fabric, they also provided that urban fabric with an identity. The oval structure and the surroundings proved, in both cases, capable of transforming each other. These ovals represent an archetypal form - in this case that of the enclosed space, an interior, a large room which can serve as work-place, playground, public square and place to live. The original function is forgotten, but the amphi-theatre-shape retains its relevance because it is so sugges-tive as to offer opportunities for constant renewal.' [1]
These amphitheatres succeed in maintaining their identity as enclosed spaces, while their content is subject to change. The same form could therefore temporarily assume different appearances under changing

The foregoing examples, and those that will be given in the following, give rise to a number of conclusions:
• In all these examples the multiple purposes that the original structure allowed for were not deliberately or intentionally built into the structure. It is, rather, their intrinsic 'competence' that enables them to perform different functions under different circumstances, and thus to play a different role within the city as a whole.

• It is certainly not true that there is always one specific form that fits one specific purpose. So there are forms which not only permit various interpretations, but which can actually evoke these interpretations under changing circumstances. So you could say that the variety of solutions must have been contained in the form as inherent propositions.

• In none of these cases does the actual structure change under the influence of its new function - and this is a crucial point: the form is capable of adapting itself to a variety of functions and of assuming a variety of appearances, while remaining essentially the same.

• The degree in which a form accommodates different interpretations passively or evokes those interpretations actively because it is in itself suggestive (as in the case of the arenas) varies from one situation to another.

they may even disappear completely from one day to the next. There is an important distinction therefore between cases in which adjustments or extensions are actually constructed, and cases in which the 'filling' relates exclusively to temporary usage, which are therefore more like 'software'. In the following examples the emphasis is on more temporary adjustments, such as those which daily usage calls for.

Amphitheatre Lucca, Italy

• The main form which we called structure is collective by nature, it is usually controlled by a governing body, and is essentially public. Control over the uses to which it is put ranges from more public to more private, depending on the commercial interests involved.

• Situations which are more or less permanent are usually accompanied by the construction of extensions or further subdivisions - in themselves often whole edifices in their own right. Changes of function can take place in the course of very long periods, of a few years, a season, a week, or they can take place daily.

The shorter the duration of a particular situation the less permanent the nature of the extensions or adjustments will be, and in the case of daily usage

Amphitheatre Arles, France

TEMPLES, BALI (255-259)

Unlike the centralistic emphasis on a single, dominating monument as in the Christian world, Hinduism, as practised on Bali, is characterized by multiple centres of attention, which finds expression in what you might call a decentralization of ceremonial sites. There are thousands of temples spread out all over the island, alone and in groups.

There are multiple levels of attention both in terms of space and in terms of time, depending on the nature of the celebration: the veneration of an ancestor, ceremonies relating to a good harvest and so on. The use of the different temples is bound up with specific occasions, so that not all the temples are used at the same time, but there is always something going on in some of them. The temples, which vary in size from small pieces of furniture to small houses, are sometimes made of stone, but usually they consist of a sort of open stall with a sophisticated wooden construction and thatched roofs on a stone base. They are, essentially, rather like free-standing covered altars in the open air, dotting the landscape. You come across disused temples, of which little more than the skeleton stands: empty stalls one or more of which are then, suddenly, furnished and decorated with beautiful draperies, with objects made of bamboo and palm leaves, and other attributes belonging to specific occasions, and always with offerings. Each individual temple therefore functions as a sort of framework which is elaborated and furnished, whenever necessary, with the proper elements to specify the particular occasion that requires observance. So each temple permits temporary appropriation to a specific end, it is dressed up as it were, to assume a certain role, after which it is allowed to revert to its original, passive state.

255

Of course this is a simplification of the actual situation, because you also find temples that contain several smaller temples, which in turn contain even smaller ones - structures within structures - which might well indicate differences in the relation to a specific ancestor between individuals vis à vis the community.

And as if all this is not enough, long rows of women suddenly appear, coming from all sides and bearing tall multi-coloured burdens on their heads: offerings of rice, coconut and sugar in an incredible variety of shapes and colours. All the offerings are placed in the little temples by way of a finishing - and edible - touch: the most transient and softest component in a sequence of attributes ranging from 'hardware' to 'software'.

256

257 258

259

When the ceremony is over and the gods have received the offerings, the edible offerings are taken home again, where they are consumed, and any leftovers at the temple

are eaten by dogs. This may strike the western, rational mind as somewhat contradictory - after all, you either give food to the gods or you eat it yourself - but in a less literal and perhaps more intelligent sense it is possible to do both: once the religious transaction has been effected the offering is just a tasty tidbit for the people and the dogs. So one and the same object can evidently perform several roles, in this case at different times when, as here, it is given a ritual interpretation on certain occasions only to be divested of that content when the occasion has passed, and thus to return from the extraordinary to the

260 261

ordinary. In Christian churches all the religious appurtenances retain their sacred importance at all times, even when the church is not in use. In the western world it is inconceivable that a house of worship should become a place where children play hide-and-seek, as in Bali where the children regularly turn the temples into their playground. An altar for a climbing-frame - it is hard to imagine. People in the West are perhaps not imaginative enough, and it is not very efficient either, to have to construct climbing-frames as well as altars, as if God would object to children climbing over his altars - no, in this part of the world we want to keep everything neat and tidy and in its proper place, so there must be no confusion concerning meanings.

ROCKEFELLER PLAZA, NEW YORK (260,261)
Rockefeller Plaza, the small sunken public square in the middle of Rockefeller Centre in Manhattan takes on a completely different appearance in summer and in winter. In the winter there are the skaters, and in the summer months the ice makes way for a terrace with plenty of seats among plants and parasols. This clearly defined space offers every opportunity for exploiting the changing circumstances of the different seasons to the full.

COLUMBIA UNIVERSITY, NEW YORK (262)
Monumental flights of steps are a staple feature of buildings which are intended to emanate a sense of importance, and thus to evoke an attendant sense of respect and awe from all who enter. In this case the building is a library, the nerve-centre of a university, a temple where knowledge is stored. And here the awe-inspiring entrance does not in any way invite a casual and spontaneous visit, while anyone who has difficulty

walking is firmly discouraged. So it is by no means a welcoming library!

It is as if anyone wishing to partake of that knowledge must be made to feel that something is expected of him in return. But however imposing the steps were intended to be, the photograph shows that they can be used quite informally, too, rather like a grandstand, if the occasion arises, e.g. when a speech is delivered. So here the architecture proves to function quite differently than expected, and even, as in this case with the students turning their backs to the library, to serve a completely contrary purpose.

On the level of form these steps derive their importance wholly from the uses to which they are put, and that same importance can, under the influence of the specific use that is made of the steps, turn into its opposite, as we see here.

It would not be difficult to cite more examples of how a large-scale form can, quite unintentionally, permit different interpretations, but what we are concerned with here are the potential applications of the established principle. If an architect is capable of fully grasping the implications of the distinction between structure and filling, or in other words between 'competence' and 'performance', he can arrive at solutions with a greater potential value as regards applicability - i.e. with more space for interpretation. And because the time factor is incorporated in his solutions: with more space for time. While on the one hand structure stands for what is collective, the way in which it may be interpreted, on the other hand, represents individual requirements, thus reconciling individual and collective.

262

3 STRUCTURE AS A GENERATIVE SPINE: WARP AND WEFT

Un precident à Alger: le viaduc
port = les Arcades sont habitées!
les camions et les autos passent dessous

Unlike in the previous examples, we are now concerned not in the first place with the different interpretations over time, but with the diversity of individual interpretations which will be able to coincide in time, thereby constituting one whole, thanks to a structure that, as a common denominator so to speak, reconciles the diversity of individual forms of expression.

The ordering mechanism contained in the following examples brings a variety of images to mind. Let us take the image of a fabric such as that constituted by warp and weft. You could say that the warp establishes the basic ordering of the fabric, and in doing so creates the opportunity to achieve the greatest possible variety and colourfulness with the weft.

The warp must first and foremost be strong and of the correct tension, but as regards colour it needs merely to serve as a base. It is the weft that gives colour, pattern and texture to the fabric, depending on the imagination of the weaver. Warp and weft make up an indivisible whole, the one cannot exist without the other, they give each other their purpose.

FORT L'EMPEREUR PROJECT, ALGIERS 1930 / LE CORBUSIER
(263-269)

The idea underlying this elongated megastructure which follows the coastline like a ribbon, is to combine a motorway and living accommodation. Above and

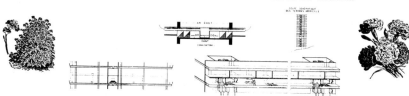

les terrains sont mis en vente, à chaque étage, terrains de 10 m. de façade, de 15 m., de 20 m., de 30 m., avec ou sans jardin.

Ainsi, à Fort-l'Empereur pourront être logés « royalement » 220.000 habitants, au fur et à mesure des besoins, et chaque architecte y fera la villa qu'il lui plaira d'imaginer.

Voici les « terrains artificiels », les cités-jardins en hauteur. Tout y est rassemblé : la vue, l'espace, le soleil, les communications instantanées, verticales et horizontales, les alimentations économes d'eau, de gaz, etc., la voirie parfaite et facile — égouts, poubelles, etc. L'aspect architectural prodigieux : une saisissante apparition ! La diversité la plus totale dans l'unité. Si l'on veut, chaque architecte construira sa villa et qu'importe à l'ensemble, si le style mauresque voisine avec le Louis XVI ou la Renaissance italienne. Le raccord sur le sol accidenté, sans dépense, aisément. Les promenades à pied déambulent au long des accidents violents du sol.

Les autos arrivent, à niveau, sur cette autostrade unique, parfaite, munie dans son dessous, de garages abondants.

On crée d'abord les terrains artificiels : autostrade + planchers des substructures au-dessous. Et l'on met en vente ces terrains pour villas avec jardin et vue illimitée. Puis on continue par des tranches successives de superstructure.

AL 3342

CITÉ JARDIN EN HAUTEUR

VOIRIE DES RUES INTÉRIEURES SUPERPOSÉES.

Existe-t-il, dans une ville du monde, une voirie aussi parfaite que celle-ci ? Aussi économique, visitable ? Toutes les tuyauteries accessibles : la distribution parfaite de l'air exact. La vidange des poubelles.

Quelles économies, quelle réforme au gaspillage insensé des cités-jardins. C'est le béton armé et l'acier qui ont fait le miracle.

le plan de la villa : rez-de-chaussée avec patio et jardin : étage ouvert sur le patio.

un exemple : une toute petite villa sur un terrain de 15×12 m.= 180 m². A vrai dire, le super

Habitants d'Alger, existe-t-il chez vous, un seul appartement dispensant ces joies essentielles ?

des super-luxes sur un paquebot. Mais il y a ici quelque chose de plus piquant. Sur le sol inaccessible de Fort-l'Empereur, on a, dans ce plan, réinstauré les principes fondamentaux du

plan de l'habitation mauresque : le contraste des hauteurs diverses, le patio ouvert sur un jardin clôturé de hauts murs ; la vue sur la mer. Ça c'est du bon régionalisme !

Page 247 'La ville Radieuse', Paris 1933/Le Corbusier

underneath the motorway there are stacked floors constituting artificial building-sites. Dwelling units can be constructed on these sites by individual owners in any style.

You could call this construction of 'sols artificiels' a bearer (Le Corbusier himself used the term superstructure), and it would obviously have to be built in a single operation as part of the motorway, and by the state. The drawing shows that Le Corbusier envisaged, on paper at any rate, the greatest variety imaginable. And certainly in 1930, in the heyday of the Modern Movement and Functionalism in architecture, this was absolutely revolutionary, even if he had somewhat naive notions about traffic, as some later commentators have contended. But it was a most extraordinary vision, which even today, more than fifty years later, inspires more architects than are prepared to admit it!

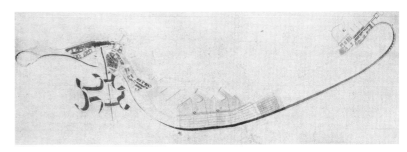

moreover makes the complex as a whole infinitely richer than any one architect, however ingenious, could ever make it.But that is not all - the drawing shows that, with such a structure, the greater the diversity in the parts, the better the quality of the whole! So chaos

265
266
267

Le Corbusier's plan for Algiers is the key to our train of thought, inasmuch as it proposes, explicitly, that the individual occupants are offered the opportunity, by virtue of the strength of the megastructure itself, to create their homes exactly as they themselves wish, or according to the ideas of 'their own' architects. While the collective structure in fact only indicates the spatial limits of each individual dwelling, the dwellings together determine the appearance of the whole.
Such a 'superstructure' creates the conditions, on the collective level, for an exceptional freedom on the part of the individual inhabitants.
The drawing - which is, incidentally, one of the most evocative that Le Corbusier ever made - shows that the most divergent designs and construction methods can coexist harmoniously, and that it is the megastructure that not only makes this diversity possible, but

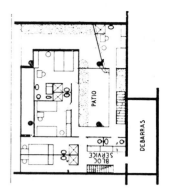

and order do seem to need one another.
The drawing also shows some run-of-the-mill
dwellings, popular housing (!) of the type that always
appears in a system in which the people themselves
have no say in the design and construction of the
houses they live in. In Le Corbusier's drawing these
dwellings do not occupy a prominent position vis à vis
the exuberance around them, and they seem to be no
more than a curious reminder of days gone by. But this
type of mass housing is the reality that we encounter
time and again, and indeed it is one of the most basic
problems that confront us. People today do not seem to
have any idea how to give expression to their own
way of living, while people all over the world have
always made the kind of houses they wanted, just as
they wore the kind of clothes they liked, used their
own tools and ate their own kind of food.
So there is no reason to assume that the capacity to
express oneself in a personal way in form is essentially any different from the capacity to express oneself
personally in language. And if we do not seem to be
capable of this any more, then we may reasonably
assume that the impotence of architecture today is
caused by a very serious disruption of social relations.
Mass housing, which is superficially in accordance with
our industrial circumstances, derives its dominant
position from the mechanism of mono-cultural
behaviour which governs our society. The least an
architect can do in a situation like this is to provide the
outlines of images that will show ways of rousing the
people from this condition of numbness.
As close as Le Corbusier's proposal (1932) brings us to
an apparently obvious solution, so far are we removed
from it today. Even the smallest steps in that direction
soon prove to conflict fundamentally with the
consequences of our institutionalized centralized
society, and we do not get much nearer to the
realization of our plans. But those few times that we
do succeed at least give us an opportunity of
demonstrating the principle, albeit in a more
theoretical than practical way.

'THE BEARERS AND THE PEOPLE; THE END OF MASS HOUSING',
1961 / N.J. HABRAKEN
I would like to mention Habraken's contribution in this
context, which in a sense fits in with what Le Corbusier
had in mind when he made his plan for Algiers. Habraken
tried, in theory at least, to arrive at a basis on which,
using the industrial apparatus that is at our disposal,
people can be offered much more freedom in their choice
of how they want to live. The bearers, specially designed
skeletal units provided by the state complete with the
basic technical necessities, can serve as construction sites
on which people can build prefabricated houses or part of
houses which are marketed by any number of firms.
Since the inhabitant can pick the type of house that he
likes out of a range of possibilities, and since he can have
certain adjustments made to suit his taste, he is thus again
actively involved in the process, in the result of which he
currently has no say.
But problems immediately arise because here too the
houses soon become wholly commercialized, and
therefore subject to the vicissitudes of competition and
marketing mechanisms. And that means that they will be
attuned to the lowest common denominator - that of
mediocrity - and so we are right back where we started.
What makes the proposal interesting is the attempt to
create the conditions for a more sensible and efficacious
exploitation of the industrial potential that our society has
so much of. Every one of us asks himself from time to time
why houses cannot be produced like cars, and, from a
technological viewpoint, it is very hard to understand why
we all have such a problem with houses.
The answer is less simple that the question, but one thing
is clear: it is especially the problem of siting with its
infinite diversity of requirements and rules that conflict
with all repetition, which is the mainstay of modern
technology. If only you could divorce the house itself as a
problem from that of the 'building site', which the state
could provide as a sophisticated urban framework, then in
theory at least one of the twentieth century's dreams could
come true. But the very few attempts that have been made
to realize that dream have not succeeded in producing a

268 269

fraction of the poetic image that Le Corbusier conjured up for us more than fifty years ago.

HOUSEBOATS PROJECT (270-273)

Houseboats, usually moored close to each other in clusters at the order of the authorities, are in Holland the most conspicuous example of (admittedly permanent) accommodation in which the inhabitants still have a large say and this has resulted, especially in terms of external appearance, in a richly diversified situation.

This freedom of expression is undoubtedly due to the absence of a traditional, official form and appearance of houseboats. From the outset the nature of this phenomenon was established by home-made solutions to the housing problem.

That this did not really lead to chaotic situations and the general untidiness that authorities are so afraid of is, no doubt, because the overall shape and size of houseboats is based on the barges on top of which they are built, and which do not vary much. Besides, they are all moored lengthwise to a quay-side, from which they get their water, gas and electricity. So these houseboats represent free and personal interpretations of essentially standard elements which are connected with the public amenities at permanent moorings.

In places where conglomerations of houseboats constitute entire floating neighbourhoods, usually on the outskirts of the cities, jetties have often been built by way of public facility: a minimal spine which provides basic necessities such as access and energy. It is this 'public spine' that aligns the diversity, so to speak, and thus introduces a certain order.

You could imagine planning floating residential neighbourhoods in areas with a lot of water, even entire cities on the water, with a network of boardwalks instead

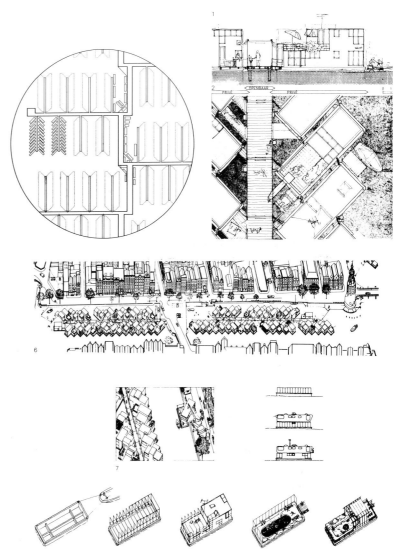

of streets providing the infrastructure. The dwelling units in such a settlement on the water would then be far more varied in appearance than would ever be possible in our ordinary towns and cities on land. And what a sense of freedom, to know that you can now and then move your houseboat to a different spot, for instance when you want to be in a specific neighbourhood for one reason or another. (This idea arose in connection with a plan for urban renewal in the centre of Amsterdam in 1970, so that people who had to vacate their homes temporarily for renovation could move to a houseboat in a canal nearby and therefore not have to leave their familiar environment against their will.)

271 272
273

270

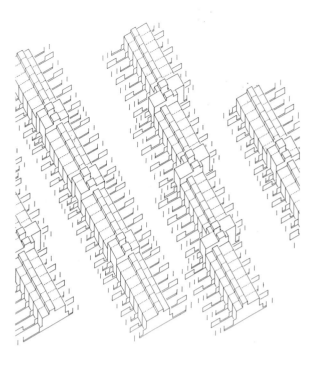

DEVENTER-STEENBRUGGE HOUSING PROJECT (274)

274ab

Only an open grid has been designed, no more than a street pattern and the basic parcelling. The houses border, essentially, on two streets, and can therefore have two front doors: the danger of excessive social control is thus avoided (should it have arisen again through the emphasis on community spirit).

So the expectation is that the different street, each derive their own specific character from the inhabitants and from their activities, so that a wide variety of solutions will manifest themselves within a pattern of identically laid-out streets.

Front and back of the parcel are made suitable for construction, by the inhabitants themselves, of extensions to the house such as a garage, shed, workspace, an extra room, a garden room, or a small shop. To make this easier low walls are erected at either end on the borderline between the parcels, as an encouragement and reminder to the inhabitants of what they can undertake themselves.

The street space is constituted by the whole to which each inhabitant makes his or her contribution: the space that the inhabitants leave and make for each other. In the street the mutual dependency that already governed the delimitation of the private areas becomes the prime factor, and indeed it should be possible for the inhabitants themselves to take any decisions that concern them collectively as inhabitants of the same street. [4]

DE SCHALM, PROJECT FOR A NEIGHBOURHOOD CENTRE (275-277)

Since the interaction between people manifests itself in the street, one can conceive of the neighbourhood centre as a street capable of accommodating a variety of potential accretions, depending on the specific needs that arise and on the available resources. The neighbourhood centre should be planned in such a way that it can evolve over the years, by virtue of its adaptability to specific needs; in other words it should always be possible to add new elements and to alter or even demolish them in accordance with changing needs.

We therefore started out from what one might call a spine, a street with a transparent roof and at right angles to a number of walls marking off intermedi-ate zones between the central street and future accretions. However chaotic the complex of components may be, the spinal street must transform the whole into a permanently ordered chaos. If

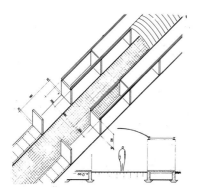
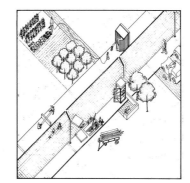
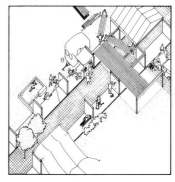

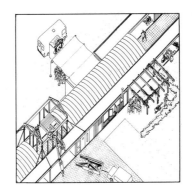
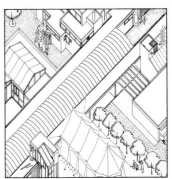

space is required for a special occasion (i.e. temporarily) such as celebrations, fairs, exhibitions, it is often much better to improvise with installations such as marquees, shelters, hangars, stalls and the like. These offer many more possibilities than permanent structures, which tend to be either just too small or far too big, and which eliminate the element of surprise. For more permanent accommodati-on use can be made of prefabricated constructions readily available on the market, such as those for building-site sheds, offices or hangars. The point is then for the inhabitants to create their environment themselves, and in this process architects cannot do otherwise than to hand the inhabitants the appropriate tools. This project, a typical product of the early seventies, raises quite a few questions now that the result has turned out to be not completely satisfactory. It is evident that the users were unable to live up to what we had expected of them. They proved unable to do very much more than order complete prefabricated building components, have them put up and do some painting. The 'light-street' has developed into a shapeless mass. Apparently the street with walls as a formal motif was not strong enough to withstand the impact of the cross-structures (the 'weft'), let alone to generate them as was originally intended.

Although this project certainly combined a large variety of elements and may well in many respects be termed a success from the viewpoint of a group venture in the neigh-bourhood itself, this is by no means manifest at the level of formal unity. What individuals achieve in their private

surroundings is not necessarily achieved by a group in a communal space. The project is an illustration of what happens, if too much freedom is given to the user. The result is disappointing compared with the greater spatial possibilities that an architect might have offered them.

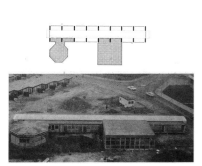

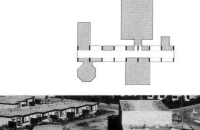
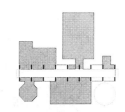

PROJECT FOR A PEDESTRIAN UNDERPASS (278-281)

An underpass running beneath a wide traffic artery
constituted an important part of the sunken pedestrian
network which was to link the city-centre with the railway
station.

This, at any rate, was what the Apeldoorn planner had in
mind at the time when the Centraal Beheer building was
being designed, and there was every reason then to
connect this future pedestrian route to the building. The
idea arose to make the underpass extra wide, so that it
could be used for more than just pedestrian traffic. In this
way it would be possible not only to avoid the desolation
which so often characterizes such tunnels, but moreover
this construction, as a public amenity, could provide
accommodation for institutions requiring space but unable
to pay commercial rents, such as youth activity centres,
rehearsal space for theatre groups, etc., as well as for
marginal selling. But why not also consider the possibility
of a covered market!

The experience with covered public spaces shows that this
idea is not realistic, and like the urban plan, it hinges on
overestimation of what is feasible.

In sum the plan amounted to the following: rather than

using the wide spans that are commonly featured in
underpasses with a view to restricting the number of
necessary points of support, a large number of columns
were to be used - relatively large columns, so that they
might serve, without further adjustment, as the
demarcation of more or less enclosed spatial units,
corners, niches, in short of such compartmentalization as
might be required. (Each column actually consists of two
separate smaller columns enclosed by a wall, which in
turn can accommodate additional niches or display
windows). The idea was to demonstrate that by adopting
the straightforward disposition of massive 'adhesive'
columns, aligned with the walking direction, the
suggestion would emanate from them that they should be
put to use - in other words, that the construction material
should be ordered in such a way as to ensure a maximum
of competence.

278 279 280

281abc

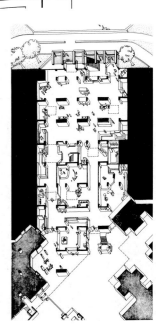

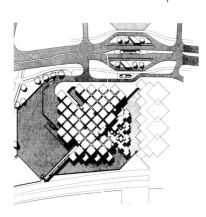

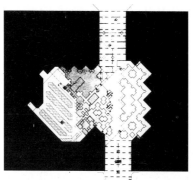

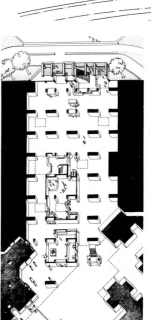

HOUSING, WESTBROEK (282-289)

The structural design of this residential neighbourhood, small in scale and only partly built as yet, is not based on principles of construction but on the nature of the actual building site. Centuries ago the area was artificially divided by a parcelling system consisting of long parallel ditches - a traditional characteristic of the local landscape, which was to be preserved at all costs.

It is common practice in the Netherlands to prepare unsuitable construction sites for building by first depositing a bed of sand several metres thick to serve as the foundation for roads, drains, etc.; this naturally erases every trace of the underlying landscape, thereby providing a clean slate, upon which an entirely abstracted plan can be realized regardless of the nature of the terrain. But in this case, grateful use was made of the 'natural' articulation of the site upon which to base the urban plan.

The main outline of the plan was to build on the narrow strips between the ditches, and because the strips were not wide enough to accommodate a street lined on both sides with dwellings and gardens, the buildings were slotted together, which yielded a profile of very narrow streets threading partially overlapping structures.

Thanks to this solution it was possible to keep the space required for the sand foundation and the infrastructure of streets and drains down to the barest minimun, i.e. as far removed as possible from the ditches (or rather little canals) in order to prevent transgression of the banks due

to lateral pressure. This specific layout was thus wholly engendered by the restrictions and possibilities of the original site.

The ditches or little canals were thus retained in the plan; the banks were reinforced according to varying methods, and where they mark the end of private gardens they have taken on a variegated appearance under the influence of their new function. Not only did the existing articulation and parcelling of the landscape yield a highly specific layout in this case, the resulting architecture in turn gave the ditches a new look.

Thus the basic structure played a crucial role in the disposition of the buildings, and vice versa: basic structure and buildings reciprocate on the level of form.

In retrospect, one could argue that the plan as it was realized does not sufficiently manifest the underlying urbanistic intentions. The main reason for this is apart

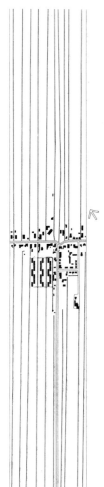

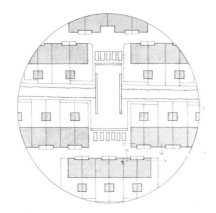

284 285
286
287
288
289

instable soil exchanged with sand-layer | poles | solid soil

typical Dutch solution

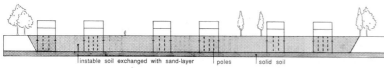

sand-layer | instabel soil | solid soil | original ditches | poles

solution using natural articulation in Westbroek

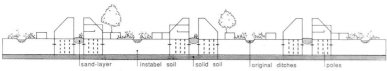

from the fact that the plan has not reached completion, that it was not carried out by more than one architect. The scale of the project was too small to permit engaging more architects, and unfortunately the truly generative potential of the basic motif - which is at least manifest in the ditch embankments - was thus not fully exploited with regard to the buildings themselves.

During the 1960s a number of plans were drawn up, notably in the circles of Team X, in which the principle of distinction between structure and complement was already emphatically included. These plans, in which the rigidity of exclusive functions and the ensuing disintegration has successfully been eliminated, can indeed be seen as anticipating and inspiring what we might now call structuralism in architecture.

FREE UNIVERSITY, BERLIN, 1963 / CANDILIS, JOSIC & WOODS (290-294)

This project, in the original version, proposed a formula for the way a modern university could be spatially organized as a network of interrelationships and opportunities for communication. Instead of starting out from the usual division into faculties, each as a stronghold in its own building, with its own library etc., the point of departure in this building was a single continuous structure functioning like a roofed academic agglomeration, in which all the component parts could be positioned in the most logical relation vis à vis each other. And because ideas change over time also the interrelationships will change, and with them the different components; it was therefore proposed to create spaces that can be erected or dismantled within a fixed and permanent network of interior streets.

This is explained in the following statements by Shadrach Woods:
'a)
Our intention in this plan, is to choose a minimum organization which provides maximum opportunities for the kind of contact, exchange and feed-back that is the real raison d'être of the university, without compromising the tranquility of individual work.
b)
We were convinced that it was necessary to go beyond the analytic study of different faculties or activities in different buildings; we imagined a synthesis of functions and departments where all disciplines could be associated and where the psychological and administrative barriers which separate one from the other would not be reinforced through architectural articulation or the fragmentary identification of the parts at the expense of the whole.

c)
The web of primary and secondary circulation and servicing retains the possibility of modification so that it can be used efficiently. In the first planning stage it exists only as an approximate network of rights-of-way. It is built only as and when it is required to provide circulation and service. It is not a megastructure but rather a minimum structuring organization. This organization keeps its potential for growth and change, within the limits of the technological and economic milieu.

d)
No one of the stems has been given greater importance than the others, either in dimension or through the intensity of activities along it. It is inherent in this plan that it should begin by being non-centric through use. The arbitrary decision of an architect as to the nature and location of 'centres'was replaced by the real choice of the people who use the system'.

(Shadrach Woods, *World Architecture*, London 1965, pp. 113-114)

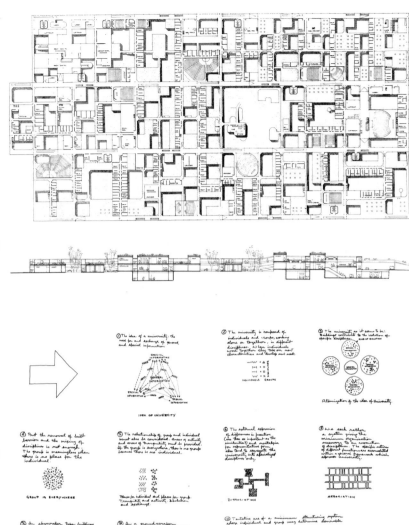

Woods was certainly addicted to 'change and growth', to the idea that change and growth (and apparently never diminution, by the way) should be treated as the most important constants - and this is the exact reverse of what we are advocating - but he has received his due in that the Free University, as it was eventually built, turned out to be an ordinary rigid structure after all.

But there is still every reason to at least take into consideration the still relevant and hence undeniably important basic idea of a minimal ordering, in this case a spatial organization necessary for optimal interchange which, on principle, generates freedom of choice in the way the basic structure is to be filled in.

Explanation with diagrams by S. Woods

290
291
292 293
294

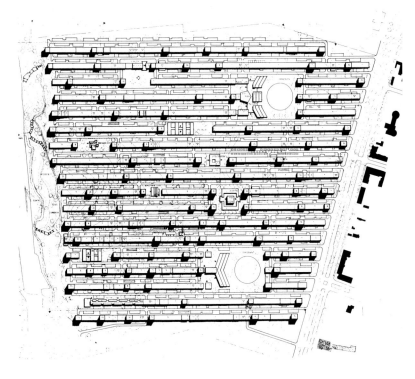

not the form of the buildings and so on. In this way a variety of differentiated dwelling forms and street spaces could arise.

The specific functions of certain areas might well change in the future, necessitating certain adjustments which, however, need not spoil the unity or organization of the whole. After all there are, scattered throughout the plan, pedestrian bridges over the motorway as well as covered cross-connections for both pedestrians and cars (depending on the specific demands of different locations).

The built-up area as a whole (consisting of dwelling structures and street structures etc.) could be viewed as a great container in which the entire age-old gamut of urban existence can be permitted to take its familiar, lively course.

Serious attempts were made to give the motorcar a fitting role, instead of starting out from what is best for the vehicle. Through-traffic has been eliminated from the area, which has already done a lot to simplify the problem. The inhabitants of this place will at last be able to walk, play, drive and park wherever they like, and they will always know where they belong.' (Stefan Wewerka, 1964)

PROJECT FOR A RESIDENTIAL AREA, BERLIN 1965 / S. WEWERKA (295-298)

'The street can be regarded as more or less the oldest element of urban planning. The street had always been the 'living room' of the people. The idea of putting the familiar urban space to use again resulted in this design. The public space must once more become the setting, with an improved spatial organization, forall the activities it has been used for since time immemorial.

Unlike the so-called building plan, the proposed zoning scheme indicates only destinations and accessibilities, but

295
296
297 298

'This project is, in essence, simply an intensive kind of plotting of the building site by means of wall-like building blocks, a grid that must still be filled in within a range of possibilities defined by certain 'rules of the game'.

Openings can be made in the walls, they can be interrupted altogether to create public spaces or squares, the heights of the blocks can vary, pedestrian overpasses can be made to link the blocks together, and so forth. On confrontation with this grid a world of possibilities opens up before the architect's eyes, in other words the grid is capable of generating or even of provoking solutions.

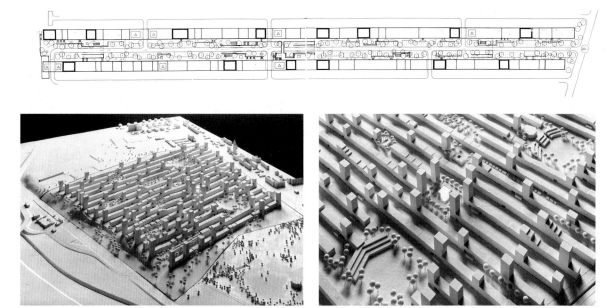

Watts Towers,
Los Angeles
1921-54/S. Rodia

The constraints of working with the proposed theme evidently do not have a restricting effect but, as catalyzing agents, actually have a stimulating effect. So the constraints of the theme in fact result in more freedom (is it a paradox that freedom and restraint generate each other?).

Different designers working independently can use the grid as a 'master plan', which they can complement with their own specific solutions. In the same way a great variety of programmes can be implemented. Within the layout, the components can develop according to their own criteria. The plan as such permits such a variety of interpretations that, regardless of what is substituted and by whom, the complex as a whole will always have a certain order.

The essence is that the grid can be interpreted on all levels - it merely provides the objective pattern, the underlying current as it were, the proto-form, which acquires its true identity by virtue of those very interpretations that are given to it, notably by the programmes that are filled in and the specific way in which that is done. Whatever is filled in, it will always be directed ordered, that is to say not ordered in the sense of 'subservience' but rather in the sense of 'inclination'. The grid functions as a generative framework which contains within it the basic inclination that it transmitted to each solution. And because the grid vests the individual components with the common inclination, not only will the parts determine the identity of the whole, but conversely the whole will contribute to the identity of the parts. The identity of the parts and of the whole will be reciprocally generative.' [3]

Apart from the exceptional quality of the plans of Woods and Wewerka as ideas, what we can learn in particular from them is that we should not concentrate our attention to the exclusion of all else on change as such, but on the structure which, in its constancy, is capable of absorbing change.

In the example given above, the image of warp and weft, the collective structure is therefore the warp, into which individual interpretations are woven as the weft. It is the collective structure, in itself meaning

299 300
301

Le Palais Idéal,
1879-1912/
Facteur Cheval

little or nothing that evoked the individual interpretations, which would not have arisen if the context had not been there. Moreover it is the structure that indicates the coherence without which there would only be an overwhelming mass of expressions - which we call chaos.

The awareness of the repressive effects of the equating of dwelling units in apartment buildings as large-scale storage systems reached a peak in the sixties. The consequence was a radical repudiation of everything that merely referred to systems and order imposed from above. At the same time much emphasis was placed on the wealth that is the product of individual expression. Think of Sam Rodia's 'Watts Towers', or the postman Cheval's 'Palais Idéal', and all the fantastic architecture that people driven by an extreme commitment succeeded in creating with their bare hands! And yet the ideal of the victory of individual creativity and dedication over everything that is imposed by the powers that be is an oversimplification.

Just as language is necessary to be able to express ourselves collectively in terms of structure, so a collective formal structure is necessary to be able to express oneself spatially in one's environment.

If there is anything that comes to the fore out of all these examples it is surely the paradox that the restriction of a structuring principle (warp, spine, grid) apparently results not in a diminution but in an expansion of the possibilities of adaptation and therefore of the individual possibilities of expression. *The correct structural theme does not restrict freedom but is actually conducive to freedom!*
So the way the structure is filled in is no more subservient to the structure than the other way round

I am still thinking in terms of warp and weft: the warp may well serve to keep the whole fabric together, but the appearance of the end-product is still determined by the weft.

But not only are structure and infill equivalent, they are also reciprocal, and so here the warp and weft idea no longer applies - in the same way that speech also makes language and not only the reverse, they therefore generate each other, and the better the quality of each, the less important the distinction between the two categories.

VILLA SAVOYE, POISSY 1929-32 / LE CORBUSIER (302-305)
It is difficult to find a better example of a 'plan libre' than Le Corbusier's Villa Savoye in Poissy: 'Les Heures Claires'.
The 'plan libre' demonstrates a consistent exploitation of the new possibilities offered by the application of the concrete frame.
Characteristic of these early examples of free plans were, besides the free-standing columns, the often curved walls which almost ostentatiously proclaimed their liberation from a load-bearing function. When confronted with such a concrete framework you inevitably expect the columns to be dispersed according to some regular arrangement governed by constructive criteria, and at first sight you are inclined to think that they are arranged as indicated in fig.a, but this is not the case at all.
It is possible that Le Corbusier did indeed start out from such a regular system, but that in the process of his design he must have felt the urge not only to adapt the walls to the positions of the columns, but conversely also to shift the columns vis à vis the walls, in order thus to obtain the correct configuration. By virtue of the

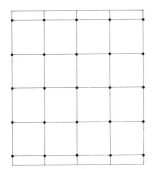 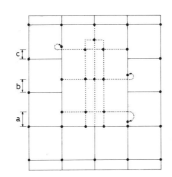 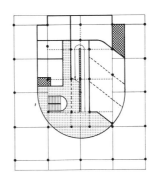 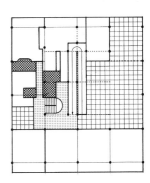

conditions that the walls and columns offer, both systems allow room for each other, and so they create the conditions of freedom *in each other*. The building, like a white machine, a spaceship from another planet landed in the midst of nature, represents like no other the mechanism of twentieth-century architecture.

303
304
305

4 GRIDIRON

Plan, Timgad, Algeria

The principle of minimal ordering of the city by a grid such as the gridiron has been known ever since town planning was invented. In towns that did not evolve thanks to a succession of events in a gradual process of growth, but developed according to a preconceived, fixed plan, the need was felt time and again, whenever the local circumstances did not automatically provide self-evident incentive for some kind of ordering, for something in the way of a grid: a 'blueprint' for what was to be done next. Whatever the primary point of departure in each specific case, there are variations on the same theme to be found throughout history which guarantee in a single formula the conditions of land distribution, also on a larger scale or in a longer term, and the accessibility of each plot of land. The starting-point is nearly always rectangular or square plots: streets enclosing blocks whose dimensions correspond with the construction method which is envisaged, although they could in principle be filled in a variety of ways, the nature of the filling depending on the nature of the period in which it is required.

306
307 308

ENSANCHE, BARCELONA 1859 / I. CERDÁ (307-310)

Ildefonso Cerdá's plan for Barcelona in the second half of the neneteenth century was aimed at ensuring a higher quality than that offered by a primary ordering of streets and blocks within which one could do pretty much as one pleased. The size of the squares was established by him in relation to certain heights of construction in order thus to guarantee adequate living conditions everywhere. He also proposed that part of the blocks should be kept free from buildings.

Nothing came of this in the plan as it was realized because, as is so often the case, the exigencies of living conditions were no match for the far greater power of the landowners and exploiters. Cerdá's proposal for a building principle consisting of strips that could alternate in direction per block, simple as it may seem, created virtually inexhaustible possibilities for variation, which would lead to an incredibly rich pattern of urban space. And this not only applies to the volumes on the abstract level, there is also the alternation with greenery which in itself constitutes an organizing factor in defining and varying the space. And we have not even referred to the further elaboration of the blocks by different architects,

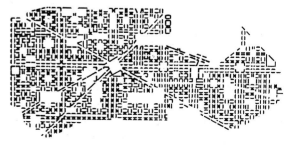

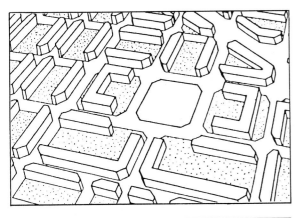

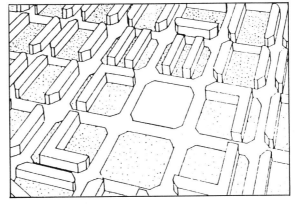

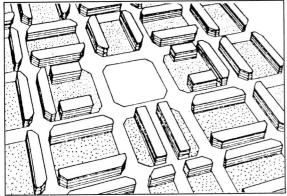

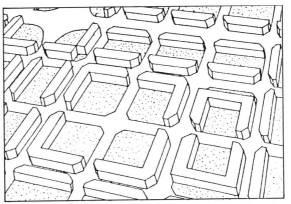

309abcde
310

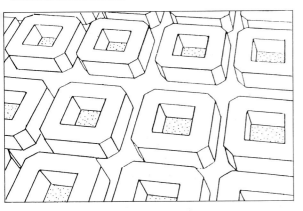

each with his own signature, which would automatically ensure that no two places within this lucid, coherent system would be identical.

The most ingenious aspect of this plan is that the corners are always well-defined, and that these 'cornerstone' buildings consistently face the intersecting streets with a diagonal façade. The four diagonals widen each intersection to form a small square, which thus provide a welcome relief from the monotony of the long streets. Even in the form in which this plan was ultimately realized, with closed block siting and much taller buildings than originally intended, the effect of this corner arrangement on the layout as a whole is still noticeable, suggestive as it was for architects - and not least for Gaudi - to depart from the rigidity of the most obvious solutions.

Casa Milà, Barcelona 1906-10/A. Gaudí

Manhattan, New York (311-314)

In the rapidly developed large American cities we find the gridiron applied in its most elementary form and with the most characteristic results. It is hard to imagine a better way to tame the wild collection of architectural forms ranging from flat structures to skyscrapers - which is almost impossible to curb in this world of inexorable free enterprise.

Manhattan is undeniably the most exciting example of all. Not only does one see the most fascinating range of architectural solutions pass before one's eyes like a greatly varied landscape, but due to the curiously elongated shape of the peninsula one is constantly aware of two contradictory features: on the one hand the wide streets along the longitudinal axis which are so long that you can see the vanishing point on the horizon, and on the other, the narrower lateral streets covering the relatively short distance from one end by the water to the other. While one experiences the vastness of the city in Manhattan, each side-street still affords a view of the water beyond. So in this case the grid contributes in a very special way to the way the urban space is experienced.

One of the first things to strike the visitor to Manhattan is the cold-blooded consistency with which the grid has been applied, until it simply cannot be continued any further, so that the somewhat frayed edges not only appear to be random but also to some extent insensitive. But remarkably enough it is also in those places that the most interesting solutions were devised. One would expect, within such a severe rectangular system, that the extremities would be allowed to terminate in a way befitting the possibilities offered by the grid.

But, as so often happens, it is the confrontation between one principle and another that reveals the nature of each. This is most evident perhaps where the regular longitudinal pattern is cut across by Broadway, the old country road which was left virtually unchanged as if it were inherent in the landscape. Broadway was incorporated into the grid as an inevitable given factor, and wherever it meets the grid it disrupts it, thereby challenging architects to find an imaginative solution to the irregularity. One celebrated example of such a solution is the Flat-Iron building on Madison Square. It is in these places that the nature of the grid manifests itself most convincingly.

The biggest misconception regarding the gridiron system is that it must inevitably lead to monotony, and that its effect is repressive. Those dangers do admittedly exist, but here are enough great examples to prove that, in a gigantic expanse of buildings, the negative aspects actually recede into the background. Whether the ordering of the gridiron will indeed expand the possibilities of variation instead of reducing them depends first and foremost on whether the proper balance has been found between regulations and freedom of choice.

311 312

The grid is like a hand operating on extremely simple principles - it admittedly sets down the overall rules, but is all the more flexible when it comes to the detailing of each site. As an objective basis it plots the layout of the urban space, and this layout brings the inevitably chaotic effect of myriad separate decisions down to acceptable propositions. In its simplicity the grid is a more effective means of obtaining some form of regulation than many a finer-meshed system of rules which, although ostensibly more flexible and open, tend to suffocate the imaginative spirit. As far as its economy of means is concerned it is very like a chessboard - and who can think of a wider range of possibilities arising from such simple and straightforward rules than that of a chessplayer?

313
314

5 BUILDING ORDER

In simple terms, you could say that building order is the unity that arises in a building when the parts taken together determine the whole, and conversely, when the separate parts derive from that whole in an equally logical way. The unity resulting from design that consistently employs this reciprocity - parts *determining* the whole and *determined* by it - may in a sense be regarded as a structure. The material (the information) is deliberately chosen, adapted to suit the requirements of the task in question, and, in principle, the solutions of the various design situations (i.e. how the building is interrelated from place to place) are permutations of or at least directly derived from one another. As a result there will be a distinct, one could say family, relationship between the various parts. Following this train of thought, one sees that there is an obvious comparison with that outstanding example of structure: language.

315 316

Each sentence derives its meaning from the words of which it is composed, while at the same time each word derives its meaning from the sentence as a whole.

Of course, every well-designed building has a consistent idea with a distinct thematic unity behind it, a unity of vocabulary, material, and building method. But here the essential thing is design based on a consistent strategy. Starting out from the components you have to go through the whole building again and again to check whether all the extremities can be brought together under the denominator of a common theme (hence putting the hypothesis to the test). That exploration in turn leads to adjustment of the hypothesis or theme.

This working method implies, in fact, filling in one's own design structure, as it were and, by feeding back the result, one eventually arrives at an ordering in which the conditions for all conceivable infills are already present - in other words, a structure which may be said to be programmed to accommodate all expected infills. In this way it is possible to aim consciously at a unity of spatiality, components, materials and colours, in such a way that a maximum of variety of uses can be accommodated.

This thought process, inspired by structuralism, attempts to square accounts with the somewhat contradictory functionalistic striving to find a specific form and a specific spatial organization for each function.

Design that seeks the largest common denominator, the 'set' of all the requirements under discussion in a particular task (i.e. the programme in its widest sense), employs a different strategy and demands a fundamentally different outlook from the architect.

ORPHANAGE, AMSTERDAM 1955-60 / A. VAN EYCK (315-321)
'The first executed structuring with a building order, in the sense of a unity in which parts and whole determine each other reciprocally, is the orphanage of Aldo van Eyck. The organization of this building, with its 'streets' and 'squares' and independent building units, is like a small self-contained city. It evokes these associations even if one is not familiar with Van Eyck's exhortation 'Make of each a place, a bunch of places of each house and each city, for a house is a tiny city, a city a huge house'. This identification with a 'small city' is perhaps in itself the most creative step, and a highly significant breakthrough. In the design phase, once this 'connection' has been made, a train of further associations is released, adding a new dimension to the quality of the communal, 'public', places. Corridors become 'streets', interior lighting becomes 'street lighting' and so on. Although a building can never be a city nor anything between the two, it can still become city-like and thus become a better house. This reciprocal house-city image leads to a consistent articulation of large and small both inside and outside in sequences of contingent units which interlock without

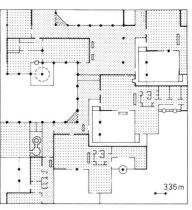

336 m

stress or effort. When this articulation is carried through to the smallest dimension, not only buildings and cities acquire reciprocal meaning, but buildings and furniture also, because large scale pieces of 'built' furniture are like small houses in which one feels yet more interiorized than in a large room. Thus each part is given the dimension which suits its purpose best, i.e. the right size through which it comes into its own.

All this has become common knowledge by now, so I wonder if there is anybody who believes not to have been influenced by it. But what I always found most amazing is that no matter how absorbing the elaboration down to the smallest part may be, the essence of the larger whole remains as powerful as ever. The whole radiates the calm of an equilibrium which encompasses an extraordinary intricacy of form and space in one single image. It seems to me that the secret lies in the inexorable unity of material, form, scale and construction combined in a building order of such clarity that I have always associated it more with classical order than with the casbah. (I know, Aldo wants both: clarity, but labyrinthian, and casbah, but organized. Neither one nor the other, but both at once, which calls for a more inclusive mechanism. By now we should be in a position to achieve this, with all the means at our disposal in the twentieth century.)

Perhaps the lintels have something to do with it also, marked as they are by the horizontal openings placed in such a way as to give the impression of a widening of the columns at the top, capital-like. The continuous lintel zone forms a horizon throughout the entire building, both inside and outside.

What thus became clear to me was that the way a landscape is set free by its horizon is akin to the way the cohesive potential of a building order can give a building a horizon from which - strange paradox - it likewise draws its freedom.

It is the dome-like roof units, the round columns and above all the lintel chain which make the penetrability of the building's perimeter from both outside and inside reciprocally possible. They invite, as it were, a play of walls around them, letting outdoor areas in and interior areas out. Duiker's open air school comes to mind. There the glass skin around the class-room's outer edge, by turning inwards away from it, leaves space for the ample loggias (outdoor class-rooms), whilst the concrete frame continues to allow you to 'read' the entire building mass. Through cantilevering, the way only Duiker knew how, the corners are rendered even lighter and more transparent.
In the Orphanage the outer skin also turns inwards to form either porch, loggia or veranda within the periphery, but the opposite occurs as well: the interior breaks out in

317 318 319
320 321

three places, doing away with the internal corners which otherwise would have constricted both movement and view of these particular places. Solutions of this kind are certainly astonishing.

My very first cursory confrontation with the Orphanage, still under construction at the time, was enough to convince me that this wonderful new building was going to be of an entirely new kind, based on a different mechanism and heralding another kind of architecture'.[8]

LINMIJ (322-331)

The workspace that was constructed on the roof of a laundering factory dating from the beginning of this century was intended as the first step in the plans to extend the premises. The expectation was at that time that successive extensions would become necessary as the different departments expanded:

1.

the impossibility of predicting which departments would require expansion at which times;

2.

the nature and investment potential of the company permitted only a limited number of building units to be

realized simultaneously;

3.

the quality of the existing premises was good enough to warrant preservation and, although somewhat gloomy and inefficiently laid out, the building would still be serviceable after incidental alterations.

In order to channel the expected growth in the future and to guard against the eventual emergence of a haphazard patchwork of extensions, it was decided to design building units based on a number of interrelated motifs. In this way it would be possible to use different combinations to create a variety of larger spaces. The fundamental principles for the design were as follows:

a.

to accommodate the constant changes within the business, each building unit had to meet a wide range of industrial requirements - i.e. it should not be too strictly attuned to a specific programme, but flexible enough to accommodate varying functions without adjustment to the unit itself being necessary;

b.

the premises should be complete and whole after each extension, regardless of the subsequent stage in construction; each new addition should therefore constitute a finished whole.

The building unit should therefore have an identity of its own strong enough to be capable of asserting itself regardless of the specific milieu and moreover to contribute to the identity of the larger whole of which it is a constituent. The rather demonstrative use of prefabricated components is in this case not a consequence of the need for repetition but actually - and this seems paradoxical - the consequence of the desire to individualize each component. The components must be autonomous in order to serve multiple functions, while the form must be chosen in such a way that the different

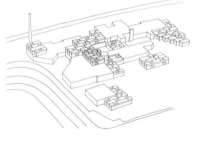

322ab
323

building units are constantly attuned to one another. The original premises were so constructed as to allow for another floor to be added on top, and were therefore sturdy enough to serve as the base for the step-by-step extensions that would eventually cover this artificial rock-formation. The new structures enhance the colour of the old, while conversely the old contributes to the creation and formation of the new. Old and new retain their own identity while confirming each other's.

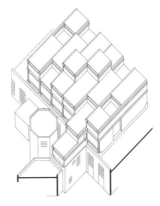

325

327

326   328

329 330 331

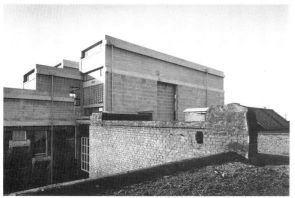

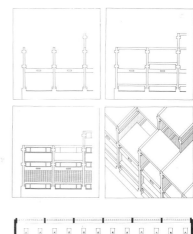

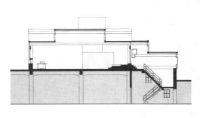

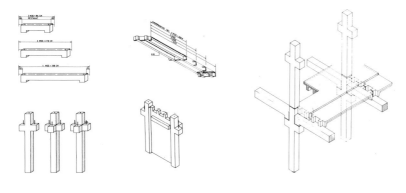

332

333 334

335

DE DRIE HOVEN, HOME FOR THE ELDERLY (332-341)
Because this complex for elderly and disabled people
consists of a combination of a nursing home section, a
section where some care is provided, and a section with
independent dwellings and central amenities, and
because different ministries each with their own rules and
regulations have responsibility for the various sections, the
overall design had to accommodate a considerable
diversity of dimensions as far as the maximum and
minimum heights and widths of corridors, rooms and
storeys were concerned. And because the combination of

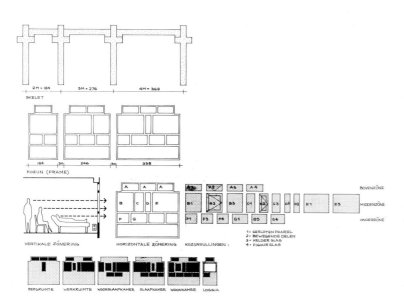

these very different categories of accommodation was
aimed at maximum interchangeability, so that residents
whose condition improved or worsened would need to be
moved from one section to another as little as possible, it
was obvious that the complex was to be conceived not as
a conglomerate of separate buildings but as an urban
area, a miniature city in which all amenities would, in
principle, be available and accessible to all residents.
These considerations led to the idea to create one
continuous structural framework, based on the same
modular unit, to meet the requirements of the highly varied
and complex programme. The smallest unit capable of
serving as the basic component for rooms of any size was
calculated to be 92 cm. The programmes of requirements
of the respective categories were subsequently fitted into
an overall building order, consisting structurally of a
system of column-, beam- and floor-elements, i.e. an order
conditioned a priori by the selected unit of measurement
of 92 cm. and thus receptive to a wide range of specific
demands.
Synchronization and standardization of dimensions
throughout the complex was not only important for
interchangeable usage, but also to arrive at the most
rational and rapid construction method, and thus to keep
the costs down to a minimum and to stay within the
budget.
In order to keep the number of construction elements down
to a minimum, three lintel sizes were chosen, which yield
three different bays: 2 x 92 = 184 cm; 3 x 92 = 276 cm;
4 x 92 = 368 cm. Adding up these bays produces
standard measurements of 5 x 92, 6 x 92 etc., like a coin
system (5-cent, 10-cent and 25-cent coins).
With the resulting 'construction kit' made up of different
elements, spaces and building masses can be combined at
will. The initial layout of this complex consisted of units
grouped around three courtyards of successive sizes,
whereby the contrast in spatial effect was further
intensified by having two- and three-storey structures
surrounding the largest of the three courtyards, three and
four storeys surrounding the middle-sized courtyard, and
five and six storeys surrounding the smallest courtyard.
The progression from two to six storeys reaches its
architectonic culmination-point in the centre of the
complex, expressed in a spatially extraverted window
above the auditorium (to which I attached great
importance as indeed to the fact that the diagonals of the
three courtyards form right angles). A great deal of
energy was spent on these features, fully confident as we
were about the programme of requirements. The latter,
however, soon changed under the influence of a rather
sudden development in the ideas about and approaches
to the care for the elderly.
While quite a lot of the new proposals could initially be

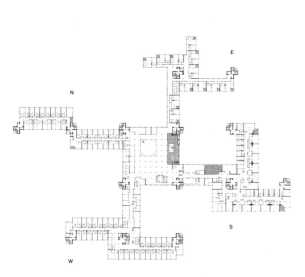

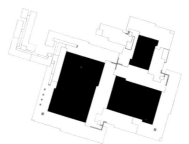

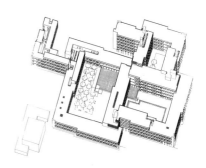

adapted by means of a number of modifications that did not entail fundamental alterations to the original plan, it became evident after a while that the closed circuit according to which the plan had been organized was too rigid and hermetic to adapt itself to all the changes that had become necessary in the meantime, and in the end the plan had to be abandoned altogether. The lesson that we learned from this experience was that if you adhere so strictly to such a specific and explicit organization of the main form, your plan is doomed to failure, and that it would in fact be far better to start out from a more open and more flexible basic structure that is capable of accommodating adjustments as they become necessary. After this failure, a new concept was developed, according to which the project could finally be realized. The first step, this time, was to establish which general facilities were relevant to the entire premises, such as

staircases, lifts, switchboards, conduit shafts, air ducts and maintenance closets. These were all concentrated in vertical shafts located at rational and regular distances from one another throughout the complex. This resulted in a constellation of towers which, on the constructional level, serve a stabilizing function within the complex as a whole.

The programme of requirements, translated into a spatial scheme, was superimposed on this 'objective' grid marked by the towers, and adjusted to the dimensions of the building site. The fixed points of support, the towers, consequently serve to bring a certain ordering into the space as a whole, while the 'construction kit' of (prefabricated) concrete elements guarantees the ultimate coherence and unity of the various components which are formed 'from within'.

The building structure of De Drie Hoven, formed as it is by identical beams and columns throughout, is manifestly present in the entire building, although the way it is filled in varies from place to place. The design-concept of such a structure is that a great diversity of fillings is possible, as the reflection of a differentiated usage, without detracting from the visual and organizational coherence

336   337ab

338   339

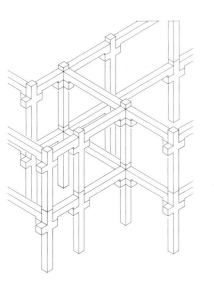

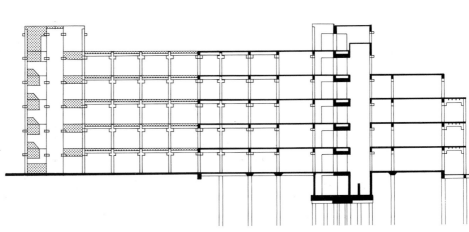

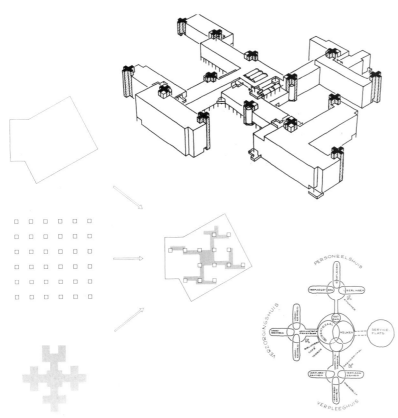

of the whole. Besides, conversions that become necessary as a result of new insights can be fairly easily undertaken within the framework of the structure which continues to perform its load-bearing function and which itself is not or hardly affected by alteration of the walls, doors and ceilings, etc.

Although it is in a sense painful for the architect on the one hand to see how the components he has designed with so much care eventually disappear or are altered beyond recognition by others and without prior consultation, it is on the other hand also a kind of triumph that his idea as far as the overall concept is concerned remains standing. You could compare the structure to a tree which loses its leaves every year. The tree remains the same, but the leaves are renewed each spring. The usage varies over time and the users demand of the building that it adapts itself properly to their insights as they evolve. Sometimes this entails a step backwards in the spatial quality, but sometimes, too, it means a step forward, an improvement on the original situation.

340

341

CENTRAAL BEHEER OFFICE BUILDING (342-353)

The idea which was proposed previously in two
competition projects for town halls in Valkenswaard (343-344)
and Amsterdam (345-346) respectively, and which finally
materialised in the Centraal Beheer office building, is that
of a building as a sort of settlement, consisting of a larger
number of equal spatial units, like so many islands strung
together. These spatial units constitute the basic building
blocks; they are comparatively small and can
accommodate the different programme components (or
'functions' if you prefer), because their dimensions as well
as their form and spatial organization are geared to that
purpose. They are therefore polyvalent.

Whereas De Drie Hoven involved a programme with a
very high diversity of spatial dimensions and spatial
requirements - which necessarily resulted in a single
building order that would allow for a great variety - in the
case of this office building, analogous to the ultimate
chosen basic principle of the square spatial unit, however
simple in the elementary sense, proved capable of
meeting virtually all spatial requirements. Thanks to their
polyvalence the different spatial units can, however, if
necessary take over each other's roles - and that is a key

to the capacity to absorb change.

Designing an office building may well be simple enough
in principle, but it was this very necessity of adaptability
that led to the assignment . Constant changes occur within
the organization, thereby requiring frequent adjustments
to the size of the different departments. The building must
be capable of accommodating these internal forces, while
the building as a whole must continue to function in every
respect and at all times. This means that permanent
adaptability is a precondition of the design. In each new
situation, to ensure the equilibrium of the system as a
whole, i.e. that it continues to function, the components
must be able to serve different purposes.

The building has been designed as an ordered expanse,
consisting of a basic structure which manifests itself as an
essentially fixed and permanent zone throughout the
building, and a complementary variable and interpretable
zone.

The basic structure is the bearer of the entire complex, as
it were. It is the main construction, it comprises the duct
system and coincides with the principal 'traffic routes'
inside the complex. The basic structure manifests itself in
two ways, notably as a continuous structure (spine), and

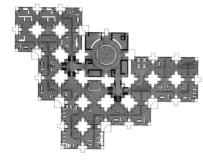

with regular interruptions along the periphery of the complex in the form of small towers (cf. the vertebrae). The interpretable zones are geared to performing all foreseeable functions, which make specific demands on the space and which therefore give rise to divergent 'complementary' solutions. It is this interpretable zone that can be filled in with the primary ingredients of the different component parts. The basic structure and interpretable zone in its entirety thus awaits complementary filling in, while remaining essentially the same: the building as a whole derives its identity from the complex of different interpretations.

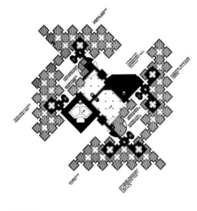

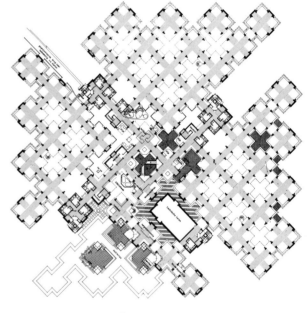

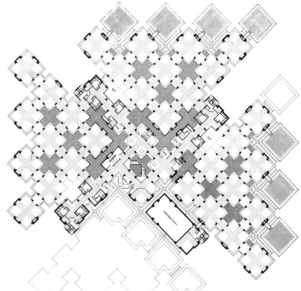

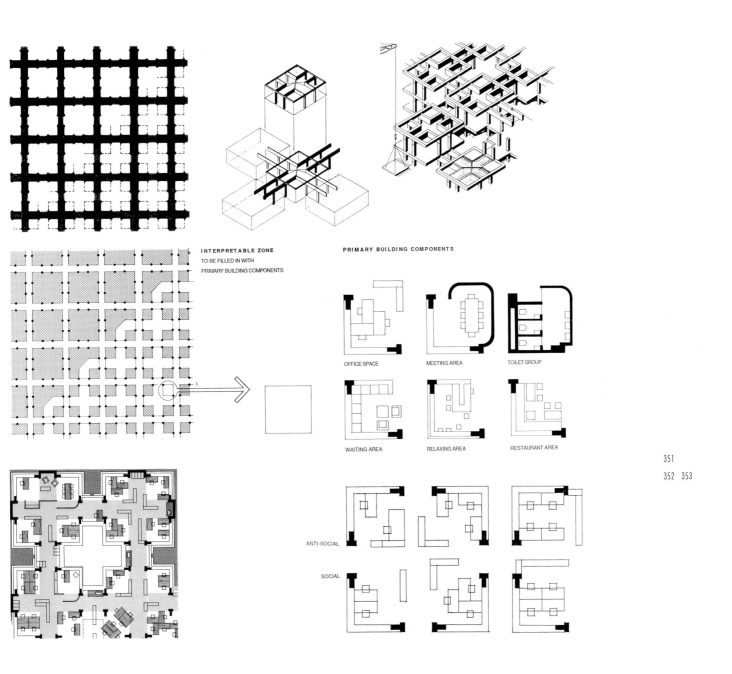

INTERPRETABLE ZONE
TO BE FILLED IN WITH
PRIMARY BUILDING COMPONENTS

PRIMARY BUILDING COMPONENTS

OFFICE SPACE

MEETING AREA

TOILET GROUP

WAITING AREA

RELAXING AREA

RESTAURANT AREA

ANTI-SOCIAL

SOCIAL

351

352 353

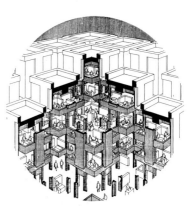

VREDENBURG MUSIC CENTRE (355-360)

From the outside the complex as a whole looks like a random form, and does not exactly live up to one's expectations concerning a self-contained building. The point of departure in the design - i.e. to avoid the effect of a 'temple' of music by integrating the structure as much as possible in the surroundings - and the ensuing principle of accessibility resulted in a peripheral arrangement composed of multiple facets. And because all these facets have been constituted of the same materials they represent, in effect, simply different facets of the same whole. In other words, more attention has been paid to the legibility of the parts than to the coherence of the whole, while the whole is represented in those parts. This means that the whole can be viewed from many different sides. The constructional elements become more independent, they are emancipated as it were, and by

virtue of the different ways in which these elements are 'assembled' at the corners the relationships that are established vis à vis each other also differ constantly. So in spite of its differentiated periphery, the uniformity of materials and constructional elements as well as the way in which these elements are joined together make the complex as a whole speak one architectonic language (although the wooden facings in the interior are an additional feature). By the application of the same basic materials inside and out, interior and exterior are put into perspective, thereby reinforcing the overall expression of accessibility.

An important role within the building order is played by the recurrent use of columns, with their emphatic and clearly recognizable form-language. They stand in grid-formation with equal distances between them, thus marking off equal areas throughout the entire building. They represent the cadence of the building, and set the rhythm of the space, just as the bars indicate the type of intervals and beats in a musical score.

The arrangement of the columns constitutes a minimal ordering system which allows for a very flexible filling in of the different parts, and which has a regulating effect on the great diversity of constituent elements arising from the complexity of the programme.

While serving to unify the whole, this column system is an

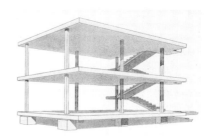

355

354

356 357 358

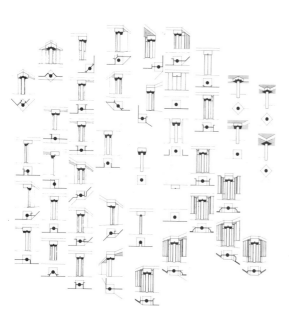

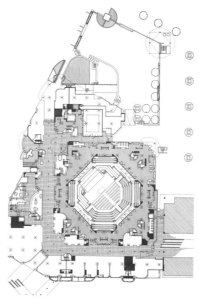

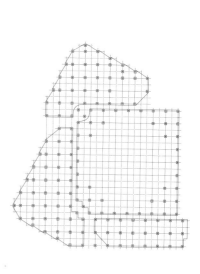

inducement to design each space according to its specific requirements and location. This principle does not essentially diverge from the 'plan libre' that was developed in the early years of this century as a new way of exploiting the full possibilities offered by the application of a concrete skeleton consisting of columns and platforms (354). Among the characteristic features of the early examples of the free plan were the often demonstratively curved walls and also the free-standing columns with their own spaces; these features contrast with the way the free plan is usually applied nowadays, with the columns serving as the starting-point for the walls. In a structure comprising a proportionately greater number of rooms or enclosed spaces, the latter 'method' is obviously more suitable.

When the columns are free-standing, round columns are undeniably preferable, if only because they adapt themselves in a so much friendlier and gentler way to the presence of crowds of people in their midst.

Standing 'in the way' everywhere yet without ever being an obstacle, the columns manifest themselves strongly, their strong personality being further reinforced by the square capitals, an 'overstatement' of the form required for the construction. The main function of these aligned capitals, is to coordinate the connections with the ceilings coming towards them from different directions and at different heights. In addition their extra width keep the adjoining wall at a distance, and so helps to create a certain spaciousness around each column. The columns in the frontages serve to keep the walls at a greater or smaller distance apart, depending on the amount of glass that is required in a specific location. The openings in the frontages are on the whole always located in the 'column zone', only very rarely do they occur as 'holes' in the wall. The columns standing freely in the spaces enveloping them constitute a motif which recurs in different variations throughout the building, and which therefore yield a recognizable and characteristic image. Indeed the column was designed to enable each place to evoke different spatial experiences, while the bare column remains the same whatever the specific location it is in. Depending on the derived openness or closedness it appears in a different guise, you could say: dressed for a different part. So the column determines the aspect of a place, while at the same time its own image is determined by that place in return. The column structure may be seen as a system that generates freedom: a 'competence' that provides an incentive for the 'performance' belonging to a specific situation, and therefore an instrument that yielded a coherent building order despite the absence of repetitive spaces.

359
360

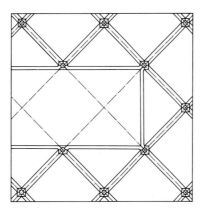

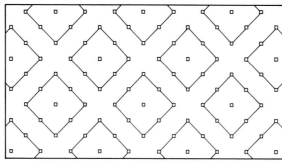

361
362
363
364

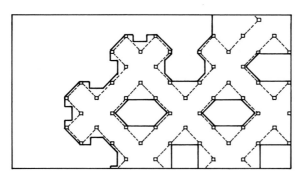

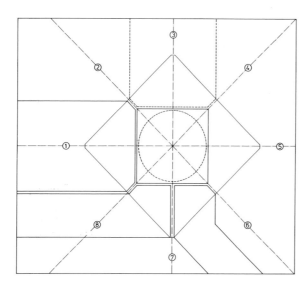

MINISTRY OF SOCIAL AFFAIRS (361-379)

Instead of a building volume with an endless succession of office floors the building has been articulated into segments; the building volume is thus divided up into several ostensibly more or less separate buildings, grouped next to and opposite each other along an elongated central zone: i.e. several small office buildings together forming one complex. Each of these more or less separate 'office blocks' consisting of a number of interconnected octagons, can accommodate one or more departments, each of which is directly accessible from the central zone.

The office units consist of one or more successive or superimposed octagonal islands of + 420 m2, in which the spaces can be arranged in many different ways. Each spatial unit accommodates an average of 32 people in rooms with 1, 2, or 3 work-areas. Although the building was designed primarily as a cell-office, it lends itself in principle also to more open organizational forms where and when the need arises.

The building appears to consist of a conglomerate of octagons strung together - at least, that is the first impression of the periphery from both outside and inside. Also the subdivision into office units follows a pattern of octagons.

From a constructive viewpoint the building is a regularly constituted skeleton made up of a large number of identical prefabricated concrete elements, which are assembled on site. These elements have been combined in such a way that a repetition of similarly identical spatial units is obtained.

The main beams, all diagonally positioned, form a continuous conduit zone across all floors. The pattern has been chosen with a view to creating consistently square spaces as secondary zones outside the primary zone of the main structure; these secondary zones could be left open in places between the floor-panels terminated by secondary edging beams.

It is the selected diagonal form of terminating these secondary zones that cuts out the octagonal shapes from the floor as a whole, as it were, and it is also here that the desired rhythmical articulation is achieved.

The chosen building structure thus makes it possible to 'fill in' the different parts of the programme according to the desired organization. The regular 'objective' disposition of columns offers much scope for variation in fillings and readjustments, so that the building will prove to be relatively adaptable to future needs.

The building structure serves throughout to introduce order, and will not in effect restrict the freedom of filling in but will enlarge it. The structure is the architectural common thread running through the entire complex, making the different components legible and thus ordering

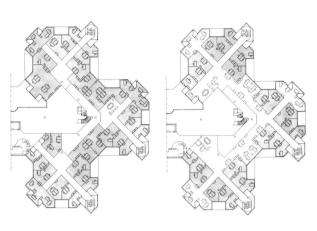

them. Apart from the spatial division and organization, the structure also generates the starting-point for the technical installations, in a pattern of similar conduit shafts throughout the building, wholly integrated into the construction.

The main direction of the office units - and that is the direction of the main beams thus constituting the primary structure - is consistently diagonal with respect to the direction of the building as a whole.

The way the central hall as a spatial main artery cuts through the entire length of the building is therefore followed by the direction of the secondary beams which, although of a lighter calibre than the main beams, perform a function that is at least as important from a spatial point of view.

One of the most intriguing design themes of this building was the integration of these two deliberately chosen primary directions. The problem boiled down to making the constructive main beams and the diagonal secondary beams come together in such a way that the latter would ensure a convincing and continuous lengthwise definition of the space. The solution to the support of beams coming from 8 directions was provided by the square column-heads, which, forming table-tops of 1 square metre and divided into 8 zones, can in principle accommodate beams from all directions. The intersection points, twenty of which were needed to be able to meet all the spatial demands of the building, were individually and collectively designed as a single plastic theme. The heavy main beams coming together from different directions and the lighter secondary beams were attuned to each other by profiling the higher beams in such a way that they unite the dimensions of both types; in addition the column-heads were not oriented to the main beams but rather to the secondary ones (which become edging-beams in the

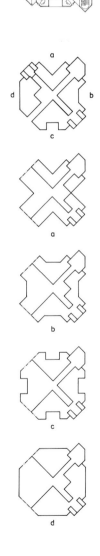

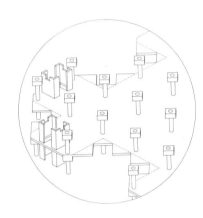

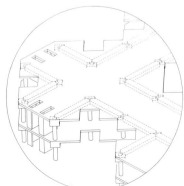

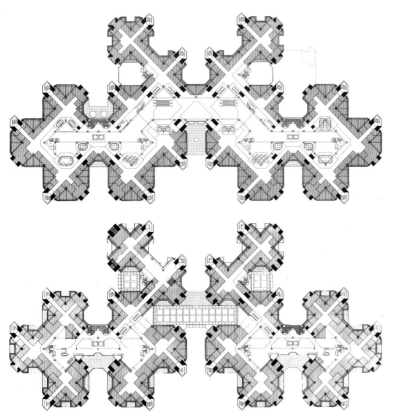

voids). The consequence of this choice of direction is that the direction of the central hall is just as strongly manifest as that of the main beams of the building. The intersections created thus sum up the entire structural principle, and so, as 1cubic metre-point where everything comes together, they represent the structural and constructive concept of the building as a whole and, by virtue of the diversity within their unity, they are the most important elements of the building order.

Thanks to the large-scale repetition of constructive elements and the possibility of extending floors wholly or partially at will, the building was eminently suited to execution with prefabricated concrete elements. An advantage was that the quality of the finish that could be obtained was high enough for the elements to serve as bare concrete. The bearing structure is essentially built up of four constructive elements: columns, beams, shafts and floors. The beams resting on the columnheads were furnished on one side with a projecting ridge which served at a later stage as a simple attachment for the 'void floor-panels'. The required degree of accuracy here was provided by prefabrication of the beams. The structure was given stability by the conduit shafts, which

368
369
370

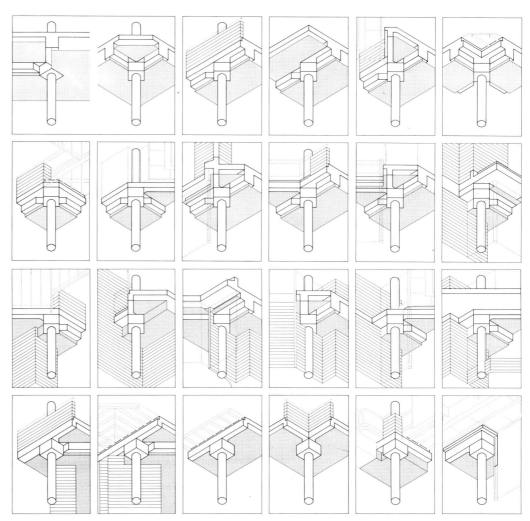

371

372 373

374 375 376 377

were poured on site. For the floors between the beams either prefab units or on-site poured concrete could be used. The parking space beneath the front of the building was executed with the same column distribution as in the office floors. The decision to adopt a system whereby pre-pabricated components can be assembled on the building site represented a considerable reduction of the cost, and this in turn made it feasible to erect such a complex structure within a limited budget.

378 379
380 381

Apollo Schools (380-388)

Both of these schools resulted from the same spatial programme of requirements set by the Ministry of Education and, having been developed from the same building order, as a common design, there are many similarities between

them. But there are also a number of important differences between the two buildings owing to the different siting and the consequently differently orientated bay windows of the class-rooms, but also as a result of the divergent principles underlying the two school communities.

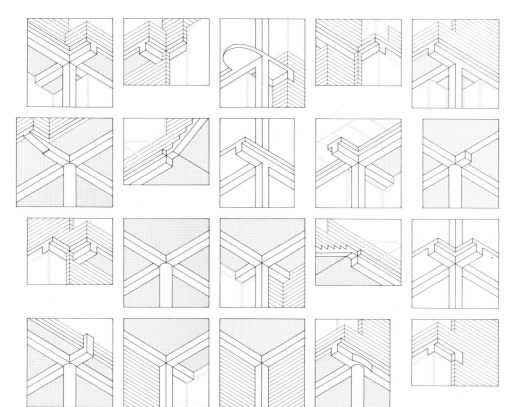

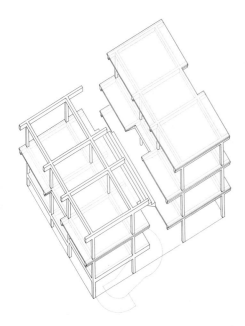

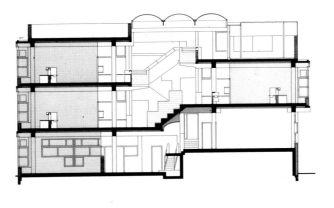

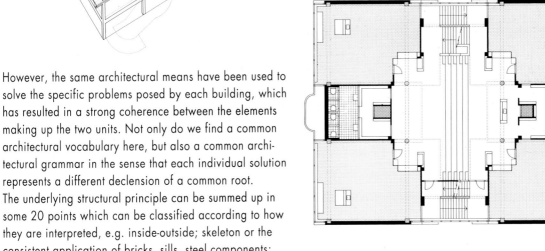

However, the same architectural means have been used to solve the specific problems posed by each building, which has resulted in a strong coherence between the elements making up the two units. Not only do we find a common architectural vocabulary here, but also a common architectural grammar in the sense that each individual solution represents a different declension of a common root.
The underlying structural principle can be summed up in some 20 points which can be classified according to how they are interpreted, e.g. inside-outside; skeleton or the consistent application of bricks, sills, steel components;

382   383

384

385   386

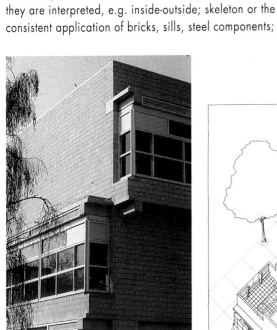

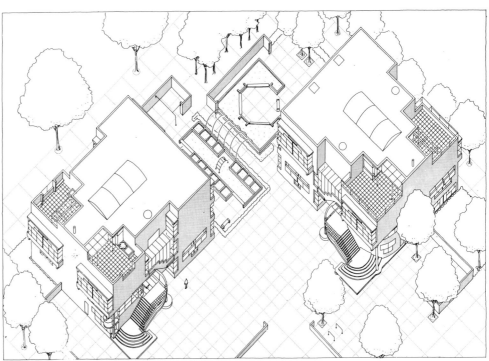

normal or oversized; crossed beams or T-junctions. All the elements are linked by a sort of family kinship, which has resulted from the consideration at the design stage of the implications of each point for all the other points, so that each subsequent step refers back to the first.

The unity of means inherent in a building order may well remind you of classification into architectural styles, according to which the ubiquitous classicist style also, ostensibly, meets the criteria that we set for a building order.

In an architectural style each element has its fixed task, and allows itself to be combined with others according to specific rules. In this sense an architectural style thus represents a sort of formal language by means of which you can express some things and not others, in the sense that each element and each combination of elements inevitably refers to a certain fixed meaning thereby leaving little or no room for interpretation. But in addition, and this has more far-reaching consequences, the technical limitations of the 'construction kit' determine its spatial potential. For instance, you cannot make cantilever - when applying classicistic principles, and therefore no open corners without a column (as in the buildings of Duiker and Rietveld) - for the means to do so are simply not provided in the construction kit.

As a matter of fact, if the history of architecture has anything to do with architectural styles it is especially that they have succeeded in throwing off its yoke. The architect derives his 'raison d'être' from the continuous efforts to break away from the conventional pattern, which he must do because what he has to say cannot be said with the means that are available.

The building order of a project is the outcome of a
more profound realization of the uses to which it will
be put, now and in the future.
The building order thus anticipates the 'performance'
that may presumably be expected of it. And from this a
'competence' is (re)constructed through an inductive
process.
In fact, therefore, each architectural assignment
contains an incentive to develop a new order, i.e. an
order emanating from the specific nature of that
assignment. Just as each order represents a specific
mechanism, it also tends to be exclusive to that
mechanism. Different aims are emphasized in different
instances, but the central issue with structure is the
paradox of an ordering creating freedom - *a horizon
throughout your plan.*

389

Man laying out fish to dry, Senegal

6 FUNCTIONALITY, FLEXIBILITY AND POLYVALENCE

In functionalist architecture the form was derived from the expression of efficiency (which did not automatically mean that all functionalist architecture was equally efficacious). In the 'functional city' and 'functional building' it was the differences that were particularly manifest. This amounted to an extreme specification of requirements and types of utility, which inevitably resulted in more fragmentation than integration, and if there was anything to which these concepts were not resistant, it was time.

Actually, the good functionalists, preoccupied and indeed obsessed as they often were by their 'international style', managed to avoid the usual pitfalls, and most of their airy, white cubic buildings are in fact suited to multiple purposes. But especially the so-called functional urbanism gives a very clear demonstration of the extent to which thinking about solutions to architectural problems has been hampered by segregation of functions instead of integration. The rapid obsolescence of all too specific solutions leads not only to disfunctionality but also to serious inefficiency.

Just think of the parking garages with sloping floors, which are still being built on a large scale. This may well be an inexpensive and easy-to-construct system, but you can never use the building for anything else, if things change - in a period when far fewer people own cars, for instance.

Flexibility became the catch-word, it was to be the panacea to cure all the ills of architecture. So long as the design of buildings was neutral, it was thought, they could be put to different uses, and they could therefore, in theory at least, absorb and accommodate the influences of changing times and situations. That at least would be one point gained, but neutrality in fact consists of the absence of identity, in other words, the lack of distinctive features. The problem of changeability, then, is not so much a matter of having to adapt and modify distinctive features, but of having those distinctive features in the first place!

'Flexibility signifies - since there is no single solution that is preferable to all others - the absolute denial of a fixed, clearcut standpoint. The flexible plan starts out from the certainty that the correct solution does not exist, because the problem requiring solution is in a permanent state of flux, i.e. it is always temporary. Flexibility is ostensibly inherent in relativity, but in actual fact it only has to do with uncertainty; with no daring to commit oneself, and therefore with refusing to accept the responsibility that is inevitably bound up with each and every action that one takes. Although a flexible set-up admittedly adapts itself to each change as it presents itself, it can never be the best and most suitable solution to any one problem; it can at any given moment provide any solution but the most appropriate one. Flexibility therefore represents the set of all unsuitable solutions to a problem.

On these grounds a system which is kept flexible for the sake of the changing objects that are to be accommodated within that system would indeed yield the most neutral solution to specific problems, but never the best, the most appropriate solution...

The only constructive approach to a situation that is subject to change is a form that starts out from this changefulness as a permanent - that is, essentially a static - given factor: a form which is polyvalent. In other words, a form that can be put to different uses without having to undergo changes itself, so that a minimal flexibility can still produce an optimal solution. In our cities of today we are confronted with large numbers of dwellings, the construction of which entails production methods whereby enormous quantities of components can be supplied - which, however, are uniform. By equating the uniformity of dwelling units - the result of those production methods - with the equality of the inhabitants, we have come to the point where uniform dwellings are assembled in monotonous, uniform building blocks.

The uniform urban plan and the uniform floor-plan are based on the segregation of functions, and it is the blind obedience to the dictates of these functions that has resulted in taking the distinctions between living and working, eating and sleeping etc. as the starting-point for conceiving the spaces for different purposes in different ways, on the grounds that different activities make different specific demands on the spaces in which they are to take place. This is what we have been told for the past twenty-five years, but even if living and working or eating and sleeping could justifiably be termed activities, that still does not mean that they make specific demands on the space in which they are to take place - it is the people who make specific demands because they wish to interpret one and the same function in their own specific ways, according to their own specific tastes.

If, in the functional city and the functional floor-plan the identity of those who conceived the idea in the first place is lost without trace, that cannot be blamed on the uniformity of the dwelling units, but on the way in which they are uniform, namely in such a way that they tolerate one particular function exclusively in one prescribed and strictly standardized concept. The houses and cities that are being built nowadays do not and will not permit any fundamental changes at all!

By collectively prescribing where people will have to put their tables and their beds - generation after generation - we are actually causing that uniformity. This collective coagulation of individual freedom of action has assigned a pre-determined purpose to every place in the home and in the city alike - and has done so in such an uninspired way that all the variations that make up identity are radically nipped in the bud. What makes the old canal-houses so livable is that you can work, relax or sleep in every room, that each room kindles the inhabitant's imagination as to how he would most like to use it. The greater diversity in the old city-centre of Amsterdam, for instance, is definitely not caused by richer or more diverse underlying principles (the principles underlying twentieth-century buildings are certainly more complex), but by sequences of spaces in which, although they are not usually very different from one another, the potential for individual interpretation is inherent due to their greater polyvalence.

Collective interpretations of individual living patterns must be abandoned. What we need is a diversity of space in which the different functions can be sublimated to become archetypal forms, which make individual interpretation of the communal living-pattern possible by virtue of their ability to accommodate and absorb, and indeed to induce every desired function and alteration thereof.'[1]

What the foregoing, and all the examples that have been cited, boil down to is a plea to design in such a way that buildings and cities possess the ability to adapt themselves to diversity and change while retaining their identity.

What we are looking for is a way of thinking and acting that can lead to a different 'mechanism' (in linguistic terms you would say a paradigm) which is less fixed, less static, and which is therefore better equipped to meet the challenge that twentieth century society in all its complexity puts to the architect. The point therefore is to arrive at an architecture that, when the users decide to put it to different uses than those originally envisaged by the architect, does not get upset and confused and consequently loses its identity. To put it even more strongly: architecture should offer an incentive to its users to influence it wherever possible, not merely to reinforce its identity, but more especially to enhance and affirm the identity of its users.

Structuralism has shown how effective this process is in language, and my persistent reference to this is because it thus indicates a direction for architecture. Even though architecture is still so often conceived as a system of communication, it is not merely a language, although there are a number of analogies, such as the concepts of 'competence' and 'performance', which do not relate to language exclusively but which are just as appropriate to the use of form - and from which we

must, in principle, also be able to derive form.

It goes without saying that efficacy must always come first and foremost, since that is the only criterion that is beyond all dispute - although it is of the utmost importance to establish what exactly is meant by the term. Certainly, there are objects and forms that have hardly more than one single purpose - usually technical appliances, and these must indeed simply function, they must just do their job, no more and no less.

But most objects and forms have, besides that single purpose for which they are designed and to which they generally owe their name at the most, an added value and potential and hence great efficacy. This greater efficacy, which we call polyvalence and which comes closest to 'competence', is the characteristic I want to emphasize as a criterion of design.

The following excerpt of a text from 1963 deals with the same basic principles. It also serves as an introduction to the next chapter.

390 391

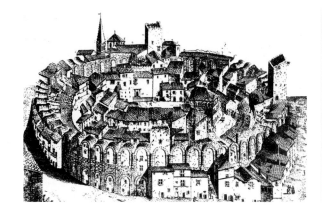

'The reciprocity of form and programme'

'The most important characteristic of a city is, perhaps, the continuous change inherent in an urban environment, which we experience as a normal, everyday situation. The city is subject to constant change, the city has never complied and still does not comply with the rules of organic growth and functional evolution, according to which man has tried to give it form. Every day, every season, and in the long term, temporary and lasting, incidental and regular changes take place: people move from one house to another and buildings are altered, with the result that shifts occur in the foci of the web of relationships which in turn give rise to other shifts in intensity. Thus each intervention in fact brings about a change in the significance of the other built forms to a greater or lesser extent.

In order that every citizen and everything of the city retain its identity at all times, it is necessary for the situation to be complete in itself at every moment in time.

The process of change must constantly appear to us as a permanent situation, that is why the changeability itself must come first and foremost as a constant factor, which contributes to the significance of each individual form. In order to withstand changes built forms must be made in such a way that they permit multiple interpretations, i.e. that they can both absorb and exude multiple meanings, without, however, losing their identity in the process.

Any uniform dwellings, therefore, must in the same period of time, like any places in the city in different periods of time, be capable of accommodating alternating meanings.

This analogy makes it clear that place and time can be eliminated and substituted by a single, focal point of departure, i.e. that meanings are capable of changing their abode.

It is equally clear that neither neutrality, which is the inevitable result of flexibility (tolerable for all, just right for no -one), nor specificity which is the consequence of too much expression (just right - but for whom?), can yield an adequate solution. It is not somewhere between these two extremes of the lack of commitment and too much self-assurance that the possibility of a solution lies, but quite aside from them: namely in a standpoint that everyone can relate to in his or her own way, a standpoint therefore that can take on a different - and hence divergent - meaning for each individual.

In order to be able to have different meanings each form must be interpretable in the sense that it must be capable of taking on different roles. And it can only take on those different roles if the different meanings are contained in the essence of the form, so that they are an implicit provocation rather than an explicit suggestion.

A form divested of the meanings that are attached to it, while possessing plurality because each meaning can be derived from it, is reduced to its most primary purpose.

If we want to respond to the multiplicity in which society manifests itself we must liberate form from the shackles of coagulated meanings. We must continuously search for archetypal forms which, because they can be associated with multiple meanings, can not only absorb a programme but can also generate one.

Form and programme evoke one another.' [3]

7 FORM AND USERS: THE SPACE OF FORM

In the foregoing the notion of structure was used as a 'framework' (of constant relationships) with the potential ability to evoke freedom of interpretation - and hence scope - per individual situation.

Up to now we have dealt mainly with urban forms that were interpreted by several people simultaneously, and consequently in collective situations, apparently collective associations were involved.

In terms of the structure and of its designers our main concern was the relation between designer and structure, with the users in effect playing a subservient role, more of object than of subject - for while we can establish that a form has been interpreted as structure, that does not explain what induced people to do so in the first place.

Now by taking form in a general sense to be a sort of structure, the relationship between form and users becomes conceivable, once more, when the users are individuals, and thus the notion of form can throw off the yoke of abstraction. This shift in the attention to what a form can mean to those whom it concerns (and who enter into relationships with it) indirectly raises the question of the relationship between the creator of the form, the designer and the users.

Starting out from interpretability as an inherent characteristic of form, we come to the question of what makes a form - as structure - interpretable.

The answer must be: the accommodating capacity of the form, shall we say its 'competence', which allows it to be filled with associations and thus brings about a mutual dependence with the users.

So what we are concerned with here is the space of the form, in the same way that a musical instrument offers its player freedom of action.

In earlier examples, e.g. the arenas, we also dealt with accommodating capacity in the literal sense, but what we have now termed 'competence' - namely the implication of accommodating capacity for meanings - sheds a different light on all forms in which architecture is involved.

'... so here we are not talking about a notion of form that presupposes and maintains a formal and unalterable relation between object and viewer. We are not here concerned with a visual appearance as a shell around the object, but with form in the sense of accommodating capacity and potential bearer of meaning. Form can be vested with meaning, but can also be divested of it by the use to which the form is put and by the values that are attributed and added to it, or indeed removed from it - all depending on the way in which users and form interact.

What we want to state is that it is this capacity to absorb and communicate meaning that determines the effect form can have on users, and, conversely, the effect of users on form. For the central issue here is the interaction between form and users, what they do to each other, and how they appropriate each other.

Designing should be a matter of organizing material in such a way that its potential is fully exploited. Everything that has been deliberately shaped should function better, i.e. it should be better geared to doing what is expected of it, by different people in different situations and at different times. In whatever we set out to make we must try to not only meet the requirements of the function in the strict sense, but also that more than one purpose may be served, so that it can play as many different roles as possible for the benefit of the different individual users. Each user will then be able to react to it in his or her own way, to interpret it personally so that it may be integrated into his familiar surroundings.

Just like words and sentences, forms depend on how they are "read" and which images they are able to conjure up for the "reader". A form can evoke different images in different people and in different situations, and thus take on a different meaning, and it is the phenomenon of this experience that is the key to an altered awareness of form, which will enable us to make things that are better suited to more situations. The ability to absorb meanings and also to abandon them again without essentially changing itself makes form a potential bearer of significance - in short, signifiable ...' [4]

8 MAKING SPACE, LEAVING SPACE

We should go about designing in such a way that the result does not refer too outspokenly to an unequivocal goal, but that it still permits interpretation, so that it will take on its identity through usage. What we make must constitute an offer, it must have the capacity to elicit, time and again, specific reactions befitting specific situations; so it must not be merely neutral and flexible - and hence non-specific - but it must possess that wider efficaciousness that we call polyvalence.

WEESPERSTRAAT STUDENT ACCOMMODATION (392-394)

The living-street on the fourth floor is illuminated by means of large concrete light-blocks. These blocks are close to the ground so that the light does not bother the inhabitants while their view from the high windows is not obstructed either. The primary function of these blocks is illumination, but by virtue of their form and placement they offer opportunities for a variety of other uses.

'As far as shape and siting are concerned these blocks were conditioned, as it were, to play a variety of roles, and they are in fact interpreted as benches, work-surfaces, and - in warm weather - as picnic tables. These light-blocks have been placed so centrally that they act as focal points in all sorts of circumstances. They are like magnets, to which things that happen in the communal walkway attach themselves, and so they can become an incentive for street-life, that multicoloured blend of manifestations of

392 393
394

individual and collective interests.

Not making any provisions means, in theory at least, that plenty of opportunities exist for spontaneous improvisation with the space and - certainly for the architect - plenty of scope for dreaming. But then - we fear - that so long as the environment is organized according to fixed meanings and the concomitant form-symbols in the sense of 'what is right' and 'what is not right', the inhabitants themselves will not be capable of doing very much of their own accord.' [4]

MONTESSORI SCHOOL, DELFT (395-417)

The panes with extra wide ledges over the doors, between class-rooms and hallway in the Montessori School in Delft can be used for placing potted plants, books, models, clay figures, and to put away assorted odds and ends. These open 'cabinets' thus constitute a framework that can be filled in according to the specific needs and wishes of each group in its own particular way.

The central point of the school hall is the brick podium-block, which is used for both formal assemblies and spontaneous gatherings. At first sight it would seem that the potential of the space would be greater if the block could be moved out of the way from time to time and, as was to be expected this was indeed a point of lengthy discussions. It is the permanence, the immobility, and the 'being in the way' that is the central issue, because it is indeed that inescapable presence as a focal point that

contains the suggestions and incentives for response in each situation as it arises. The block becomes a 'touchstone', and contributes to the articulation of the space in such a way that the range of possibilities of usage increases.

In each situation the raised platform evokes a particular image, and since it permits a variety of interpretations, it can play a variety of different roles, but conversely also the children themselves are stimulated to take on a greater variety of roles in the space. The children use it to sit on or to lay out materials during handwork classes, music lessons and all the other activities which take place in the school hall. Incidentally, the platform can be extended in all directions with a set of wooden sections, which can be drawn out from the interior of the block to turn it into a real stage for proper theatrical dance and music performances. The children can put the different parts

395 396 397
399
398 400

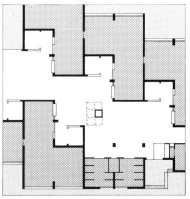

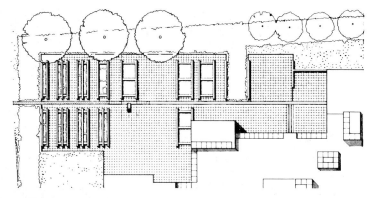

401 402
403
404 405
406 407 408

together and take them apart again themselves, without help from the teacher. During the lunch breaks the children play games on it and around it, or they huddle together there to look at their picture books, while there is in fact plenty of space all around them. To them it is an island in a sea of shiny floor-space.

The floor in the hall of the kindergarten section has a square depression in the middle which is filled with loose wood blocks. They can be taken out and placed around the square to form a self-contained seating arrangement. The blocks are constructed as low stools, which can easily be moved by the children all around the hall, or they can be piled up to form a tower. The children also use them to make trains. In many respects the square is the opposite of the brick platform in the other hall. Just as the block evokes images and associations with climbing a hill to get a better view, so the square hollow gives a feeling of seclusion, a retreat, and evokes associations with descending into a valley or hollow. If the platform-block is an island in the sea, the hollow square is a lake, which the children have turned into a swimming pool by adding a diving board.

The space behind the school building is articulated and divided into a number of separate oblong spaces by low walls. The strips between the parallel walls are intended primarily for gardens and sand-pits, but they could also be used for other purposes. Like each separate compartment, this walled area as a whole may be seen as a framework, that can be filled in, in different situations.

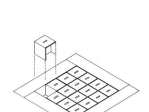

409 410 411
412 414
413
415 416 417

This ordering constitutes a fixed frame of reference, for individual and collective initiatives.
The material that has been used for the low walls to mark off the separate compartments consists of perforated building blocks, which in turn provide smaller openings or compartments that can be used in different ways. Some ot them, for instance, become flower ports surrounding a small garden plot, while others, around a sand-pit, for instance, turn into containers sunk into a counter for the sale of 'ice cream'. Or sticks can be put in the holes - and there you have the beginnings of a tent ... In short, the handy format of the perforations themselves offer endless opportunities for informal usage.

Trees go well with market places, and they make the area less bare and desolate on the days when no market is being held. Since there was already a car-park under the square raised boxes of bricks were constructed to hold the minimum amount of soil needed for the trees to grow in. The size of these boxes and the distances between them were determined on the basis of the market-stalls, so that the trees would serve as fixed points for the positioning of the rows of stalls with sufficient space in front and behind each row.

The market vendors who were allocated, or who chose, spaces next to the tree-boxes, use them for extra, informal display-space. As a result, the boxes often take on quite an exotic appearance, which even, in a way, recalls the temples of Bali.

The construction of the tree-boxes served as a good opportunity to install the necessary electrical facilities for the market as well as for street lighting in the same operation. The tree-boxes have been designed in such a way that they provide seating in the shade on days when there is no market - the principle of multi-purpose design that, as far as we are concerned, should underlie everything we do to the urban environment.

418
419 421
420 422

VREDENBURG SQUARE (418-422)

When the decision had been taken to re-organize the space of Vredenburg square in Utrecht to accommodate the market which had traditionally been held there, it was proposed to plant trees on the square.

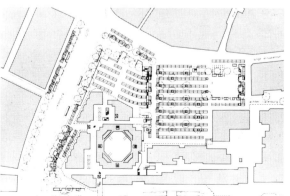

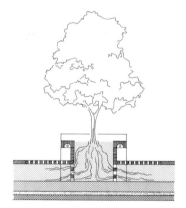

The examples cited in the foregoing centred on the application of components which function temporarily in certain 'usage situations', after which they revert to their original state, only to undergo new metamorphoses later, as the need arises. You could say that the relationship between those features and the users is temporary, with the appropriation by those users being similarly temporary and therefore casual. In a context of areas that require looking after, you could go a step further by leaving quite a lot of the components in an unfinished state, so as to offer the users the opportunity of finishing them in the way most suited to their particular needs and preferences.

DIAGOON DWELLINGS (423-445)

'The idea underlying the skeleton houses, eight prototypes of which have been built in Delft, is that they are in principle unfinished. The plan is, to some extent, indefinitive, so that the occupants themselves will be able to decide how to divide their living space - where they want to sleep, where to eat and so on. If the family circumstances change the dwelling can be adjusted accordingly to meet new needs, and even to some extent enlarged. The actual design should be seen as a provisional framework that must still be filled in. The skeleton is a half-product, which everyone can complete according to his own needs and desires.

The house consists basically of two fixed cores, with several split levels constituting the dwelling units which can accommodate a variety of functions: living, sleeping, study, play, relaxing, dining, etc. In each unit, i.e. level, a section can be partitioned off to make a room, the remaining area forming an indoor balcony running along the entire living-hall (void). These 'balconies', which can be furnished according to the tastes of the individual members of the family, constitute the living area for the family as a community of people. There is no strict division between living and sleeping areas (with the imposition of 'going upstairs'). Each member of the family has his own part of the house - the large communal living-room.'[4]

423

424 425

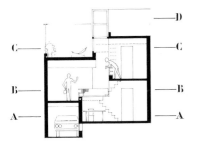

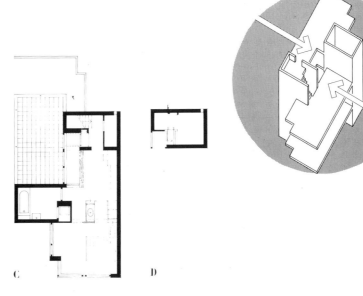

A   B   C   D

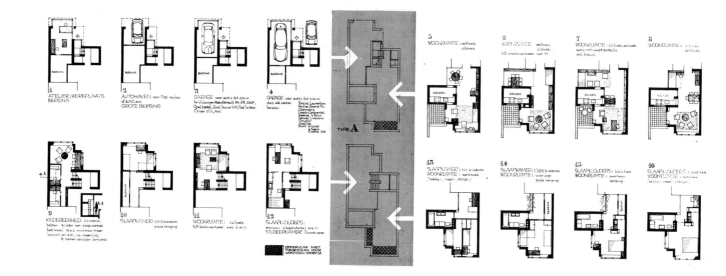

'Architects should not merely demonstrate what is possible, they should also and especially indicate the possibilities that are inherent in the design and within everyone's reach. It is of the utmost importance to realize that there is a lot to be learned from how occupants respond individually to the suggestions contained in the design. Housing is still designed according to what local government bodies, investors, sociologists and architects think people want. And what they think cannot be other than stereotyped: such solutions may well be roughly adequate, but they can never be wholly satisfactory. They are the collective interpretation by a few of the individual wishes of a multitude. What do we really know about everyone's individual wishes, and how should we set out to discover what they are? The study of human behaviour, however painstaking and thorough, can never penetrate the thick skin of conditioning which has formed that behaviour and which suppresses a truly personal exercise of the will. Because we can never learn what each person really wants for himself, no one will ever be capable of inventing for others the perfect dwelling. In the days when people still built their own homes they were not free either, because every society is, by definition, no more than a basic pattern to which its members are subservient. Everyone is doomed to be as he wants others to see him - that is the price the individual must pay to society in order to

426

428

427 429

belong, and so he is both possessor of and possessed by collective patterns of behaviour. Even if people build their own houses they cannot escape from this but, everyone should at least be free to give his personal interpretation to the collective pattern.' [4]

How much one has to do with one's neighbours depends to a great extent on the type of boundary there is between the gardens. A fence is essentially a means of obtaining maximum isolation from each other. Absence of all boundaries, on the other hand, means being seen constantly by one's neighbours, being unable to avoid one another. Simply providing the rudiments of a partition between adjacent premises, by way of an invitation to which everyone can respond as he wishes, provides an incentive and legitimates the measures which everyone would like to take, but which they would otherwise hesitate to take on their own.
A low base of perforated blocks provides the foundation for a brick wall, but it can also serve as the support for a wooden fence.' [4]

The raised terrace at the back created possibilities for personal interpretation. Firstly the stairs, which were restricted to the absolute minimum during construction, could be replaced by alternative arrangements for access to the garden.
Secondly there is the open space under the small terrace, deliberately left unenclosed in spite of the usual decision to shut off such areas - a decision that architects tend to take in order to avoid clutter and untidiness, without their realizing the potential advantages of such an extra, sheltered little place. Finally, this small terrace, bounded by walls on three sides, is eminently suitable for a lateral extension to the living-room.

430
431
432 433

'Adjacent roof-terraces facing each other are in this case separated by a metal bar structure, by way of a summary demarcation between the two areas. Railings and bars invite one to hang things from them or to attach things, especially lightweight, temporary materials such as canvas

or reed matting. Here again, we find the base of perforated blocks, which can very well be used to put plants in them.' [4]

The challenge offered by these unfinished roof-terraces yielded a great variety of solutions - one inhabitant even used his to build a complete greenhouse (which resulted in a pitched roof after all!). This particular idea had not occurred to the architect himself. The structure was dismantled after a few years to make space for an extra penthouse-room - the important thing being not so much the ingenuity of the construction as the actual fact that

alterations of this kind and on this scale are indeed feasible.

At the front, next to the entrances, a tiny 'yard' was suggested architecturally by the presence of a vertical concrete beam. Because the beam itself serves to support the balcony above and the space behind the beam is open, there is not an actual sheltered portico, although it would be quite easy to construct one by, say, installing a glass roof. And depending on the individual inhabitant's needs and tastes, and on what the situation inspires in his or her imagination, the space can even be closed off completely to serve as a bicycle shed, but it can also be used to make an extension (admittedly a very small one) to the entrance hallway inside.

Viewed from the living-room above, the concrete beam marks a space that could, in principle, be turned into an outdoor living space to which access is provided by the 'window' - deliberately positioned and proportioned in such a way that, depending on personal interpretation, it can be used either as a large window or as a small door. Garages were not formally provided for in the plan, although this would not have been unusual in this type of housing. But the carport-like space at street level can be used as such, and even garage-doors can quite easily be installed - but this space can equally well be used to create an extra room: an office, study or workshop which can be made directly accessible from outside if necessary. So many people leave their cars out of doors anyway, and a great many people attach more importance to the luxury of an extra room than to prolonging the life of their car by a few years.

'Windows can be designed as a framework that can be filled in according to the choise of the occupants with either glass or closed panels. The framework itself is

440 441
442
443

a constant factor, and represents, you might say, the context and order within which each individual's liberty and all liberties together can be taken as an integral part of the whole. The framework is devised to accommodate all conceivable infills within the limits of certain regulations, in the sense that the sum of all the different infills will always amount to a coherent whole.'[4]

444

'One could draw the conclusion from all this that all we have to do is devise bare cartridges, as unemphatic and neutral as possible, so as to allow the inhabitants optimal freedom to realize their specific desires. However paradoxical this may seem, it is highly questionable whether such a degree of freedom would not result in a sort of paralysis, because while so very many alternatives present themselves, it is still extremely difficult to make the choice that will prove to be the best one for you. It is rather like those huge menus that offer such an infinite variety of dishes that one's appetite is dulled rather than whetted. When there are too many possibilities to choose from it can become virtually impossible to reach a decision, let alone the best one - too much can be just as bad as too little.

Not only is it a prerequisite for every choice that the range of possibilities can be grasped, (and is therefore limited), but also the chooser must be able to visualize the alternatives one by one in terms of his own way of thinking, he must be able to conceive of them in terms of his own experience, in other words, they must elicit association, so that he can compare them mentally with propositions of which he was already conscious or which can be raised from his subconscious experience. By comparison of the image evoked by the new stimulus with the images already collected in previous

experience, its potential can be assessed and can consequently become an extension of his familiar world, and thus of his personality. So if the mechanism of selection necessitates recognition or identification of images already stored in experience, it is of the utmost importance that everything that is offered should evoke as many associations as possible. The more associations can be evoked the more individuals will be able to respond to them - that is, the more chance there is that the associations evoked will be of specific relevance to the user in a given situation. Each form therefore, rather than being neutral, should contain the greatest possible variety of propositions which, without imposing any one specific direction, can thus constantly bring about associations. An incitement is necessary to motivate and stimulate man to adapt his environment to his own needs and to make it his own. And so we must confront him with stimuli that will elicit interpretations and usages in the way best suited to his own purposes.

These 'stimuli' must be so designed as to evoke images in everyone's mind; images which, through being projected into his experiential world, will result in associations that encourage individual use, that is to say, the very use that is most appropriate for his situation at that particular time.

The focal point in this whole story, and the examples cited here are intended to emphasize this, is that people in their dependence on themselves and on each other, and the fundamental restrictions this imposes, are unable to liberate themselves from the systems of signification and the underlying systems of values and valuation which confine them, without some help from outside. Freedom may well hold great potential for many but there must be a spark to get the engine running.

Take, for instance, a dark space or niche - for most people it will suggest a secluded and safe corner, but for each individual it has a different significance, a relevance to his particular circumstances: it can be just a secluded corner to relax in, for quiet study, for sleep, for use as a darkroom, or just as storage for food or other private belongings.

If a house is to have the capacity to evoke all these different kinds of associations and be able to accommodate them, it must have such a secluded corner somewhere - and in the same way, small rooms, tower rooms, attics, cellars, and windows under eaves induce other kinds of associations. The richer the variety of what is offered, the greater the capacity of the house to meet the most richly variegated desires of the inhabitants.

The starkness and poverty of most new housing
manifests itself in this respect, sadly contrasting with
what an old house has to offer - possibly in
contravention of the building regulations. One need
only think of the infinite possibilities that old houses
offer for converting and furnishing in as many ways as
there are people. Even if, as in a new building, they
are based on a stereotype, they still have much more
to offer because of the greater richness of stimuli for
new associations, which make it possible for its
inhabitants to truly appropriate the space.' [4]

9 INCENTIVES

Design geared to maximum 'incentive' quality calls for a new and different approach on the part of the architect. What is required is a shift in the focus of attention: the architect must switch his habitual concentration from the building programme, which usually reflects only a collective interpretation, to the multiple situation, individual or collective, as it arises in the everyday reality of everything that we build. To bring this variegated assortment of data to the surface the architect has only one means at his disposal: his imagination. He must use his imagination to the full to be able to identify himself with the users and thus to understand how his design will come across to them and what they will expect from it. This specific imaginative capacity, which may be seen as an indispensable part of the architect's normal competence and which should as such be acquired like any other

skill, is the only means of getting through to what are in fact basic facts: the programme behind the (building) programme.

How one should go about processing all these facts, which must ultimately result in a design that will indeed be capable of inducing associations among the users, is a different story, but some of the more concrete aspects of this process, which pertain to the 'anatomy' of a building, can help to explain directly or indirectly the 'inducement' or 'incentive' quality of the architectural features dealt with in the examples given in the previous chapter.

Certainly in those cases where we deliberately leave something unfinished because we expect the users to be capable of doing a better job at finishing it than we would, the basic form that is employed must, on the technical and practical level, lend itself to such purposes.

Anatomically speaking all incomplete parts must not only be receptive to adaptation and addition, they must also, to a certain extent, be designed to accommodate various solutions, and should moreover

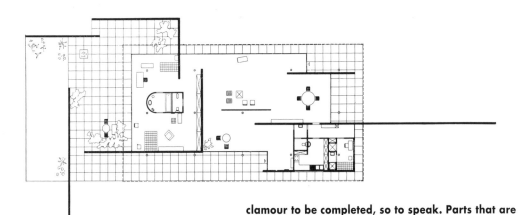

House at Berlin Building Exhibition /Mies van der Rohe

clamour to be completed, so to speak. Parts that are not explicitly self-contained but rather exist in relationship with other components, must be formed in such a way that they can indeed be fitted together or combined, in other words that they induce the user to take such action. In the most literal sense, too, the semi-finished product must consist in an inducement - and that is something which can only be achieved if that was your idea from the very start.

The most elementary principles, e.g. that it is easier to add onto something straight than onto a slanting or curved plane, play a major role here, especially when you can reasonably assume that there will be no architect around to help when the decision must actually be taken.

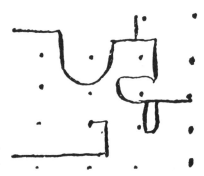

'plan libre'/ Le Corbusier

COLUMNS

For the erection of walls or partitions rectangular columns are not necessarily better as a starting-point, but they are certainly easier to work with than round ones, and it is important to bear that in mind, especially in cases where the columns constitute the cornerstones of the organization of the space. And this is indeed nearly always the case - except in the early 'plan libre', where free-standing columns define their own space irrespective of dividing walls. The columns in the Centraal Beheer office building as well as in De Drie Hoven were profiled in such a way that they have a maximum 'slotting' capacity to accommodate adjoining walls and low partitions, while also the proportioning was wholly geared to such purposes. In the Music Centre (which may be characterized as a sequence of large spaces merging into one another with relatively few partitions) the columns are round. (448,449) Round, free-standing columns in a large space where many people come together function most satisfactory in a crowd, where they are unobstructive and do not stand in the way. In the Apollo schools square columns were used wherever adjoining walls occur, while the four free-standing columns in the hall are round (450). They stand, rather aloof, in the midst of the bustle of activity, where they can be read as intersections of the spatial construction.

Not only the form but also the dimension of component parts and of course the dimension of the spaces between the different parts determine their accommodating capacity, which in turn strongly influences the range of possibilities as to the disposition of the furniture. Consequently it is often better to make a column slightly larger than strictly necessary for the construction, if that yields more 'attachment surface', thereby increasing the possibilities of utilization.

448 449
450

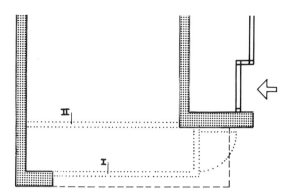

(will a bed fit in the niche, or is it just too big?).
In the skeleton dwellings which are 'conditioned' as much as possible to accommodate additions and alterations, the piers on either side of the floor section that could be designated as garage space were positioned in relation to one another in such a way that there are multiple potential solutions in the way of frontages or garage doors. A less obvious solution has been chosen here with a view to increasing the range of possibilities. Such a 'starting-point' poses a problem, to which each user can find the solution that suits his purposes best.

Diagoon Dwellings

PIERS
In addition to columns, especially piers, which occur in every building in many forms, can serve a variety of purposes, depending on where they are located and on the space they leave open: take for instance a chimney breast, the kind that you find interrupting one of the long walls in so many old houses, and which you cannot ignore when you are furnishing the room: indeed, the pier as such marks the space and provides a starting-point, since the space on either side strongly affects the possibilities and limitations of the room as a whole

451 452
      455
453 454

If you have an eye for these things you can see examples everywhere of alterations and additions to houses which the inhabitants themselves have made in the course of time, probably without prior permission from the authorities or landlords, and usually very successfully.
Such additions are especially likely to have been made in places that offered incentives in that direction, such as balconies which 'clamoured' to be roofed, and particularly loggias, which could quite easily be enclosed.

De Drie Hoven,
Home for the Elderly

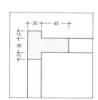

Centraal Beheer
Office Building

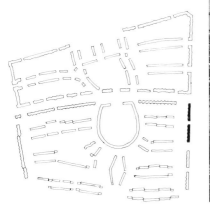

*Hufeisensiedlung,
Berlin-Britz, 1925-27/
B. Taut*

456 457 458

459   460

HOUSING, BERLIN 1925-27 / B. TAUT (456-460)

It does not seem likely that the features that encourage
that sort of addition or alteration were deliberately
included by the architect, although you would be inclined
to think so in the case of Bruno Taut's housing complex in
Berlin - which really looks as if it was designed to
accommodate all the alterations that the inhabitants have
made since the houses were built.

Bruno Taut, in the early days of anonymous mass housing,
was undoubtedly one of the first architects to side
unequivocally with the users. It was not until much later,

when we had got to know all the oppressive effects of
endless rows of identical dwellings, that proposals started
to be put forward to try to do something, as an
architectural principle, about that soul-destroying
anonymity.

De Drie Hoven,
Home for the Elderly

461
462
463 464

Montessori School,
Delft

PERFORATED BUILDING BLOCKS

Such incentives are inherent in concrete perforated building blocks, representing as they do a basic and at the same time extreme example of reciprocity of form and usage. The holes in these blocks just as literally demand filling in (at least if the blocks have cavities on one side only - otherwise they become windows).

In situations where perforated building blocks were applied, as on the living balconies in the home for the elderly De Drie Hoven, or in the apartments in the Haarlemmer Houttuinen housing scheme in Amsterdam or in the Kassel housing project, they were always soon put to use - mostly as flower pots. Of course, people who wanted potted plants or window-boxes anyway would easily have found other solutions for their greenery, but since these blocks look unfinished on their own and clamour to be put to some kind of use, so to speak, they are an incentive to do something with them.

By adopting the principle of reciprocity of form and usage as a starting-point, the emphasis admittedly shifts to what one could describe as greater freedom for the users and inhabitants, but this should not be taken to mean that the architect should, as a consequence, follow the instructions of those users as to what he must do - and especially as to what he must not do.

When we indirectly advocate giving the users a greater role to play in the shaping of their surroundings, the objective is not primarily to encourage more individuality, but rather to redress the balance between what we ought to make for them and what we should leave up to them.

Offering 'incentives' which evoke associations in the users, which in turn lead to specific adjustments to suit specific situations, in fact presupposes - notwithstanding the shift in emphasis - a more thoroughly considered design based on a more detailed and more subtle programme of requirements. The point in creating incentives is to raise the inherent potential as much as possible, in other words: to put more into less, or to make less out of which more can be drawn. For each situation the following could be said to apply: incentive + association = interpretation.

In this question the 'incentive' itself is a sort of constant, which produces a variety of interpretations through varying associations. And if we substitute 'competence' for 'incentive' and 'performance' for 'interpretation' we find ourselves back with the linguistic analogy again, as described in (Incidentally, who can help noticing the miniature, rudimentary arenas in the perforated blocks?)

Just as the architect's stand 'vis à vis' a collective structure is interpretative - i.e. that of the user - so his stand 'vis à vis' the users of his architecture is that of making his design interpretable for them. An architect must be quite clear about how far he should go and where he should not impose: he must make space and leave space, in the proper proportions and in the proper balance.

10 FORM AS AN INSTRUMENT

'The more influence you can personally exert on the things around you, the more you will feel emotionally involved with them and the more attention you will pay to them, and also, the more you will be inclined to lavish care and love on the things around you.
You can only develop an affection for things that you can identify with - things on which you can project so much of your own identity and in which you can invest so much care and dedication that they become part of you, absorbed into your own personal world. All that care and dedication makes it seem as if the object needs you, not only can you decide to a large extent what happens to it but the object itself gets a say in your life as well; this kind of relationship too may evidently be seen as a process of mutual appropriation. The more involved a person is with the form and content of his surroundings, the more those surroundings become appropriated by him, and just as he takes possession of his surroundings, so they will take possession of him.
In the light of this reciprocal appropriation of people and things it is fair to state that the incentives that are offered by us as architects represent an invitation for completion and 'colouring' by the people who live there, while on the other hand the people too extend an invitation to the things to complete, colour and fill in their own existence.
Thus user and form reinforce each other and interact - and such a relationship is analogous to that between individual and community. Users project themselves onto the form, just as individuals show their true colour in their various relationships with others, while playing and being played upon, and thereby become who they are.
Form directed towards a given purpose functions as an apparatus, and where form and programme are mutually evocative the apparatus itself becomes an instrument. A properly functioning apparatus does the work for which it is programmed, that which is expected of it - no less, but also no more. By pressing the right buttons the expected results are obtained, the same for everyone, always the same.

A (musical) instrument essentially contains as many possibilities of usage as uses to which it is put - an instrument must be played. Within the limits of the instrument, it is up to the player to draw what he can

from it, within the limits of his own ability. Thus instrument and player reveal to each other their respective abilities to complement and fulfill one another. Form as an instrument offers the scope for each person to do what he has most at heart, and above all to do it in his own way.' [4]

The following text from 1966, originally published in Forum 7-1967 under the title 'Identity' can serve as a summing up:
'In the design of each building the architect must constantly bear in mind that the users must have the freedom to decide for themselves how they want to use each part, each space. Their personal interpretation is infinitely more important than the stereotyped approach of the architect strictly adhering to his building programme. The combination of functions which together constitute the programme is geared to a standard pattern of living - a sort of highest common factor, more or less suitable for everyone - and inevitably results in everyone being forced to fit the image that we are expected to project, according to which we are expected to act, to eat, to sleep, to enter our homes - an image, in short, which each one of us only very faintly resembles, and which is therefore wholly inadequate.
In other words, it isn't at all difficult to create a lucid architecture if the requirements that it is supposed to meet are obscure enough!
It is the discrepancies that arise from everyone's individual need to interpret a specific function, depending on the circumstances and place, in his or her own way, that ultimately provide each one of us with an identity of one's own, and because it is impossible (and has always been impossible) to tailor everyone's circumstances to fit exactly, we must create this potential for personal interpretation by designing things in such a way that they can indeed be interpreted.
It is not enough merely to leave room for personal interpretation, in other words to stop designing at an earlier stage. This would admittedly result in a greater degree of flexibility, but flexibility does not necessarily contribute to a better functioning of things (for flexibility can never produce the best imaginable results for any given situation). As long as there is no real expansion of the choices open to people, the stereotyped pattern will not disappear, and this expansion can only be achieved if we start out by making it possible for the things around us to play a variety of different roles, i.e. to take on different colours while remaining true to themselves.
Only when all these different roles have been taken

into consideration by giving them priority in the design stage, i.e. by including them as important issues in the programme of requirements, can we expect that each individual will be induced to form his or her own interpretation of the issue concerned. The different roles, being given priority by way of provocation, will be suggested without being made explicit.

Within the framework of the conditioning that has been given to the form, the user gains the freedom to choose for himself which pattern suits him best, to select his own menu as it were; he can be truer to himself, his identity is increased. Each place, each component, will have to be attuned to the programme in its totality, i.e. to all the expected programmes together. If we condition the form to accommodate an optimal diversity of usage, then infinitely more possibilities can be extracted from the totality, without this necessarily detracting in any way from the primary designation of the project. The 'returns' can be increased by the possibilities of usage which are embedded in the design as intentions under the surface.' [3a]

Paris, Parc des Buttes Chaumont

466

C INVITING FORM

that arises, in other words, it must not only be accommodating but also stimulating - and it is this fundamental and active adequacy that I would like to call 'inviting form': form with more sympathy for people.

When you look at one of the vast number of books on architecture that are being published nowadays and you see all those glossy photographs, taken without exception in perfect weather conditions, you can't help wondering what goes on in the architects' minds, how they see the world; sometimes I think they practice a different profession from mine! For what can architecture be other than concerning oneself with situations in daily life as lived by all people; it's rather like clothing, which must after all not only suit you well, but also fit properly. And if it is the fashion nowadays to concern oneself with outward appearances, however cleverly vested with references to higher things, then architecture is degraded to sculpture of an inferior sort. The point is that whatever you do, wherever and however you organize space, it will inevitably have some degree of influence on the situation of people. Architecture, indeed, everything that is built, cannot help playing some kind of role in the lives of the people who use it, and it is the architect's main task, whether he likes it or not, to see to it that everything he makes is adequate for all those situations. It is not only a matter of efficacy in the sense of whether it is practical or not, but also of whether what we design is properly attuned to normal relations between people and whether or not it affirms the equality of all people. The question whether architecture has a social function is totally irrelevant, because socially indifferent solutions simply do not exist; in other words, every intervention in people's surroundings, regardless of the architect's specific aims, has a social implication. So we are not in fact free to go ahead and design exactly what we please - everything we do has consequences for people and their relationships.
There is not that much an architect can do, which makes it all the more important to make sure that few opportunities there are are not missed. If you think you can't make the world a better place with your work, at least make sure you don't make it worse. The art of architecture is not only to make beautiful things - nor is it only to make useful things, it is to do both at once - like a tailor who makes clothes that both look good and fit well. And, if at all possible, clothes that everyone can wear, not just the Emperor.
Everything we design must be adequate for every situation

1 THE HABITABLE SPACE BETWEEN THINGS

By approaching the designed object as an instrument rather than as an apparatus, as we did in the previous section of these studies (part B), we were in fact already advocating what amounts to a greater efficiency. Having discussed examples of the ability of form to play different roles under changing circumstances not only by creating the necessary conditions but also by actually encouraging such differentiated usage, this section will deal with extending this idea to a general principal. For what we need is an expansion of the possibilities of all the things we design so that they will be more useful, more applicable, and so more suited to their purpose, or suited to more purposes.

If something is geared very specifically to a certain aim it functions the way it has been programmed to function, i.e. as it was expected to function. This is the sort of functionalism that the functionalists talked about, but it is also the minimum of utility that can be expected of architecture. And in order to achieve more than that minimum in the diversity of situations as they arise I am pleading for form and space with a greater 'accommodating' potential, like a musical instrument that sounds the way the player wants it to sound. The point is to increase this 'accommodating potential' and thus to make space more receptive to different situations. Once you start looking for them it is easy to find even in the most unexpected corners examples of usage that the designers (if any) certainly never envisaged.

People use their surroundings in every situation as best they can, and quite often the things around them, quite unintentionally, offer unexpected opportunities which are then grasped 'in passing' as it were.

467

"Irregularities' such as differences in level occur everywhere, and instead of going to great lengths to minimize them we should rather concentrate on trying to form them so consciously that they can be maximally exploited. Parapets, railings, post and gutters are forms of articulation and represent increased possibilities for attachment. They can be used as primitive elements of what we could call the basic grammar of architecture. Occurring as they do in diverse shapes and sizes they are a constant stimulus for usage in everyday life.

The most elementary provision to enable people to take possession of their direct environment is probably the provision of seating (the opportunity to *seat* oneself having everything to do, linguistically, with *settlement*). A place to sit offers an opportunity for temporary appropriation, while creating the circumstances for contact with others. Not only would an ordinary domestic sofa or chair be incapable if withstanding such varied and casual usage, it would also fail to stimulate such usage.
Objects that present themselves explicitly and exclusively for a specific purpose - e.g. for sitting on - appear to be unsuitable for other purposes. Extreme functionality in a design makes it rigid and inflexible, that is, it leaves the user of the designed object too little freedom to interpret its function as he pleases. It is as if it has been decided a priori what is to be expected of the user, what he may and what he may not do. The user is thus subservient to the form and the concomitant a priori 'agreement'; he is only capable of using the object, of appropriating it temporarily in a way, if what he wants to do with it corresponds to what the form dictates.
What a sofa dictates can be regarded as the sum of what those responsible for its existence have to offer: the furniture makers, the buyers, an ideology, a society, a culture. The concept 'bench' is maintained by a series of associations which are so powerful that the user has little chance of seeing beyond those associ-ations to pick out what he needs most at that moment - and that may well be a table rather than a bench, or just a place to put down a tray with coffee things. In the case of a chance encounter that need may be no more than an opportunity to rest one's foot: a small gesture which can be a sign to someone else that you are not averse to the idea of more personal contact. If the response to this first tentative and as yet non-committal gesture was not displeasing, then both parties can successively assume more permanent positions, always in keeping with the degree of commitment or non-commitment that each wants. ' [4]

RAISED SIDEWALK, BUENOS AIRES (468)
'There where the sidewalk is so high that you can sit on it or lean against it, in streets with a steep incline, for instance, such a place, if favourably situated (as on a corner), can become a place where people meet and linger. This is where young football players find a ready audience, and a place any street vendor wanting to draw the attention of passers-by will want to make use of: an obvious spot, but with the natural advantage of some seclusion for the display of his wares.' [4]

468

469

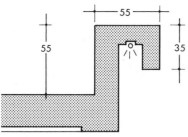

WEESPERSTRAAT STUDENT ACCOMMODATION (470-472)
'A long, broad parapet should look fairly unobtrusive at
first sight, just somewhere to pause, to lean against or to
sit on, for a fleeting moment or for a longer conversation
as the case may be. Sometimes it serves as eating-space
when the restaurants is crowded, and it was used for
laying out a buffet supper one Christmas.' [4]

**For contact to be established spontaneously a certain
casualness, non-committalness, is indispensable. It is
the certainty that you can break off contact and
withdraw as soon as you like that encourages you to
carry on. The establishment of contact is in a way
rather like the process of seduction, with both sides
making equal claims on the other in the knowledge
that retreat is possible at any time.
Here too the associations that are evoked in us by the**

**images we all store in our consciousness - collective
associations, we could say - play a decisive role. Just
think of a courting couple which is readily imagined
sitting on a bench, with all the attendant associations
of bonds for the future and the situations that appear
to arise inevitably, as a result.' [4]**

LA CAPELLE, FRANCE (473)
'It does not take much for things to serve as a sort of
structure to which everyday life can attach itself. The
simple railing where elderly people find support when
going up or down a stepped street is, for every child in
the neighbourhood, a challenge to demonstrate its agility.
It serves as a playground climbing-frame and, in summer,
is sure to be used for building huts and hideouts.
In Holland, moreover, you can be sure that housewives
would use such a railing for beating the dust out of their
carpets. A straightforward iron railing is literally 'at
hand', for a wide range of uses, for all sorts of ordinary,
everyday situations, and it transforms the street into a
playground.
The designed, purpose-built playgrounds which are
scattered throughout the city are, for the time being,
indispensable places of refuge for children. But, like
prostheses, they are also a painful reminder of how
severely the city, which should itself be a playground for
its citizens and children, has been amputated in this
respect.' [4]

470 471
472

473

HIGH COURT, CHANDIGARH 1951-55 / LE CORBUSIER (474-477)

The 'Brise-Soleil' constructions which are featured in so much of Le Corbusier's later architecture, consist of a fixed concrete grid made up of horizontal and vertical planes; besides screening off the sun, of course, the honeycomb-like structure with its deep niches serves other, less obvious purposes too. What fascinated Le Corbusier himself about this structure was no doubt primarily its strong plasticity, and I would not be at all surprised if he never really considered the possibility that it could prove useful for a variety of other reasons besides its expressive plasticity and its screening properties, thereby adding an extra quality to the building as a whole.

In the foregoing examples the quality arose from more or less chance factors, in any case it did not result from deliberate design, but it must also be possible to turn such quality into an explicit requirement of the design brief. Meeting this extra qualitative requirement need not cost much extra money, it can ensue as a matter of course once you put your mind to it. What this amounts to is doing more with the same material, organizing it differently, giving more prominence to what was already there - it's a matter of priorities.

474 475

476 477

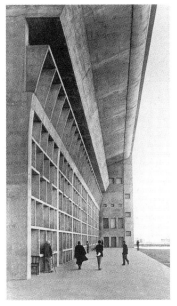

478

479 480

VREDENBURG MUSIC CENTRE (478-482)

A theatre lobby can never have too much seating. Only a comparatively small proportion of the audience find an 'official' seat during the intervals, so the more informal seating accommodation there is, the better.

In order to meet extra seating requirement masonry plinth courses were constructed wherever feasible: less comfortable than an upholstered bench, no doubt, but no less serviceable for that. Another typical problem during an interval is finding somewhere to put down cups,

glasses and bottles. The solution tends to be to use any flat surface that is available. Providing such space exclusively for that purpose would probably be taking things too far, it is sufficient to make the top of parapets, balustrades, partitions etc. wide enough, e.g. by adding a wooden ledge, for this minor although persistent problem. On the upper level of the shopping arcade the metal balustrade curves outwards at regular intervals to provide space for a small bench, from where one can just oversee, looking from side to side, the arcade below in both directions. The raised back - a little too majestic perhaps - was the concession that had to be made to the building authorities, since the regulations applying to the height of parapets had to be strictly observed; the more natural and somewhat more elegant design of the model that preceded the definitive version was turned down.

At present these seats are now removed because they supposedly attract too many 'vagrants' who make themselves at home in this sheltered mall, especially at night; they leave a lot of rubbish behind and there are many complaints by passers-by about harassment. This is a problem in cities all over the world and it must be a bitter paradox that a welcoming gesture also invites the

The Dutch Railways have a commitment to maintaining well-designed and clean public premises. The large numbers of young people hanging around in Rotterdam's Central Station were recently confronted with a 'discouragement' policy taking the form of, among other things, pointed steel rods fitted onto the stone seating space. This rather dire adjustment is part of the Dutch Railway's own campaign against litter and defacement! (Bouw 11, 1987)

presence of less desirable guests. Once you open the door you must let everyone in! the tendency to make things as impersonal and unassailable as possible is not surprising, but the consequences are often absurd.

483

481 482

DE EVENAAR, SCHOOL, (483-490)

The stairway up to the entrance of the new primary school 'De Evenaar' in Amsterdam has been given an extra articulation to make the access from street level to the school more fluent. The juxtaposition of the two flights of steps thus suggested bending the railing components vis à vis each other. This gave rise to the decision to make the parapert elements on the landing curve in such a way as to produce two small places to sit. Certainly the form here (like the corner seats in the Music Centre gallery) is rather dominant and by no means fortuitous, yet in both cases it is quite a logical outcome of the given situation. Here the form explicitly offers its function, unlike in the case of the curved perforated steel sheeting on the upper landing, where, however, children soon discover the implicit seating opportunities.

484 485
486
487 488

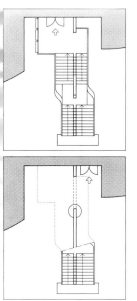
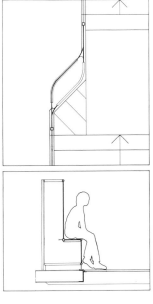

APOLLO SCHOOLS (491-493)

'Window sills, shelves and ledges in a classroom all offer opportunities to display the children's handicraft products which are not only usually fragile, but also numerous. It is especially this sort of thing that enables children to appropriate a space, to make themselves at home in it. That is why we add ledges etc. wherever feasible and suitable.' [10]

489 490

491

advantages. At the entrance to a nursery school, e.g, parents gather to wait for their chuldren to take them home. It would be a bit exaggerated to install special benches just for these wainting parents, and it is even doubtful whether they would be really wanted.

All the more appropriate, then, is the informal seating-space offered by these discs, which one you might well be grateful for when it turns out that one has to wait longer than expected. During the children's recess the discs are used to leave coats and bags on - a better place for them than on the ground in a corner, surely... And last but by no means least this column inevitably serves as 'home' to hide-and-seek players.'[10]

'Colums today seldom have a either a separately defined base or the traditional capital of the columns of the classical orders. They simply dissapear into the floor. But there are situations where a widened section of the column just above the floor offers interesting extra

492
493

ST. PETER'S SQUARE, ROME, SINCE 1656/ G.H. BERNINI (494,495)
'Each of the countless columns of the fourfold colonnade
of Bernini's Piazza San Pietro in Rome has a square base
large enough for one to sit on quite comfortably, while the
columns themselves are so thick as to provide shelter to
those seated there. These multiple 'seats' bordering the
oval, just where the most seclusion is provided, offer
informal hospitality to everyone, even when the rest of the
piazza is deserted. How many of the columns now at the
design stage all over the world offer a like additional
quality to those who will later have to live with them?' [6]

St. Peter 1754/
G.P. Panini

494
495

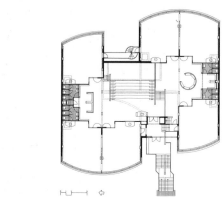

496
497
498

DE EVENAAR, SCHOOL (496-498)

Parapets bordering staircases are very often placed slantwise, following the direction of the hand-rail. This is indeed in many cases the most obvious solution, whereby an indication of the presence of this the stairs is given in a quite logical way. But in a situation where a parapet is so positioned that it offers a view of something, as in 'De Evenaar', it invites people to lean their elbows on the top, or even to sit on it. Wherever something is going on people want somewhere to pause and watch - and that itself is enough reason to try to let the architecture of the location contribute to potential seating capacity. So in this case it was a good idea to have, instead of the usual slanting parapet, a parapet divided into stepped sections with horizontal coping that is wide enough to lean your elbows on or to sit on. And if, as in this case, the wall is of masonry, the stepped design is much easier to execute, since there is no sawing of bricks to be done. So the execution, quite unintentionally, recalls elaboration of Berlage and Loos.

APOLLO SCHOOLS (499,501-503)

'Every kind of step or ledge by a school entrance becomes a place to sit for the children, especially when there is an inviting column to offer protection and to lean against. Realizing this generates form. Here again we see that form generates itself, and that is less a matter of inventing than of listening attentively to what men and objects want to be.' [10]

Of some kinds of spaces we know beforehand that they will be gratefully used, and bearing that in mind it is important to make the periphery of the building as inviting as possible, by activating each component wherever possible - and that includes, for instance, the space in front of the kindergarten entrance under the staircase leading up to the school proper. Such spaces very often degenerate into dark and smelly corners where only rubbish collects and cats roam, but no people. By making the flight of steps rise from a raised platform this situation can be avoided, while giving the area under the staircase a more positive value. It is the most literal form of making the space between things more habitable.

We must take care not to leave any holes and corners behind which are lost and useless, and which, because they serve no purpose at all, are 'uninhabitable'. An architect must not waste space by the way he organizes his material, on the contrary he must add space, and not only in the obvious places that strike the eye anyway but also in places that do not generally attract attention, i.e. between things. The foregoing examples show how you can increase the functionality of an architectural design by consistently

499

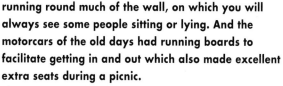

running round much of the wall, on which you will always see some people sitting or lying. And the motorcars of the old days had running boards to facilitate getting in and out which also made excellent extra seats during a picnic.

The extension of the usable space by the addition of (informal) extra horizontal planes represents the reward for making more explicit what was in fact an implicit requirement. And if this added value is seen primarily as yielding an enlargement of the capacity for seating and for putting things on, this may seem a somewhat limited advantage at first sight. But the point here is the designer's or architect's commitment (both in general and in particular) to create this added value wherever possible, as the users will turn such extras to further advantage.

Such intensification of the material should, ideally, become second nature to the architect, a question of handwriting rather than an extra, less a matter of what you design than of how you design it. It is to the content that we should be adding, and as little as possible to the design (the danger of superfluous projections and fussiness is ever-present).

A prerequisite for creating inviting form is empathy, the way hospitality is based on anticipating the wishes of one's guests. Increasing the 'accommodating potential' amounts to a greater suitability for what is required of form; a form therefore which is more orientated to people's needs in different situations, and which consequently has more to offer.

The habitable space between things represents a shift in attention from the official level to the informal, to where ordinary day-to-day lives are led, and that means in the margins between the established meanings of explicit function.

Montessori School, Delft

taking account of the in-between space.

Admittedly we come across instances of this kind of extra quality quite often in our surroundings without any architect having deliberately intended them, but still it is fair to say that we should on the whole try to make objects more substantial, less two-dimensional - by thinking more in terms of zones. Freestanding walls, if they don't reach the ceiling and are sufficiently thick, can serve as shelves for putting things on. One of the striking things about Italian churches in particular is that they have a knee-high projecting stone plinth

500
501
502 503

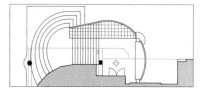

'Picnic on the beach',
Florida (1941)

504

505

506 507

'Les dames du bois
de Boulogne' (1925)

Betondorp, Amsterdam 1922/D. Greiner

Cité Industrielle,
1901-04/T. Garnier

2 PLACE AND ARTICULATION

Right Dimensions

The first consideration of decisive importance in designing a space is what that space is intended for and what not, and consequently what the proper size, is to be. The first and most obvious conclusion is: the bigger the space the more possibilities it will offer. This would imply simply making everything as big as possible. Of course that does not work. In a kitchen that is too big you have to fetch and carry much more than strictly necessary. It's simply a question of expedience, of having everything you need around you within easy reach. Different activities and uses require different spatial dimensions. A space big enough for playing pingpong is not necessarily suitable for a small group of people sitting round a table holding a conversation, for instance. What dimensions to give a space is always a question of sensing the required distance and proximity between people, depending on the situation and the purpose of space. The right balance between distance and proximity is an important point in seating arrangements, especially seating around a table: not so far apart as to discourage intensive contact when that is called for, nor so close together as to make one feel crowded. Feeling crowded can even have a paralyzing effect: in a full elevator shared with mostly strangers you will always find that conversations become stilted and soon peter out.

HAARLEMMER HOUTTUINEN HOUSING (508-510)

The small pavement gardens at the front, enclosed by a low brick wall, are no bigger than the living-balconies on the upper floors. They could hardly have been even smaler, of course, but it is by no means certain that they would have been better if larger. They are just big enough to offer sufficient space for a small company of people, and the needs of different families in this respect do not appear to vary much. There has to be enough room for a few chairs around a small table, which can be round, square or oblong but which seldom deviates from the

508
509

standard size. (All this is just as predictable as the fact that the width of the average pavement is inadequate.) The balconies of the upper-floor apartments are relatively spacious, unlike the usual situation where the people downstairs with front gardens have more space at their disposal than the occupants of the upper floors. Half of the area of these living balconies is roofed: partly by a glass awning and partly by being set back in the façade. An added advantage of the latter is that there is just enough room for a door on the side leading to the adjoining kitchen, which further contributes to integrating exterior and interior living spaces. The partition between two adjoining living-balconies is lowered to parapet-height over a distance of 60 cm. at the front, so that neighbours can easily communicate with each other if they wish.

VINCENT VAN GOGH, 'THE POTATO EATERS', 1885 (512)
Rather than taking the rules of minimal dimensions drawn up by housing authorities and building regulations officers as a spatial standard of measurement, you could take the space occupied by people sitting around a table as a sort of unit. This theme is frequently dealt with by painters, who with their keener eye for composition often take such a unit as their spatial starting-point. A lamp hanging over the table accurately defines the centre of attention. The light it sheds around it makes the people and their attributes together shape the space, so that there is ultimately a fusion between people and place. The way this 'last supper of the poor' shows how people and space complement each other makes it a particularly instructive lesson in architecture.

A room that is too small for its purpose is inadequate, but so is a space that is too large, because although it may be big enough to hold a lot that does not mean

that it necessarily fits properly so as to give the people in it the right feeling - like clothes which fit well, neither so tight as to be uncomfortable nor so loose as to hamper one's movements. Most architects, when they are not restricted by rules and regulations, tend to make spaces too large rather than too small. Everything is kept as open and spacious as possible, thereby precluding the usual and understandable objections, but the architects fail to realize that there may be possibilities that are in fact taken away by their grand gesture, that they are making more things

510 511
512
513

De Drie Hoven,
Home for the Elderly

impossible than possible. **The larger the dimensions, the more difficult it is to use them to best advantage. Aren't all those urban planners and architects constantly trying, under political pressure or not, to reserve more and more space for separate tram zones,**

Place Clemenceau, Vence, France & Rockefeller Plaza, New York

Bibliothèque Nationale, Paris & Amphitheatre, Arles, France

514 515
516 517

bicycle zones and other areas designated to traffic - all these facilities having in common that the houses have to be placed further and further apart as if they were children's clothes that have to be let out?
Wherever traffic space is squandered the buildings become isolated, standing far apart. This makes it impossible for an urban space to evolve organically from building heights and distances and thus to create a measure of intimacy and seclusion. That atmosphere of intimacy does exist in some old city centres, where the traffic is not allowed to reign supreme. And unless there is more contact and understanding between opposite sides of the street (can they still hear them-selves speak with all that traffic noise?) we can forget about reasonably functioning public space altogether.

DE DRIE HOVEN, HOME FOR THE ELDERLY (513)
'Instead of the usual seating accommodation by the window in hospital wards, every two bedrooms share a sitting-room in the space created by widening the corridor. Low brick partitions enclosing the fixed seats separate the space from the actual corridor, giving some seclusion from the people walking to and fro while

offering a view of what is going on. This arrangement encourages casual contact between the staff, even when they are very busy, and the residents. People sitting there have a sideways view down the corridor, while the windows of the bedrooms at the back can be opened, thereby also allowing for some contact.
Tese niches, which were smuggled through the barrier of strict square-metre standards, can easily accommodate four people (at the most six). It is a place to receive visitors, to eat a meal, and quite often there's a TV set or radio. The rear wall has as much shelving as possible, which offers space for the residents to put treasured possessions for which there is no room in the bedrooms. The size of these spaces and the way of furnishing create an impression of a basic living-room, just right for the number of people living there. If they had been much larger they would certainly have been less functional.' [7]

What use is to be made of a space decides what the right proportions are to be, and since the architectural and spatial conditions of a place encourage certain forms of usage and discourage others, architects have a tremendous influence, whether they like it or not, on what can and will take place in a space. Their decisions as to size alone are enough to dictate what a space is right for and what not.
Spaces such as the arenas described earlier (in parts A and B), Rockefeller Plaza, the public squares of Venice, and also such interior spaces as the Bibliothèque Nationale in Paris, are of a size that is attuned to usage in a variety of situations which, however different, resemble each other in that they are focused one common activity. Of course the skaters on Rockefeller Plaza, like the readers in the Bibliothèque Nationale, tend to be immersed in their own activities, but just as the skaters share a common audience, the readers share an all-pervading atmosphere of concentration.
This applies to large spaces and small ones alike: the dimensions have to match what is going to take place there (or conversely, what goes on there has to match the dimensions). We must see to it that the dimensions of space, large or small, are appropriate for the functions they may be expected to serve.

Provide that place

Although architects have always been preoccupied by 'place', it was Aldo van Eyck who first formulated the concept in such a way that you cannot ignore it. From among the many of his texts that deal with place and space, two well-known statements are quoted here.

'Whatever space and time mean, place and occasion mean more. For space in the image of man is place, and time in the image of man is occasion.'
'Make of each a place, a bunch of places of each house and each city, for a house is a tiny city, a city a huge house'. Aldo van Eyck, 1962

MONTESSORI SCHOOL, DELFT (518-520)

'Whenever a class of nursery-school children are left to their own devices they tend to form small groups, smaller than you might expect; and it so happens that these castle-builders and pretend-fathers and mothers feel much more at home in smaller spaces than in large ones. Bearing this in mind it seemed a good idea to have several smaller sand-pits instead of one large one. (Whenever you see nursery-school children playing together in a large group you can be sure that a teacher is behind it all, monitoring this communal activity.)

The Montessori school in Delft has a sand-pit divided into several small compartments - just right for sandcastles. Children of sandcastle age usually play on their own, or in twos or threes; four toddlers rarely play together in a group, and five or more seldom or never.

In large sand-pits the more expansionist-minded youngsters can all too easily disturb the concentration and intimacy of the others, simply because there is no demarcation of claimed space. So here the size of these small sand-pits matches and even enhances their use. The right size is made up of the totality of dimensions that are attuned to the expected usage, while conversely a certain size will attract the usage that is best attuned to it.' [7]

This sand-pit as a whole, having been subdivided into a row of compartments in order to accommodate the use it is designated for as well as possible, presents an elementary example of the principle of articulation.

518
519
520

Articulation

Space should always be articulated in such a way that places are created, spatial units whose appropriate dimensions and correct measure of enclosedness enable them to accommodate the pattern of relations of those who will use it.

How a space is articulated is a decisive factor: it will determine to a high degree whether the space will be suitable for a single large group of people, say, or for a number of small, separate groups.

The more articulation there is the smaller the spatial unit will be, and the more centres of attention there are the more individualizing the overall effect becomes - that is, that several activities can be pursued by separate groups at the same time.

That so much emphasis is laid on the articulation into small spatial units is often interpreted as a disregard for the larger scale, but this is a misconception. It is not so that a large boldly articulated space necessarily discourages use by a single central group, just as,

Area is the same in A, B, C and D

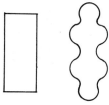

conversely, a large unarticulated space does not necessarily create the conditions for different uses at the same time.

It is in fact possible to articulate a space in such a way that it is suitable for both centralized and decentralized usage, in which case we can adopt both the large-scale concept and the small-scale concept, depending on how we wish to interpret the space.

But what we are talking about is merely the principle; it goes without saying that the nature of the articulation, such as its 'wavelength' and its quality - that is, *how* the principle is put into practice - determines the potential of the space.

521

522 523ab
524

'We must articulate things to make them smaller, that is to say no bigger than necessary, and more manageable. And because articulation increases applicability, the space expands at the same time. So what we make has to become smaller and at the same time bigger; small enough to be put to use and big enough to offer maximum potential for use.

Articulation, then, leads to 'expansion of capacity' and thus to greater yields from the material available. Less material is therefore needed, thanks to its greater intensity.

■ All things should be given the right dimensions, and the right dimensions are those that enable them to be as workable as possible. If we decide to stop making things of the wrong size it will soon become clear that almost everything should be made quite a bit smaller. Things should only be big if they consist of a massing together of small units, for oversized proportions soon create distance and detachment, and by their persistence in designing on too large, grand and empty a scale, architects have become large-scale producers of distance and alienation. Largeness based on multiplicity implies greater complexity, and that complexity enhances the interpretative potential thanks to the greater diversity of relations and the interaction of the individual components that together form the whole. [4]

CENTRAAL BEHEER OFFICE BUILDING (522-527)

The articulation of space was the principle underlying the design of the Centraal Beheer insurance office. Point of departure was the tenet that all work, as well as all recreational activity, takes place in small groups, not individually but not collectively either. A study of the situation showed that all the different components in the programme could be interpreted as spaces, or places, of 3 x 3 m, or of multiples thereof. And because things in practice are never so precisely numerical, the necessary margins were taken into account to allow for overspill into the circulation areas. If this building can be said to have the potential not only to absorb far-reaching internal changes but also to give the impression that it could also be designated for quite different purposes, then that is due to the articulation. So, when for instance an art exhibition is mounted in the building (as is done regularly), the environment can quite simply and easily be transformed into a space with gallery-like qualities.

However, the dream of a constructed space attuned to every conceivable programme of usage was not fully realized here, although it seems within reach.

The secret of articulation into a diversity of places is, indeed, that this dream can never be fully realized. For the size of the spatial units we call places is based on the spatial needs of what we might call the patterns of social interaction. The building, then, can serve as a basic struc-ture only for those purposes that more or less match it. The range of possibilities of a building is determined by the

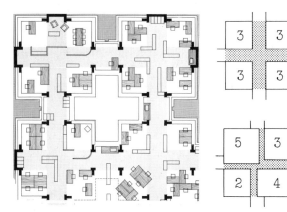

525
526 527

Foyer Vredenburg Music Centre

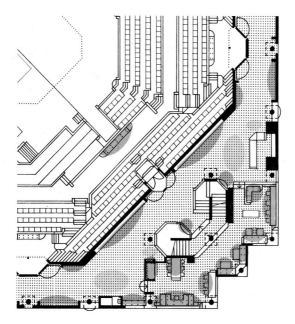

528

529 530

definitive place

possible place

density of its structure and the articulation derived from it. While it functions very well as an office building, it provides quite an unsatisfactory environment for a company party with all the staff, for instance, so it is not surprising that for such events use is made of the larger hall-space of the adjoining building. This hall forms an integral part of the complex as a whole and is therefore easily accessible.

One could measure a floor-plan according to the capacity it has for creating places, and with that an impression is obtained of the potential of the floor space for accommodating more or less separate activities. The traditional floor-plan in Dutch housing comprises two connecting rooms, separated from each other by built-in cupboards enclosing sliding doors. Many people over the years decided to remove these

obstacles in order to obtain a single, large space. However, they found that the new bigger space was not only far more difficult to organize and furnish, but also that the extra space provided by the new arrangement proved to be disappointing. The old, articulated, arrangement had offered more stimuli for the creation of places as well as more spatial differentiation. So by articulating a space there appears to be more room, while the 'place-capacity' can be increased as the occupants' need for differentiated usage grows.

HOME CONVERSION,
A small-scale and by no means spectacular conversion of a standard dwelling was undertaken to adjust the downstairs floor to a more differentiated usage, so that more activities can take place there independently of one another. The original floor plan followed the conventional pattern of kitchen, dining room and living room; after adjustment to the needs of a family with more differentiated occupations the ground floor contains at least three extra workspaces as well as an extra table and chairs in the kitchen. The additional space of forgotten corners was used to increase the number of places, thereby increasing the capacity of the communal living space as a whole.

**'Place-capacity' is a quality of that part of the floor space that is not needed for getting from one place to another. A major criterion for the quality of a floor plan is that the available floor space is used as efficiently as possible, that there is no more circulation 'space' than strictly necessary, i.e. that the space is organized in such a way that optimal place-capacity is achieved. It is easy to test a floor plan for its place-capacity, by checking to see which areas are essential as circulation zones or which areas will in all probability be used as such, and subsequently by establishing which remaining areas meet the minimum requirements of 'place'. Then you can consider whether the dimensions of the places and the degree of openness or seclusion do indeed correspond with the kind of use that will be made of those places.
By continually assessing your floorplan by means of such place-charts, increasing the place capacity of your spaces becomes second nature.**

Private house V. Horta

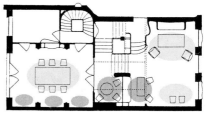

Dwelling, Amsterdam

A: original

B: after conversion

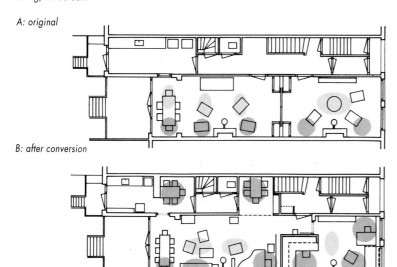

E

196 LESSONS FOR STUDENTS IN ARCHITECTURE

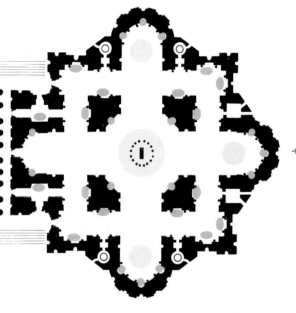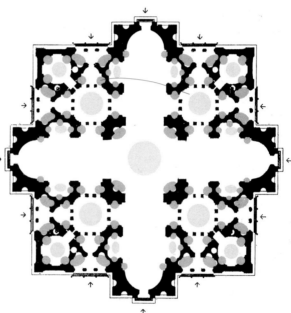

ST. PETER'S, ROME, SINCE 1452 (531-534)

When we look at one of the first plans attributed to Baldassarre Peruzzi* preceding Michelangelo's plan according to which the church was eventually constructed, we are struck by the fact that the articulation is intricate and imaginative even though the plan is not much more than a diagram. We see a series of spaces which yield an amazingly rich pattern without the broad lines of the whole being lost. It seems as if we are dealing with a completely different scale from that of the plan of Michelangelo.

The part which you would initially be inclined to call the main space is hardly different in its articulation and proportions from the spaces situated next to it. Consequently, one can not really speak of a main space or of secondary spaces any more. No single part dominates any other here..

The constructed plan of Michelangelo is, it is true, essentially the same in principle, but the measurements have been altered which created different proportions with the result that the central space became dominant. The other spaces have been given a subordinate role and their enclosure has been reduced to such an extent that it is extremely unlikely that anybody would still take it into his head to use them independently of the main space. This main area seems to absorb the rest, and this effect would undoubtedly be increased if we also took the section into consideration, by comparing the height of Michelangelo's plan with an imaginary one in the same height-width proportion for the Peruzzi plan.

You can see here what a change of articulation does to space: how the interplay of a few changes of measurement is able to alter a space to such an extent that it loses its enclosing capacity where smaller separate

*This plan was proba-
bly designed in colla-
boration with Braman-
te. The many plans of
St Peter's have been
attributed to as many
different architects, and
it is impossible to say
exactly who designed
which plan, as informa-
tion from different
sources show.
Sources: L. Benevolo,
Storia della Citta/
Norberg Schulz,
Meaning in Western
Architecture/Pevsner,
An Outline of European
Architecture/ Van Rave-
steyn, 'De doorbraak
naar de St. Pieter te
Rome', in Forum 1952

groups are concerned.

This concept of enclosing capacity or 'place quality' is concerned with the degree to which a space is capable of being inviting to larger or smaller groups, depending on its proportions and form. This seems to be based on the exact balance of enclosure and openness, intimacy and outlook, which ensures that there is sufficient focus on various places to enable people to be involved with each other, even they realize that they are all together in one large spatial whole.

'If we compare different plans of St Peter's such as those attributed to Bramante, Peruzzi, da Sangallo and Michelangelo, we also see that whereas they hardly differ from each other in principle, there are definite differences in articulation and also in the extent to which the central space dominates.

The differences between these plans are subtle but rather vital, as far as 'possibilities' for use are concerned. So the proportions of the central space in relation to the rest in the 'official' Bramante plan are just that bit different from those in the plan of Peruzzi, making the central space of the former much more important. Moreover, the four spaces in between the towers and the central space - churches in themselves as it were, miniature copies of the whole - which are so typical of the Peruzzi plan, are missing. Instead, these places became as it were the entrance hall and thus more of walking-through spaces. The four semi-circular narthexes at the extremities of the central space have also disappeared (they reappear, by

the way, in another plan attributed to Bramante).

All in all, this does mean a great loss of enclosing capacity for distinct groups. Thus you can see that the exceptional quality of the Peruzzi plan is derived primarily from this insertion of another complete spatial world in between the towers and the main space. Moreover, the proportions are inter-related in such a way that both the independence of all the parts and their interdependence remain in perfect balance.' [6]

VREDENBURG MUSIC CENTRE (535-539)

As a place where people come together a music centre represents an exceptional venue for meeting and maintaining contacts. The building may be expected to be spatially organized in such a way that it at least offers ample opportunity for social contacts. (This is especially a matter of correct articulation, that is, the adaption of proportions that will accord with the pattern of relationships between users throughout the premises.) The dimensions therefore have to match the size of the groups that people form naturally, in different places and situations. One must be free to choose whether to join a group or to remain alone, to be seen or to stay in the background, to go and talk to certain people or to avoid them.

While all attention in the auditorium is focused on that one central event taking place before a single group, before and after the performance that single mass disintegrates into a large number of small groups. In

535

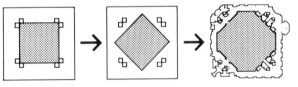

points, through which the visitors are led naturally to the foyers on all levels.

There is a large number of buffet counters divided over the different floors, so that it does not take too long to be served during intermissions. In addition to the stairs inside

536
537
538 539

spatial terms this calls for a large number of places, interconnected yet with some degree of separateness, quite unlike the situation in the auditorium. The fact that the number of people using the building at the same time is very large calls for only one vast undivided space. It is only in the auditorium itself that a single, undivided space is needed to accommodate a very large number of people at the same time. The seating arrangement consists of balcony-like compartments interspersed with a large number of aisles and stairs following the amphitheatre shape from top to bottom; exits are located at many

the auditorium, the different levels are connected, outside the auditorium in the foyers, by staircases located symmetrically in pairs at the four corners of the central volume. Instead of a few large staircases we opted once again for a larger number of small staircases just wide enough for two or three people to use without interrupting their conversation. In designing the foyer area, which encloses the main auditorium like a tenuous skin, maximum use was made of the possibilities afforded by each place, such as a view of the square outside or into the arcade, or conversely seclusion all round.

In the early stages of the plan, it looked as if the space surrounding the main auditorium would be laid out simply surrounding the auditorium in the conventional manner. But in the course of the design process it was gradually transformed into a succession of spatial units with a variety of qualities, where daylight alternates with artificial light, high ceilings with low ones and the occasional concave one, where there are niches with wall tapestries and wider areas along the route - all of which contribute to the creation of a rich assortment of places. Even someone taking the narrowest passage from one point to another passes through an area that is much more than a mere circulation zone. The foyers are dotted with places to sit: informal ones like low walls but also proper wooden benches with small tables as well as the more intimate niches with cushions. Where the foyer widens there are large round tables with chairs around them. The diversity of qualities was accentuated in places by lining the timber finishings with soft materials: the tapestries by Joost van Roojen, which lend intensity to the smallest corner.

Walking through the building, the assortment of places range from introverted corners where you can withdraw from the crowd, and places where you have an overall view of everything that is going on, to areas from where you have a view of the interior of the auditorium or of the town outside.

In this way articulation increases the range of spatial perceptions. In addition, the variegated design of these essentially small spatial units contributes to the accommodating capacity of the whole, as people are more inclined to spread out than in, say, the undifferentiated open space of a hall. [5]

540 541

The concept of scale, which is used indiscriminately merely to denote size, has to do with whether a designed space or building is thought of as too large or too small, whether it is larger or smaller than what we are used to. The adjectives 'large-scale' and 'small-scale' say nothing about actual measurements; some things are very large and others very small simply because they need to be so, which does not make them necessarily too large or too small.

The important thing to bear in mind is articulation - thus the confusion surrounding the concept of scale need no longer cloud our vision.

Take an ocean liner - is it a large-scale or a small-scale construction? It is of course a very large vessel (although a mere speck on the ocean), and would not fit in a street, say, but still it is made up of a large number of small cabins, cubicles, corridors and stairways - all of them units of far smaller dimensions than their counterparts on land.

By 'articulation' we usually mean: the rhythmical, or rather metrical, definition of walls and façades giving rise to a certain plasticity. This is a recurrent theme throughout the history of architecture, and not without reason, for it is the element of plasticity that has proved, time and again, a most effective means of expressing the external characteristics of a building and a particular architectural style. And, as metre in music arranges the piece into segments thereby giving it lucidity, so the metric element in architecture makes distances and sizes intelligible. The size of objects is far more difficult to guess if they are flat and unarticulated than if they are divided up into units whose size is familiar to us, so that we can see the whole as the sum of its parts. That is also the reason why something of very large dimensions can be reduced by graphic arti-

culation to proportions that are more easily grasped, so that it seems less vast and more perceptible- in other words, less like a massive monolith. Articulation can, therefore, serve as a means of increasing legibility, and can thus make an essential contribution to the perception of space. But it can only do so on one con-- dition: namely that what we perceive on the graphic level corresponds with the spatial organization suggested by the overall image. So if the exterior of a building indicates a division into several smaller spatial units which bear no relation to the interior arrangement, as is still all too often the case, this type of articulation serves no other purpose than to decorate the façade, and consequently to introduce an element of meaningless plasticity. Indeed, the historic façades of old houses that have been drawn together and converted into offices or hotels, say, are thus reduced to mere urban decor. It is only when graphic and/or plastic elements in the façade actually refer to the divisions of the space inside that they help us to understand how that space is organized and what sort of pattern is followed.

In architecture all means must be aimed at forming and consequently confirming the enclosed space in such a way that it is ready to accommodate a social pattern of the utmost variety and richness.

*Statue of Liberty,
New York 1883/
Steel structure, G.Eiffel,
sculptor, Bartholdi*

542 543

544 545

*San Marco Square,
Venice*

3 VIEW 1

We must always look for the right balance between view and seclusion, in other words for a spatial organization that will enable everyone in every situation to take in the position of his choice vis à vis the others. In the section devoted to articulation the concept of partition inevitably received more attention than that of combination, separation more than unification. Yet the openness of the different places is just as fundamental as their separateness, indeed the two are complementary, so that enclosedness and openness can each exist only by the grace of the other; they relate to each other dialectically, as it were. The degree in which places are separate or open vis à vis each other, and the way in which that is done, lies in the hands of the designer, and consequently you can regulate the desired contact in a particular situation in such a way that privacy is ensured where

that is required, while the range of vision of 'the other' does not become too restricted.

By introducing differences in level the scope of possibilities is expanded, but with different levels we must take into account that those who are higher up

look down on the ones standing below; the positions are therefore not equal, and we must see to it that the 'lower-downs' have the opportunity to avoid the gaze of the 'higher-ups'.

MONTESSORI SCHOOL, DELFT (546-549)

The idea behind the difference in levels in the classrooms is that while some of the children are painting or modelling in the lower section of the room, the children in the other section can do work that requires more concentration, undisturbed by the others who are engaged in less arduous activities. The teacher, standing up, can easily oversee the entire class.

Although it might have been better, from the teacher's viewpoint of keeping an eye on what is going on, to put the 'workers' in the lower section, this was not done so as to avoid giving the hard workers the feeling of being 'sent down'. In this case there were additional reasons for this arrangement, such as the location of the 'self-expression' area close to and flush with the corridor, and also the requirement that the 'normal' class section be illuminated directly through the windows in the façade.

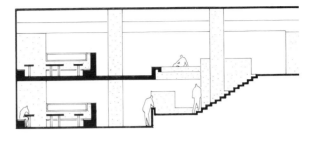

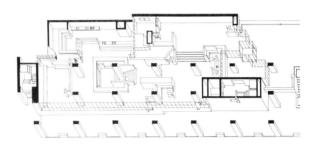

WEESPERSTRAAT STUDENT ACCOMMODATION (550-552)

Obviously it is the lines of vision that govern a proper division between areas that stimulate visual contact and those that offer more privacy; the way we deal with the height of spaces, especially in spaces with raised sections, is therefore of prime importance. The spacious landing on the stairs is just so much higher than the lower-lying dining section (this area is currently in use as a disco) that people sitting on the low parapet are on the same level as the people walking past in the dining area. This makes it easier to enter into casual contact.

550
551
552

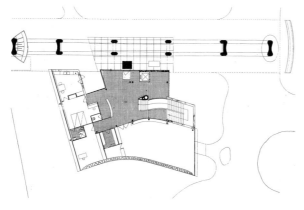

Pavillon Suisse, Paris 1932 / Le Corbusier, (553-558)

The passage-like landing after the first six treads of the stairs - which sets back the actual staircase - provides a space from where you can see over the wall of the communal living room, and so also be seen. This opens up the view of anyone going up or down the stairs, while offering a certain degree of privacy to those in the living room from the gaze of people entering the hall.

BALCONIES

Balconies are often made to extend along the full width of a building, and that is not a bad idea from the point of view of cost and constructional convenience. A disadvantage, however, is that such balconies cannot be very wide - for one thing because they take light away from the underlying storeys. Although such an apartment in such a building has a respectable number of square metres of extra space on the balcony, there isn't very much you can do with this long and narrow space. If the space were of a different shape - more like a square, for instance - it could easily hold a table and several people sitting around it having a meal together in the open air. Square balcony space also offers more seclusion simply because of its depth, and can also easily be partially screened off. Besides, part of the living room thus comes to lie directly adjoining the exterior façade, which results in a space with plenty of light but also one from which you can see directly onto the street instead of having to go out onto the balcony first.

553 554
    559
555 556
557 558

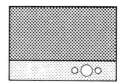 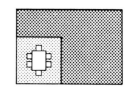

Pavillon de l'Esprit Nouveau, Paris 1925 / Le Corbusier (560-564)

If there was ever an architect with a keen eye for this kind of elementary spatial organization then it was Le Corbusier. All over the world there are examples of how he, looking through different spectacles, as it were, took old clichés apart and turned them into new 'spatial mechanisms'.

Don't forget that in his design for the 'ville radieuse' - although it has since been repudiated, not without reason, for the lack of urban space provided for in the plan - dwellings all have loggias, large two-storey-high exterior rooms. He showed an example of such a loggia-like balcony in the 'pavillon de l'esprit nouveau', built for the International Decorative Arts Exhibition in Paris in 1925 and now reconstructed in Bologna Italy. However, when he was faced with the practical requirements of designing large housing projects such as the 'Unité' in Marseille, he was obliged for financial reasons to settle for conventional narrow balconies, but these, too, were well thought-out and more spacious than is usual nowadays.

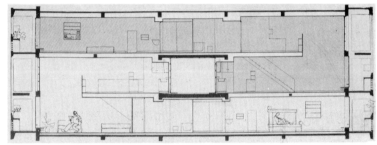

l'Unité d'habitation,
Marseille 1945/
Le Corbusier

560 564
561 565
562
563 566

Pavillon de l'Esprit
Nouveau,
reconstructed in
Bologna, Italy

imposes social contact, but at the same time we must never impose the absence of social contact either. The architect is not only a builder of walls, he is also and equally a builder of openings that offer views . Both - walls and openings - are crucial.

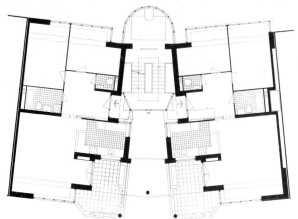

567

568   570

569

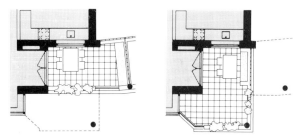

Using elementary principles of spatial organization it is possible to introduce a great many gradations of seclusion and openness. The degree of seclusion, like the degree of openness, must be very carefully dosed, so that the conditions are created for a great variety of contacts ranging from ignoring those around you to wanting to be together, so that people can, in spatial terms anyway, place themselves vis à vis others as they choose. Also the individuality of all must of course be respected as much as possible, and we must indeed see to it that the constructed environment never

DOCUMENTA URBANA HOUSING, (567-570)

xIn the section of this housing project, the theme of stairwells by way of 'vertical streets' was combined with the principle of balconies as exterior rooms. The very spacious balconies are juxtaposed on each floor in such a way that they alternately project to the front and to the side so that the vertical space is not restricted by an overhanging balcony of the floor above.

So these balconies comprise a loggia-like secluded part as well as a more open and extraverted terrace-like part either with two storeys of vertical clearance or open to the sky. The secluded part is screened off on one side by non-transparent glass bricks. This design enables you to sit outside without being observed and without being obliged to take notice of the neighbours, or, if you prefer, to choose a more 'outgoing' position with a view of the other balconies and in full view of them, too. So you are free to decide whether you want to be alone or perhaps to chat with the neighbours - if only to borrow some sugar or to comment on the weather.

LiMa Housing, (573-579)

The themes we had developed in Kassel were taken up again in the Lindenstrasse building project in Berlin, the city with the largest and most intensively used balconies, where Hugo Häring designed his lovely spacious balconies. The number of dwelling units was greater in the Berlin project than in Kassel, and the different demands of the specific situation resulted in a variety of juxtapositions and alignments which exploit the different advantages of the location to the full.

*Housing,
Siemensstadt, Berlin
1929-31/H. Häring*

571   572

573

574   575

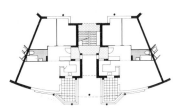

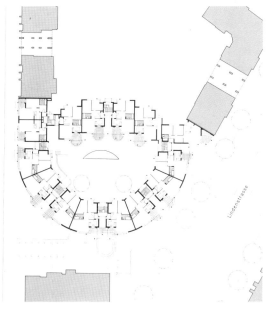

576 577 578

579

THAU SCHOOL, BARCELONA 1972-75 / MARTORELL, BOHIGAS & MACKAY (580-583)

'The main staircase of this multi-storeyed school rises in one direction along the façade, giving access to the successive floors at different points in the building: the entrances are not located one above the other vertically. As the staircase extends across the entire front, the space overhead is highest at the bottom of the stairs. Since the different floors are open facing the stairs, each floor has a full view outside through the glass façade - and hence also of the people on the staircase. The layout of each floor is clear at a glance; there is constant contact between people walking up and down the stairs and others pausing (sitting or leaning). Instead of the conventional superimposition of spatial units we have, here, a unified whole with the staircase serving as a means of bonding the floors together; it is an illustration of how you can offer spatial support to what the children in different classes have in common. So here both coming and going becomes a communal, daily activity, with a reasonable chance for everyone to catch a glimpse of a friend in a different class.' [9]

580

581

582 583

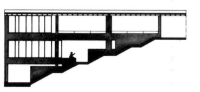

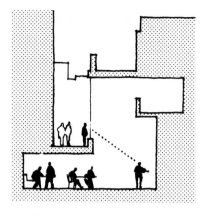

This can be regarded as an attempt on a limited scale to bridge the gap between everyday life on the street and a space that is usually tucked in among the other service areas in the background.

The point is to draw the attention of the people who work in the building to the visitors and vice versa. A similar situation is to be found in the Centraal Beheer office building where you can see into the dish-washing area and watch your plates being cleaned, while the people doing the cleaning - not the most attractive of jobs - need not feel banished and excluded from contact. [13]

DE OVERLOOP, HOME FOR THE ELDERLY (587,588)
Like De Drie Hoven, the other housing project for the elderly, De Overloop, has a village-square-like space in the centre where all the communal facilities are located. In this case the residents can also take their meals in the central area, or tea and coffee at various times of the day. In short this is where everything happens and where an escape from the isolation of the individual dwelling units is offered.

We started out from the idea that all the 'interior streets' with dwelling units should converge on the central space

584 585
586
    588
587

VREDENBURG MUSIC CENTRE (584-586)
The unofficial heart of the building is the artists' foyer. This is where the musicians and technicians get ready for the performance, and also where they unwind after it, often until very late. This space, which is almost constantly used, is situated near the dressing rooms, store rooms and other service areas. There is a visual link with the public passage above, so that passers-by can catch a glimpse of what is going on behind the scenes downstairs in the Music Centre, while the people in the artists' foyer need only look up to see the world outside.

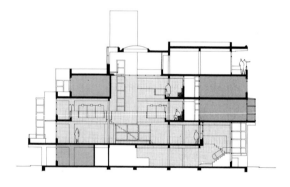

so that the residents need to walk only a short distance to get there. And since none of the floors was to be excluded, this central space had to extend vertically up to the top of the building. The large void thus created also contains the lifts with vertical windows through which the residents can be seen entering or leaving the central hall. The lifts are the most commonly used means of vertical transport, but there are also staircases.

These staircases are differently situated on each floor, their location being determined by variation rather than by repetition of direction and visibility in the space. This sets them apart from the secondary staircases situated at the end of each wing which follow the normal stairwell principle.

PARC GUËLL, BARCELONA 1900-14 / A. GAUDÍ, J.M. JUJOL
(589-591)

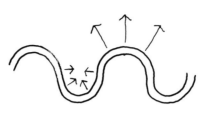

Gaudí's meandering parapet bench enclosing the main terrace in Barcelona's Parc Guëll curves in such a way that your view depends entirely on where you choose to sit. Where the parapet curves inwards you can sit facing each other in a semicircle, and where it curves outwards you have a view of the large central area which, although enclosed by the sinuous parapet, gives an impression of being the outside. The 'turning-points', that is, the arcs marking the transition from concave to convex, offer an ambiguous vantage-point. The bench with its continuous S-shape constitutes a constant succession of extroverted and introverted places in all gradations and with adequate back-support throughout; seen in its entirety it embodies a wide range of qualities which make it just as suitable for a family picnic as for a moment of more solitary relaxation, e.g. to contemplate the scene on the main terrace in front of you, or to wait for someone. This bench consists of a continuous fascinating ribbon of coloured pottery sherd designs (probably not only by Gaudí himself but also by his student Jujol) a twentieth-century collage avant la lettre. Regardless of the colour of their clothes, everyone who sits there is taken up quite naturally into the larger whole, thereby for a while becoming part of a magnificent composition.

SOCIOLOGY OF SEATING
There are many situations where you find yourself facing other people or with your back to them - which is something the designers of various means of public transport, such as trains, trams and buses, must take into account. This proximity to people who are for the most part complete strangers can lead to forced contacts, but it can also lead to more animated encounters, which may be very brief but which can also be more lasting. The way of organizing the seating in such situations is essentially no different from the way an architect deals with the organisation of a building. In the old days the trams had benches along both sides of a wide aisle, so that everyone sat with their back to the windows facing the central aisle; the result was a communal space like a waiting-room where you could cast a casual eye over the other occupants without any embarrassment.

But more often than not the aisle is crowded with standing passengers who obstruct your view entirely. The greater passenger capacity was no doubt the main reason for this arrangement, which is still to be seen in the subways of New York and Tokyo. An additional advantage is that both sitting and standing passengers can move closer together as the need arises to make room for more passengers: the space allotted to each passenger is not

589 590
591

592 593

prescribed but depends on a fluctuating demand.

Trains usually have benches across the carriage for two or three people facing each other or back-to-back in pairs. The design of the traditional D-trains, with their separate compartments like so many small rooms with glass-panelled sliding doors along a narrow corridor, enables you to make a more leisurely choice of your travelling companions - for this remarkable arrangement means that you may have to spend several hours in fairly close contact with strangers. Once you have found a seat you see little of what goes on in the rest of the train except for passengers joining or leaving the company in your compartment and others walking past in the corridor in search of a seat and at every station.

Once inside the compartment you have a full view of your fellow passengers sitting across the narrow aisle, or you can look out of the window or at the passengers in the

corridor, which offers the only standing-room on the train. Modern trains and buses, like planes, have rows of seats all facing the front, as in a traditional classroom. Even though you are sitting quite close to the other passengers, you will probably not have any contact with them except perhaps with your immediate neighbours. The growing popularity of this kind of seating arrangement whereby contact with others is virtually non-existent reflects an unmistakable trend toward individualism in other environments, too. The same is to be seen on railway platforms and other public places where there is a concentration of people waiting: the old-fashioned long benches have nearly all been replaced by individual seats separately mounted at 'café' distances from each other. This new form of sitting side by side in a row yet separately was invented to protect users from being bothered by those sitting next to them, and to prevent people from lying down on the benches. But the result is also that two people cannot sit close together anymore, nor can people move up to make room for others: distances have all been fixed beforehand, and so the use that is made of the seating is no longer flexible.

Places that are used by a lot of people over a short period of time, such as cafés, counters, company restaurants etc. are furnished with a large number of identical tables or counters which have been designed with space-saving in mind. Consequently you always sit in a company of six or eight people, the size of the group being dictated by the size of the table. However, even in these situations more variety - as in normal restaurants where groups of different sizes must be seated at the tables - would suit the pattern of social interaction of the users, better too.

Many people would prefer a small table, many others a large one: a small table for 2, 3 or 4 people when you are in the company of friends or a larger one for 6 or 8 people if you want to be more anonymous (so that at least you don't feel you have to introduce yourself to the others or ask their permission to 'join' them). And then there must also be places where you can sit on your own in such a way that it is obvious to the others, so that you need not feel embarrassed about reading your newspaper or just

594
595 596

Weesperstraat
Student
Accommodation

remaining silent. Tables by windows are especially suitable for this kind of usage because, even if there is no view to speak of, you can easily sit facing away from the others, thereby indicating your wish for privacy quite clearly. For those people who are alone but would like to enter into contact with others, very long tables would be a good solution. The contacts that take place at such a table are random in the sense that it is not its length that determines which groups take their seats there.

Of course the shape of a table, too, can exert a strong influence on the pattern of social interaction. Think of the equality of position offered by a round table as opposed to an oblong one.

APOLLO SCHOOLS (597-602)

Schools are still being built today along the old lines of a row of classrooms along a corridor with coat-pegs and the occasional 'work-corners'. There are often external reasons for such a plan, and the classrooms themselves may be well-designed and may function accordingly. But you must realize that, with this type of arrangement, each classroom becomes a self-contained, separate unit with at best a reasonable relationship with its immediate neighbours. Children in different classes see each other in the corridor when the lessons start and finish - and at those times it is usually very full - and, if they are lucky, there is also a communal hall where they can meet.

In a situation where the classrooms are grouped around the communal space, so that the children leaving the classrooms automatically converge in the centre, there would be much more opportunity for casual and spontaneous contact between children of different ages. It would stimulate ideas for doing things together, if only because both teachers and children of different classes would get to see more of each other. The school halls in the two Apollo primary schools have a split-level amphitheatre-like organisation, which greatly increases the range of visual contact. Situations of players and audience arise easily and spontaneously: children sitting on the treads of the stairs connecting the two levels soon start behaving like an audience, thereby challenging the players on the lower level to give what you might call a performance.

The split-level design of the central space not only gave rise to the adoption of the amphitheatre idea, it also provided a point of attachment for the six classrooms, disposed in two groups of three with maximum mutual visibility. This visual link draws all the classrooms together in a way that would not be possible with a strict division into superimposed storeys.

The hall space functions rather like a big communal classroom, where the teachers also have their own place (with a corner screened off for the school head) on the top

'balcony'. The location of this teachers' corner, and its open and inviting nature - the children can go right up to them at any time - gives the hall space as a whole the quality of a large living room. The glass skylight panels provide maximum visibility when looking down from the balcony into the hall, even when the classroom doors are shut. The stairs to the uppermost level were designed to be as transparent as possible so as to avoid obstructing visual contact and to let the daylight entering through the skylights penetrate into the recesses of the space.

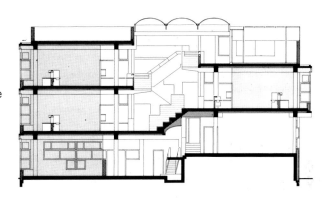

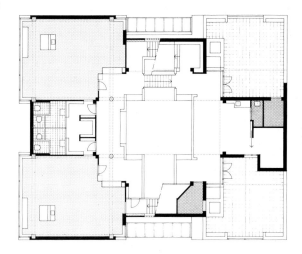

597
598

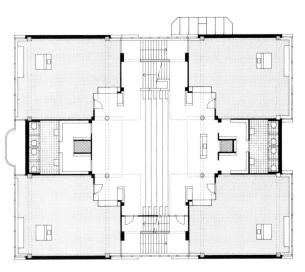

Whatever an architect does or deliberately leaves undone - the way he concerns himself with enclosing or opening - he always influences, intentionally or not, the most elementary forms of social relations. And even if social relations depend only to a limited extent on environmental factors, that is still sufficient reason to aim consciously at an organization of space that enables everyone to confront the other on an equal footing.

Ignoring this potential of architecture amounts in the end to less freedom for the inhabitants. However, the aversion shown by many architects to sociological and psychological approaches is in a sense understandable. For here we are, surrounded by the failures of a past period, with its social utopias such as 'spaces for social interaction' and other romantic, useless (at any rate never used) notions invented by architects who believed they could simply predict the behaviour of people. Architects in general have a predilection for theatrical simplifications. Attunement to psychologically and socially inescapable factors was never a prime concern in architecture. Carefully calculated dimensions, a correct articulation and the right proportion of openness and seclusion are the starting-points for the shift in attention to the 'habitable space between things'. Social architecture does not exist, but that does not mean that we can ever afford to ignore the implications of how people relate to each other, and how they react in different situations.

The mere choice between a door opening outwards or inwards is in itself an indication of this inescapable responsibility - for the direction in which the door opens will decide whether everything that goes on in the room can be seen in one glance upon entering, or whether those inside the room have the time to prepare themselves for your entrance.

Admittedly we have only talked about details up to now, but there are so infinitely many details in every building that they might well all together be just as important as the grand gesture of the architecture in its entirety. For us a building is the sum of all those small gestures which, like the thousands of muscles in a ballet dancer's body, together create a unified whole. It is this grand total of decisions, provided they are taken with proper consideration and due care, that can result in a truly welcoming architecture.

599

600 601
602

4 VIEW II

Bringing the outside world inside.

'It is the principle of shelter that receives special emphasis in the history of the origins of architecture, as it gradually acquired an increasingly articulated form, from hut to house, in the course of human history and of the rise of the city. For us the history of the view is just as important as that of shelter. And what we mean is, apart from having a view of one another, having a view of the outside world. Just as spatial relations influence personal relations, so they determine the way we relate to the environment. But instead of maintaining the opposition of interior-exterior as a fundamental contrast, we know, in the twentieth century, that interior and exterior are relative concepts, and therefore depend on where you stand, and in which direction you look.

It is no coincidence that the character of twentieth-century architecture is so much more open than it has ever been in the past. Not only do we now have the means with which to achieve this, there is also more need for openness. We have opened all the windows and so we have embraced the outside. And if Holland can be said to have played a remarkable role in modern architecture, as it developed along with the new twentieth-century consciousness in a natural process, as it were, then that is hardly surprising considering the openness that has always been and still is a characteristic feature of Dutch society. That you can look straight into Dutch living-rooms and can almost take part in what goes on inside is a tradition that never fails to amaze visitors to this country, and it shows that the Dutch are less hampered by fear of the outside world than people in many other countries, where private property and homes tend to be sealed off from the outside world.
The exceptionally large expanses of glass in our buildings, which are possible thanks to the mild climate and perhaps to our feeling of mutual dependence, at any rate reflect an extraverted interest, an open-

603

**mindedness about the opinions of others.
If Holland is a country of openness and of smallness,
then that is the expression in terms of form and space
of the way we relate to one another, of how we treat
each other and how we have managed, inside and out,
to maintain a reasonably harmonious social
environment, in the sum and in the parts!'** [7]

VAN NELLE FACTORY, ROTTERDAM 1927-29/ M. BRINKMAN,
L.C. VAN DER VLUGT (603-609)

'One of the most lucid examples of the Nieuwe Bouwen
(as the Modern Movement was called in Holland), and
certainly the biggest in this country, is the Van Nelle
factory in Rotterdam. Its huge dimensions are never
overwhelming and the building not only shows what is
going on inside but is also designed so as to give those
who work inside as wide a view as possible, not only of
the world outside but especially of each other. The curved
exterior of the office section cannot have been solely due
to the adjacent traffic route, nor was the layout of the
building volumes the determining factorin this particular
solution. That Van der Vlugt opted for this magnificent
enclosing curve - thereby going against the convictions of
his collaborateur Mart Stam - is impossible to explain in
rational terms*. But what he succeeded in achieving this
way, and that is what concerns us here, is that office and
factory are within sight of each other.
This idea recurs in the staircases, which project so far
from the building that you can see all along the façade
from each landing. The staircase on the right of the
entrance to the office section is quite unique. It bursts out
as it were, cutting across the façade almost as if it was
simply too much for the building to contain. The stairs take
you out of the building, and offer a view of the façade,
the sports fields beyond, and what used to be open
polderland in the distance. The widest panorama of all is
to be seen from the circular roof structure, which recalls

the command-bridge of a ship. But this highest point with
its impressive view of the harbour installations on the horizon is not there only for those in command but also for all
the factory workers. The building as a whole, originating
as it did from a sort of rational but wide-angled approach,
signified a clean break with the past, and offered a
glimpse of a new world, with better relations between
people. What makes this building so spectacular is,
besides the fact that it looks like a great transparent
machine, that it brings the principle of un-hierarchical
relationships into rational architectural organization.' [7]

*'The chocolate-box on
top of the factory was
designed and drawn by
me, much against my
own wishes. Nor did I
have much sympathy for
the concave wall of the
office section - but Van
der Vlugt was in
charge.' (From a letter to
Bakema, 10 June 1964,
as cited in: J.B. Bakema,
L.C. van der Vlugt,
Amsterdam 1968)

604 605

606 607

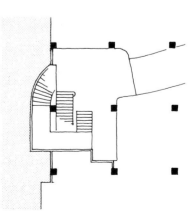

When you read Le Corbusier's description of the building, which he visited in 1932, you realize that it would probably have been impossible to make this dream come true anywhere except in Holland:

The spectacle of modern life

608

609

'*The* Van Nelle *tobacco factory in Rotterdam, a creation of the modern age, has removed all the former connotation of despair from that word "proletarian". And this deflection of the egotistic property instinct towards a feeling for collective action leads to a most happy result: the phenomenon of personal participation in every stage of the human enterprise. Labor retains its fundamental materiality, but it is enlightened by the spirit. I repeat, everything lies in that phrase: a proof of love.*

(...) *The glass begins at sidewalk or lawn level and continues upwards unbroken until it meets the clean line of the sky. The serenity of the place is total. Everything is open to the side. And this is of enormous significance to all those who are working, on all eight floors, inside. Because inside we find a poem of light. An immaculate lyricism. Dazzling vision of order. The very atmosphere of honesty. Everything is transparent; everyone can see and be seen as he works.*

(...) *The manager of the factory is there in his glass office. He can be seen. And he himself, from his office, can see the whole illuminated Dutch horizon, and, in the far distance, the life of the great port.*
The immense refectory continues the pattern, The managers, the highest and lowest administrative grades, the workers, male and female all eat together here in the same great room, which has transparent walls opening onto endless views of meadows. Together, all together.

(...) *I found it fascinating to observe the faces of those factory girls. Each one of them was an expression of the life within: joy or the opposite, a reflection of their passions or their difficulties. But, there is no proletariat here. Simply a graduated hierarchy, clearly established and respected. This atmosphere of a well-run, diligent hive is attained by means of a universal and voluntary respect for order, regularity, punctuality, justice and kindliness.*

(...) *An example of everyday reciprocity: I keep up the place in which I work; my work interests me; so the trouble taken is a source of joy! A virtuous circle for once! All are united in a compact solidarity; all bear a larger or a smaller share of the responsibility; participation. Participation. That was how the Van Nelle factory was created. The architect was given a year in which to draw up a provisional plan; then they spent five years working out the final form. Five years of collaboration: meetings to discuss every problem individually. And it was not only the directors and the architects and the managers who were at those meetings. The heads of the various departments were also present, as well as a skilled workman or clerk representing each of the specialized functions to be performed in the factory. Ideas can come from anywhere. In matters of mass production, it is well known how vitally important a minor short-cut can turn out to be. There are no small things, there are only correctly designed things that work.*
Participation!
I can truly say that my visit to that factory was one of the most beautiful days of my life.'

(Le Corbusier, *La ville radieuse*, 1933, pp. 177-179)

RIETVELD-SCHRÖDER HOUSE, UTRECHT 1924 / G. RIETVELD
(610-614)

'At the very heart of the Nieuwe Bouwen in Holland was Rietveld's Schröder House, hardly bigger than a public housing unit of today, articulated in components, each one as if it belonged to a piece of furniture.

The design is often described as a three-dimensional Mondrian painting, but quite apart from the fact that Mondrian's paintings are not concerned with extending beyond the flat plane, such a comparison does not do justice either to Mondrian's ideas or to those of Rietveld. While Mondrian tried to harmonize the different weights of specific colours (as Schönberg composed colour-sounds), and in so doing may well have painted models for true democracy, Rietveld on the other hand, working with building materials which possess physical weight, makes them weightless, so that new interrelationships can be established and the new aims be achieved. From a distance and from the outside these aims seem abstract, intended as a sort of objective composition of planes and lines, and indeed this is the quality that tends to receive most emphasis in the many publications devoted to the Schröder House. But from the inside all the different components, separately and vis à vis each other, prove to be within the reach of everyday gestures.

The space is exploited to the full, not only inside but also in the peripheries: each area is wholly attuned to the purpose it is expected to serve, with each corner, window or door being fitted with so many benches, cupboards,

610 612
611 613
614

niches and ledges that they blend unnoticeably into the furniture. Although the house is actually quite small - the main floor consists of just one room which can be subdivided when necessary - the infinite articulation of the space makes it both very large and very small.

This house, with all its features, big and small, working together to create a truly habitable, friendly completeness, shows what kind of nests people would build if they could, but besides that it offers a balance of seclusion and extraversion.

Since the Schröder House Rietveld never built anything that came quite so close to a utensil. As far as this is concerned he may well have been strongly influenced by Mrs Schröder, for whom and with whom he designed the house. That he was so prepared to listen to her shows his true nature and his profoundly right attitude to architecture.

The idea underlying the design of the house culminates in the glass-enclosed corner of the living story. When the big window in the corner is opened it is truly a window on the world. Because the corner is not obstructed by any support the space shaped by the walls at right angles to each other is allowed to expand outside, thereby creating a unique spatial experience. The sensation of being both inside and outside at the same time- a greater relativisation of interior and exterior is hard to imagine. This was indeed a most radical break with all that had existed before, and it symbolizes for many of us the excitement of the new technological possibilities.

Yet this window, paradoxical though this might seem, is simply a product of a carpenter's workmanship. Rietveld himself had to go to a smith to order an extra long window fastener. Technically, in fact, the entire Schröder House could have been constructed with the means of a century earlier. Unlike Duiker and Van der Vlugt, who sought inspiration from new techniques, Rietveld made primitive and timeless designs: the carpenter's dream of a different world.

The small bench outside by the window of Rietveld's study, under the balcony, to the left of the front door, was designed for Mrs Schröder, so sitting there she was still in contact with Rietveld when he was at work inside. The way in which the projecting planes of balconies and walls form a habitable space here thanks to the right combination of shelter and contact, with both inside and the garden, is actually classical: what is new here is only the form it takes'.[7]

Thanks to the open corner in Rietveld's Schröder House you are not, when inside, separated from the outside world, you are in the middle of it all. Also the glass circle on top of the Van Nelle factory brings the inside world outside and the horizon inside. Both of these

solutions are typical of the Nieuwe Bouwen and both - as radical as they are - are based on the absence of load-bearing construction elements in the periphery of the building. It is the principle of the cantilever which was made possible by the application of reinforced concrete, that produced this new, unprecented experience of space.

But however airy the construction of a building may be, and however the opposition between inside and outside is relativized by for instance recesses in the façade, that extraordinary new sensation of transparency and lightness can only exist when the constructive corner-column is absent, and when the façade is so thinly constructed that it apparently has only itself to support. The most consistent, and also the most beautiful, are the open corners in Duiker's buildings. The way the load-bearing structure of the Technical School in Scheveningen and of the Zonnestraal Sanatorium, and of course of his Open Air School in Amsterdam complements the thin glass exterior has never been seen before or since, but the influence of these unparalleled buildings is still felt today, all over the world.

DE OVERLOOP, HOME FOR THE ELDERLY (615-619)

A residential building for the elderly constituting a self-contained organizational unit (where many of the inhabitants tend to stay on the premises due to impaired mobility) almost inevitably assumes the nature of a bastion. In this case the location, not in the heart of the residential neighbourhood but on a residual site on the edge of town at the foot of the dyke along the Veluwe Lake, further emphasizes this undesirable effect of reclusiveness.

While the spatial organization of the interior can be

615

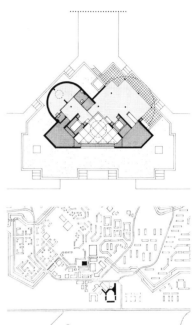

616 617
618
619

designed with an eye to maximum openness for the residents, the design of the exterior should at least see to it that the complex as a whole does not look more withdrawn than necessary.

Passers-by should be able to get a glimpse of life on the premises, but especially the residents themselves should have ample opportunity of maintaining visual contact at least with the outside world. To express this idea as explicitly as possible the location of the communal space, used for receptions and festive gatherings, was located so as to have the best possible view over the Veluwe Lake up to the horizon.

With its large windows on three sides and the suggestion of roundness due to the semi-circular roof projection the structure looks more like a ship's bridge than a tower room, thereby referring also to the ship-like buildings of the Nieuwe Bouwen movement.

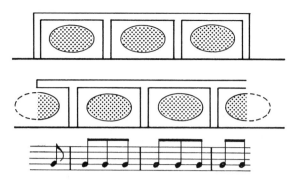

That the angle of vision is expanded by opening up a corner is a definite advantage, but it is not the only one. After all, bays added to or projecting from a façade enable you to step outside, as it were, so that you have a view up and down the street below.

But when this open corner is not an addition, because it is the actual corner of the building that has been opened up, the effect is that the building seems lighter, less massive at the very points where one would expect strength. This change in the equilibrium results in a shift of emphasis, and thus alters the rhythm of the structure te become open at beginning and end, as in many musical compositions an upbeat. (620)

620
621
622

Opening up corners where wall and ceiling meet, as in the Delft Montessori school (621,622,625) and the conversion of a private house in Laren (624), or the application of the low parapet in the Amsterdam student home (623), make the range of vision expand - even when that is not literally

the case - by virtue of the shift in focus of attention, drawing the eye upwards or downwards or to the street outside. The quality of the light entering through the windows changes, too: where it enters, unreflected, from above, it brings with it the quality of the outside, which is

623
624
625

especially important in areas (such as the communal area in the school) where you want to relate more directly to the world outside than, say, in the classrooms.

De Evenaar, School (626-629)
By placing two adjoining classrooms behind a curved section of the façade they become a sort of communal bay. The wall dividing the classrooms comprises at one end, where it meets the façade, a sliding partition. When it is closed, the two spaces are both visually and audibly separated, but when it is opened the two classrooms easily blend into one area embraced by the bay. Besides, the view of the outside world from each classroom is considerably widened when the partition is opened.

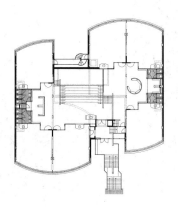

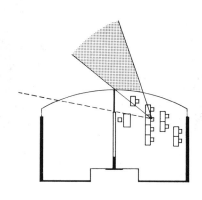

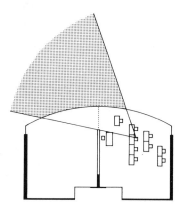

The effect of opening up the corner between two walls is even stronger when the corner between wall and ceiling is removed: this revolutionizes the traditional spatial paradigm as it manifests itself especially in the structural framework (where walls and ceilings/floors meet). The 'windows' are no longer openings in a wall or roof-plane - and therefore basically framed objects - but they actually constitute the open transitions between planes, thereby making the overal image less massive and 'stabile' and consequently less separate from its environment.

So the Nieuwe Bouwen brought the outside world inside into our familiar surroundings, which were thus dematerialized and rendered transparent. The architectonic space was expanded, and if this modern architecture reminds one of ships and birds, that is not only due to the formal idiom inspired by the universally admired functionalism of modern naval architecture, there is also and especially a deliberate allusion to the sense of freedom evoked by a view embracing endless space, and at the same time to the inevitable awareness of vulnerability.

Open Air School, Amsterdam 1927-30/J. Duiker, B. Bijvoet

630
631

Zonnestraal Sanatorium, Hilversum 1926-31/J. Duiker, B. Bijvoet, J.G. Wiebenga

5 VIEW III

has also enlarged the domain in which architecture manifests itself, and hence also the space of architecture. 'The truth' no longer exists. Depending on our standpoint and on our objectives we experience a layered reality, and so it is up to architecture to 'reveal' more, to make the different levels of experience transparent, as it were, and thus to shed more light on how things work and how they are interconnected. Whatever meaning is attached to the experience of space, in the twentieth-century world it certainly embraces more than a purely visual perception. The exposure of unsuspected layers of meaning by twentieth-century art and science has changed our way of seeing, and therefore also the way we feel. The world has changed because we now see things in a way we did not see them before, or rather, in a way we did not realize we were seeing them. We are capable of seeing so much nowadays that we cannot content ourselves with superficially pleasing appearances and decorative architecture. The space of architecture also comprises an answer to the other phenomena and layers of meaning present in our pluralistic consciousness.

632

633 634

Window on the world

The expansion of the architectonic space by the Nieuwe Bouwen movement is only one part of the story of the twentieth century. Our thinking in terms of relativity

WORLD EXHIBITION PAVILION, PARIS 1867 / F. LE PLAY (632)
More often than not buildings are portrayed in full sunlight, but here the opposite is the case. And with the reversal of day and night it seems as if interior and exterior, too, have switched roles. Like a great lamp the rounded structure illuminates the space in which it stands, stretching out its glass overhanging roofs with lights suspended at regular intervals in a welcoming gesture so that you are virtually in the building even before you have passed the actual threshold. The overall transparency of the structure in itself is an invitation to enter this modern palace containing a huge range of goods for the new consumer market, like a radiant planet affording a view of the new world.

CINEAC CINEMA, AMSTERDAM 1933 / J. DUIKER (633,634)
'The evocation of a view of a new world is especially strong in the Cineac newsreel cinema designed by Duiker & Bijvoet. Intended as an information machine that you can enter casually, in-between visits (to the shops, to catch up on what is going on in the world in pre-television days), the building itself also presents itself as a totally new structure geared in every detail to performing the function of *a window on the world*. Apart from the storey-high illuminated sign (an edifice in its own right) and the smooth transition from the street to the interior of the cinema (achieved by a glass awning and by restoring to the street a precious corner of the premises), it is especially the curved glass façade above the entrance that attracts attention.

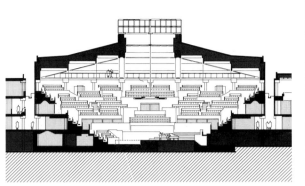

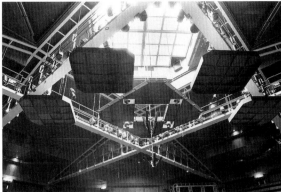

Thanks to the glass wall rounding the corner of the first floor the room containing the film projectors becomes visible from the street, while the operators (in the days before automated projection) in turn are offered a view of the street. Duikers prime concern, here, was probably to demonstrate the technology of the projectors, but as a result, instead of being hidden away in a corner, the people responsible for keeping things running are given a place in the centre of attention, within the cycle of everyday life and in full view of it. So here the architect's concern for the essential requirements of this purpose-built cinema, situated on a tiny, left-over, awkward site, gave rise to a fundamentally different spatial organization'.[7]
'The tall illuminated sign was demolished in November 1980, and the glass porch was covered over with wood. Only the curved glass wall was preserved, except that the original mullions have been replaced with thicker ones (as

also happened years ago in the Open Air School). Thus, the last of Duiker's great works has been irreparably mutilated, and the number of relatively intact examples preserved from this period of history, spanningbarely twenty years, is growing alarmingly small.
Since they cannot be put in museums like old cars and even trains and ships, and are not old enough to be eligible for the protection given to ancient buildings, only a few photographs will be left to convey an impression of these wonderfully light constructions. Who will still be able, in future years, to describe what emanated from them and the feeling they evoked?' [8]

VREDENBURG MUSIC CENTRE, (635-642)

'The large box-shaped skylight on top of the Music Centre lets in enough light to be able to give performances during the day without artificial lighting - when the sky is

635 636

637 638

clear, at any rate. But even when additional artificial lighting is necessary you still have some idea of what the weather is like and whether it is early or late in the day - at least you can tell whether the sun is shining outside, and the musicians do not have to rehearse in an artificially lit space.

The possibility of holding daylit performances adds yet another alternative to the already generous range of lighting facilities, while conversely the skylight also acts like a beacon to the outside world, a signal of the activities the Music Centre has to offer.' [5]

The dominant feature of the building is the main auditorium with 1700 seats which, following the amphitheatre shape, offer an excellent view of the central stage.

The hall itself is virtually symmetric in design. In a concert hall excellent sound is of course a prime objective, but a good view is complementary to good sound! Seeing musicians perform helps listeners to distinguish tonal subtleties, especially if those listeners have not (yet) received any musical training themselves. And if the listeners can also distinguish their fellow listeners that will

639 640

641

enhance the emotional involvement of the audience as a whole, which in turn inspires the musicians.

While the quality of modern recordings allows people to listen in the privacy of their own living rooms to renditions that are seldom acoustically equalled in live performances, it is the shared experience that makes concert-going such a special experience. Besides, it is in the concert hall that you can see the heroes and heroines of the record sleeves at work.

The design, more like that of a theatre-in-the-round than a traditional concert-hall, makes this auditorium suitable for the numerous other types of music in which the actual performance plays a more central role than in so-called classical music. Besides, the platform can be enlarged to include the ground-floor seating area, thereby making proper in-the-round performance possible.

'The auditorium is equipped with the full range of theatrical lighting facilities with controls installed - visible to the audience - on the bars overhead. Besides being suitable for a wide range of musical performances, the concert hall should, ideally, actually contribute to the quality of what goes on inside it by enhancing the general atmosphere and working conditions.

Besides offering possibilities of adjustment with respect to size and position of the platform as well as to the seating arrangement and capacity - i.e. technical and organizational flexibility, the space must have the capacity to adapt itself to the degree of openness or intimacy called for by a particular performance. And what it always boils down to is: what is offered in the way of involvement of listeners with each other and with the musicians.

The amphitheatre shape of the auditorium not only offers everyone in the audience a good view of the musicians, it also offers members of the audience a good view of each other, and that, in combination with the spacing of the seats and the articulation of the space, makes it possible for an atmosphere of unity, of communion even, to arise, which would have been unthinkable in a more conventionally designed concert hall with rows of seats behind one another all facing the same direction. Thus the building adapts itself to the specific nature of the event taking place, not only by making the auditorium itself adaptable (flexible, in mistaken architectural jargon) but also by giving it polyvalence: not only by providing a suitable environment for performances ranging from classical orchestral and chamber music to jazz, variety and circus (with live lions!), not to mention the experimental performances with different sections of the orchestra positioned in the extreme corners, but also by giving the space itself the role of an instrument upon which all these different events can be played.' [5]

■ **Our architecture must be capable of accommodating all those different situations which affect the way a building is understood and used. Not only must it be capable of adapting itself to changing weather conditions and different seasons as well being suitable**

642

for use during both day and night, it must be deliberately designed to respond to all these phenomena. The architect must take into account all those different types of usage, as well as the feelings and wishes of all sorts of categories of people: of all ages, each with its specific pattern of expectations, its own possibilities and restrictions. The definitive design must be attuned to all the intellectual and emotional data that the architect can imagine, and it must relate to all the sensory perceptions of the space. The perceptions of space consist not only of what you see, but also of what you hear, feel, and even smell - as well as the associations thereby evoked.

Thus architecture is also capable of showing that which is not actually visible, and of eliciting associations you were not aware of before. If we succeed in producing architecture that is so layered that the diversity of realities as embedded in the different layers of consciousness is reflected in the design, then the architectural environment will moreover 'visualize' these embedded realities and will thus tell the users something 'about the world'

643

644

Villa Savoye, Poissy, France 1929-32 / Le Corbusier
(643-647)

The large enclosed outdoor living room of this villa is undoubtedly the most impressive example of the constructed exterior space which is to be found in nearly all of Le Corbusier's designs. Thanks to the fact that this interior landscape is situated on the periphery of the volume and that it has the same horizontal window-arrangement as the adjoining living areas, the terrace also offers a view of the exterior landscape. Le Corbusier's roof terraces are neither gardens nor interiors: they represent a completely different spatial entity with a highly specific quality of its own.

The plant-boxes, too, create a mere illusion of a garden. They are certainly too big to be treated like flower-pots, but they are not the same as garden flower-beds either, although in his sketches Le Corbusier included a far richer variety of plants than most other architects, who tend to think of plant-boxes in terms of a mere detail with which to fill up empty parts first of the drawing and subsequently of the actual building ... Here they are more like the seed-beds in nurseries that can be covered with glass, and that is indeed how they could be used by green-thumbed inhabitants. This association is further strengthened by the inclusion in the plant-box of a light, and it is this integration of two such apparently unrelated components that makes the design so exceptional.

645
646

647abc

Framing skylights in a terrace floor in this way makes them less vulnerable, and also less of an obstacle. Looking up from the space below, the overhanging greenery gives you some idea of the terrace overhead. Unlike the conventional skylight showing a stark rectangle of sky to the observer below, Le Corbusier's skylights fringed with plants offer a less abstract view of the world outside, and even, sometimes, a glimpse of someone out on the terrace looking down or tending the plants. What Le Corbusier did here, as he so often did in his outstanding works, and what a mere detail such as this illustrates, is to combine essentially modest elements in such a way that they are complementary by virtue of the space each gives the other.

What we see here is a better organization of the component parts, so that the rectangle of light, in all its abstractness, takes on the quality of a proper view. For Le Corbusier there was no gulf between formal order and informal application. He was evidently just as concerned with the organization of daily routines as with the composition of the grand gesture. It is the interaction of ten thousand minor details, like all the elements making up a complex machine, that gives rise to poetry. And that is precisely what too few architects today seem to realize (or too many architects seem to be incapable of creating).

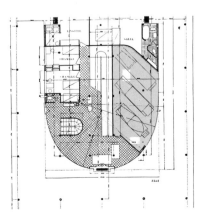

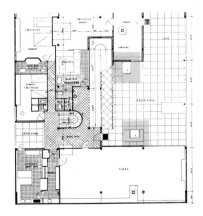

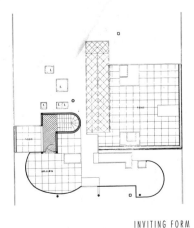

So, only a relatively small portion of the walkway as a whole connecting the two sections of the wooded park is underground, whereby the passage through the actual tunnel is relativized to become a mere incident on a longer trajectory. So you walk at a sort of safe distance through the carcass of a primordial reptile of corrugated sheet-iron, your steps on the wooden boardwalk hollow-sounding: a feeling of secrecy. Besides, halfway along the tunnel there is an opening overhead, in the middle of the motorway (which is something more underground passages should have). The tunnel itself has been reduced to a mere section of a longer route, a relatively brief interlude in a stroll in the park. The effect of the bridge is to shorten the tunnel, simply by prolonging the crossing from one area in the park to the other. And, as so often, the most eventful route is also the shortest connection between two points.

PEDESTRIAN UNDERPASS, GENEVA, SWITZERLAND 1981/
G. DESCOMBES (648-652)
In Lancy, near Geneva, Georges Descombes designed a pedestrian underpass connecting the two sections of a park cut across by a motorway. The corrugated iron constituting the actual tunnel is exposed to view at either end. But there is also a slender steel footbridge in the tunnel, under which a stream runs from one section of the park to the other. This bridge, much longer than the actual tunnel, extends into the park at each end at some distance from the motorway-ramp.

648

649 650 651

652

CHAPEL, RONCHAMP, FRANCE 1955 / LE CORBUSIER (653,654)
The chapel of the Notre Dame du Haut in Ronchamp is usually cited as an example of expressionism in building by the master of expressionist architecture, Le Corbusier. The roof is shaped like a huge basin, from which the water escapes through a single spout like those we are used to seeing in cathedrals, but more organically formed. It takes some time for the collected rainwater to drain away after the shower has moved away over the hill-tops: it gushes forth with tremendous power, its fall being broken by pyramid-shaped points in another concrete basin on the ground under the spout.

The following excerpt is from a text written upon the death of Le Corbusier on 27 August 1965: 'Everything an artist lays his hands on changes its course, Le Corbusiér was never involved in form alone, he was always concerned with the mechanisms of what lay before him; he would alter the bed of a stream to change the direction of the water, so that the water would render that different course visible and become a different body of water; the water would thus become clearer and more true to itself, while at the same time the direction, too, would become clearer and truer.

So the building tells us something about the water passing over its roof and the water tells us about the building; and in this way both water and water-covered surface shape each other by telling us about the other and about themselves.' [2]

ALHAMBRA, GRANADA, SPAIN, 14TH CENTURY A.D. (655-657)
By conducting the water over the stone steps, where it forms a sequence of little cascades down the channel from one tread to the next, these flights of steps in the Alhambra assume an extraordinary form. The light reflected by the surface of the stream as well as the sound intensify the image of a stepped descent, and that is perhaps why such a pedestrian feature as a flight of steps suddenly strikes one as something special. But it is not only our awareness of the phenomenon of steps that becomes more acute, also the phenomenon of water is

653   654
655

656 657

658

intensified by this felicitous combination - the same liquid substance that we tend to take for granted cannot escape notice in this pronounced form.

The small round ponds with fountains carved into smooth marble are artificial pools of water like the pools that form

on any paved surface, but here their presence has been formalized and made permanent by means of a minimal architectural intervention. A primary architecture with water - next to marble the richest and most refreshing material imaginable in this warm Andalusian garden!

MOSQUE, CORDOBA, SPAIN, 786-1009 (658,659)

The courtyard of the mosque in Cordoba is shaded by orange trees growing in circular depressions in the pavement. These circles are connected by means of channels, thereby forming an efficient irrigation system for the trees. In the relatively large hollows the water has ample opportunity to be absorbed by the soil; the narrow connecting channel is only for easy transportation of the water from one tree to the next. This design derives its beauty not from the simplicity of form as such, but from the fact that the form shows so clearly how it functions. You could say that form in this case not only follows function, but that it actually is the function. Not only does the circular form combine beautifully with the shape of the trees to create a graphically interesting design, it also matches the swirl of the stream of water far better than a square shape would have done (which would also have corners that would be more difficult to sweep clean).

Architecture can say something about certain phenomena such as time or water, which in turn make a statement about the architecture: they become mutually explanatory. By showing how things work, and so by bringing them to the surface, the world around us can be read, can be decoded, as it were; architecture must explain, unveil.

Essentially this amounts to a battle against reduction and the alienation that goes with it, the alienation that we can see encroaching upon us on all sides, making us ever more subservient to an environment which has less and less meaning for us and over which we have less and less control. We should aim for the most readable form, i.e. form with the greatest expressive force.

Rainwater transported in pipes hidden from view tells us nothing about what is going on, and so this remains an abstract system that can, at best, be expected to function noiselessly. In the same way, when we enter a tunnel under a river we must simply assume that we will get out at the other end eventually: we cannot see what we are doing. Conversely, crossing a bridge is always self-evident, while there may even be ships passing below us, making us aware of its dual function. Abstraction of form thus goes together with reduction of information about the way it works.

Something similar takes place in closed lifts: when you are in them you can only rely on the number lighting up on the panel to tell you where you are, and even

that depends on the country you are in, with the ground floor being called first floor in some countries, and the confusing use of initials to indicate street level in others. The entire system is based on the reliance on codes: you can't do much about it yourself except wait and see whether you will find yourself where you want to be.

The tendency in architecture to make form more abstract in an effort to achieve simplification always implies the risk of losing expressive force. This price is all too readily paid for a superficially pleasing and graphically aesthetic overall image. The temptations of 'less is more' all too easily leads to too little being achieved at too great a cost. Opinions may differ as to what is superfluous and what is essential, but simplicity can never be attained by mere omission ... 'du sublime au ridicule il n'y a qu'un pas'.

Regardless of whether the result is sheer simplicity or complexity, we must always strive after the form with the richest articulation of references, so that the maximum scope of possibilities and experiences is offered. The expansion of the architectural space in the course of the twentieth century has meant that the materials we use and the way we organize them reveal more than there is to see.

The complexity of the task represents several realities simultaneously, and all those realities must be accommodated as aspects within the plan. They constitute, so to speak, a multiple large-scale

659

programme by way of a richly variegated substance underlying the specific, straightforward requirements stated in the design brief.
The more levels of experience - as aspects - are taken into account in our design the more associations can be made, and therefore the wider the range of experiences for different people in different situations, each with his or her own perceptions.

PRIVATE HOME, BRUSSELS 1896 / V. HORTA (660-664)
'As in all the large private houses designed by Horta, this house, which he built for his own use (now the Horta Museum), has a central staircase around which the entire vertical structure is formed. The main living areas on the first floor, with different levels front and back, are not closed off from the staircase: instead of having to walk down corridors to the separate rooms, the staircase itself

660

661

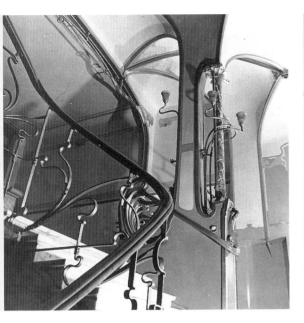

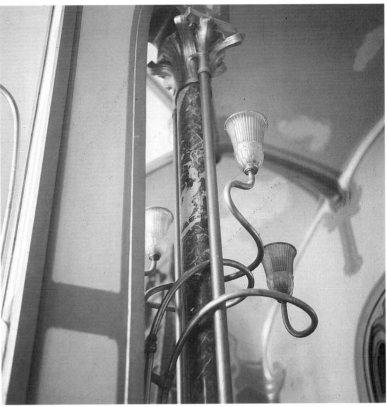

leads one through the different areas of the house. The stairs are very wide on the ground floor, and become narrower as they rise. It seems quite logical that the stairs to the more private areas on the upper floors need not be as wide, and an added advantage of the stairwell becoming more open towards the top of the house is that the light entering through the glass skylight can penetrate deeper into the building. The proportions of the staircase make one aware on every floor of the height of the building, thereby giving the building as a whole spatial coherence and unity.' [9]

We have become used to having electricity in every room, with the wiring hidden from view somewhere in the walls, but that reduces the phenomenon of electricity to something we take for granted and never stop to think about. And the heating, being regulated automatically, is

something we only notice when it doesn't work. The most striking thing about the lamps Horta designed for the hall area in his own home is of course the similarity to flowers. But to Horta himself the plant-like form represented more than mere ornament: it was a way of organizing the energy requirements in a functional manner, whereby the load-bearing structure of the building is combined with a distinct system of conduits for gaslight and heating. Each component in this integrated system functions independently of the others, and can be seen to perform its own task within the whole.

662 663

664

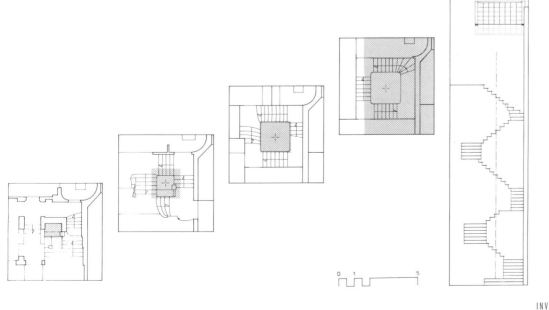

0 1   5

1. Metal faced solid
sliding screen
2. Steel framed glass
sliding door
3. Wooden guide track

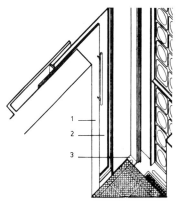

contrast in material between the glass façade and the massive stone wall beside and above it.

But I cannot imagine anyone, upon entering that house for the first time, not being awed by the space that opens itself up to him beyond that wall of solid glass. To me this house - one single space really, like an articulation of places merging and overlapping from one level to the next, without distinct partitions - was a completely new experience when I first visited it. I entered a spaceship, out of this world, with wonderful panels of curved metal which you could turn or slide aside just with your finger, mysteriously, to open up a space which had temporarily been hidden from view. Rather different, to say the least, from the normal world, where rooms are shut with heavy wooden doors swinging on hinges in door-frames set in stone walls.

And then the pair of parallel sliding doors, one of them solid and the other transparent, which you can move independently to enable you to get precisely those gradations of sound and visual contact that you want in a specific situation. The openness with its acoustic transparency makes each remote corner audible, and, together with the unusual quality of the light filtering through the glass bricks, diffuse and serene like indirect lighting, evokes an extraordinarily peaceful and airy atmosphere. So this was how I envisaged the new world of the twentieth century: and it was here that I first recognized, in architecture, the sense of space that Picasso, Braque, Léger, Delaunay, Duchamp, had evoked in me.

The allusion to a new era was further affirmed, so it seemed, by the mechanical and often literally machine-like character of all the components in the way they evoke strong associations with an industrial world, in which parts of buildings, like the parts of motorcars and aeroplanes, are produced in factories, and then assembled.

You had always wondered why buildings could not be assembled in the same way, out of perfected components - and here this was actually what had happened: the train windows that slide up and down, lightweight aeroplane

665 666
667

MAISON DE VERRE, PARIS 1928-32 / P. CHAREAU, B. BIJVOET, L. DALBET (665-677)

668 669

The most striking thing about this house is not the exterior. When you first see it, tucked away in a courtyard, it certainly doesn't look the way you would expect a house of glass to look. Besides, you can hardly see anything of the interior from the outside: the big glass brick façade sits there, almost like a windowless wall, in the middle of the old architecture, adapting itself to the shape of the surroundings. With its unemphatic exterior, the house sets itself apart from its surroundings only by a spectacular

staircases, cogs and wheels exposed to view showing how the windows open and close, and attention everywhere for the smallest detail; everything invented and constructed on the basis of entirely new principles. This is how you imagined an architecture made up of prefabricated structural components. The dream that such a wealth of solutions could be within the reach of all seemed to be coming true at last.

The technique with which this house was designed and constructed down to the smallest detail calls to mind the symbolic perfection of a Rolls Royce and now, after more than fifty years, with everything still functioning equally smoothly, we still fall for it. And this is not really that surprising either, for its delights lie not only in the beauty of each solution as such, but derive from the implication that it would be possible to repeat them.

So it all looks more like the form of a technique than the technique of a form. And we can still imagine that the technology of our time will be capable of producing an architecture in which each element within the composite whole can be understood for what it is and why it has been made that way. But why has the course of industry taken so little notice of the potential of this technique?

While there are plenty of buildings with industrial implications on the formal level, and which therefore perpetuate our dream, the architectural components that are industrially produced do not resemble them, and they lack the feeling of Chareau, Eames or Piano.
The interests of the construction industry and the paths it treads in practice do not always coincide. The construction industry would rather produce trash with built-in obsolescence, or prostitute itself with perfect prefabricated concrete elements which hide behind a mask of ridiculous vaguely classicist mouldings: we are

670abc
671 672

673

capable of so much - and therefore also of grossness. No, the 'Maison de Verre' remained a dream, and the new world of industrial production still has not learnt how to manufacture constructional elements with the same degree of perfection as, say, modern electronic equipment.

It is the misleading paradox of this house that the idea of industrial production is not confirmed by the industrial reality: things that look as if they are reproduceable are not necessarily so. Architecture seems, time and again, incapable of bridging the gap between idea and reality the way art does.

674
　675
676　677

'Only rarely does architecture succeed in escaping its ostensibly inescapable fate - that of seeking to assert itself in one trend or another, instead of exposing the superficiality of trendiness and replacing it by a truer reality. And architecture, it seems, tends to be too material to be ideal, and instead of attacking existing reality it does the oppposite: it does its utmost to affirm it. We can only speak of art when an entirely different mechanism is at issue, when a different paradigm replaces what is familiar and within easy reach. What makes this house a work of art is that it makes us look at the world around us with different eyes: it is through the change in our vision that it can change the world. On second thoughts the 'Maison de Verre' is more like a complex of unique pieces, an extremely delicate equilibrium of ideas such as can probably arise only once, at a single moment in history; a hand-crafted product, which, with more emphasis on the connections between the various elements than on the elements themselves, is closer to Art Nouveau than to modern industrial thinking.

Take, for instance, the feeling you get when you see the way in which the electricity is conducted through free-standing vertical pipes and columns on which the switches are mounted, and which therefore, instead of coming out of the wall randomly, becomes visible and intelligible as an autonomous system in its own right: that is the spirit of Horta. Here you see the true functionality, arising from Art Nouveau.

But also the spatiality of this house becomes less amazing once you've been inside the big houses designed by Horta. There, too, you already find, as a concept, the principle of the continuous, articulated space, which can be expanded or contracted at will by means of adjustable

elements, and in which there are no corridors, halls or staircases in the conventional sense any more, so that the hierarchy of serving and served spaces starts to fade, and each area becomes living space.

When the Dalsace family was still living there, the house was indeed a large living space with, even in the remotest corners, that touch of Annie Dalsace's caring hand and her deep love of architecture, by which and for which all this came about. So this house, with all its perfect metal constructions, radiated a special kind of warmth, which somehow defies description.

Perhaps the most remarkable thing about it was that the atmosphere it breathed was so unlike the highly exclusive, ostentatious atmosphere that you usually find in such a wealthy environment. Complete equivalence reigned in this space, the same care being lavished on the most everyday kind of utility goods as on the priceless art

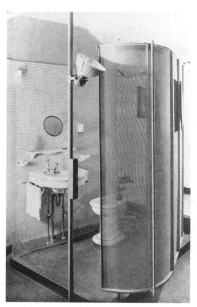

objects by these elegant and imaginative people in their ever-hospitable environment: a wonderful dream come true of a new, lighter and more transparent world.' [11]

The way a building is put together, i.e. how it works, should be 'legible' to its users: instead of a layer of stucco covering everything up, for instance, it is better to show the actual building bricks, the beams, columns of steel or concrete, and the lintels over the windows. It might not be such a bad idea to leave at least some of the 'innards' of the building exposed to view, too, to make people more aware of the effort that goes into creating a satisfactory dwelling. In fact, our utilitarian objects in general could do with a more straightforward and lucid design. In the nineteenth century, with its techniques firmly rooted in the craft tradition, this was obviously not as important as it is today, with the increasing alienation - also in architecture - of man from his environment. People have been proved wrong time and again in simply trusting that things in the world will be organized with their best interests in mind: we must be able to see for ourselves what is going on.

VAN EETVELDE HOUSE, BRUSSELS 1898 / V. HORTA (679,680)
Horta's characteristic railings, which are also to be seen in the Van Eetvelde house (now an office), first of all make us think of long sinuous creepers. But on closer inspection this ironwork proves to be composed not of continuous curving rods but of a large number of quite small components which, while describing perfect curves in combination, are all separately attached to the upright supports.
The holes for attachment are positioned in each metal strip in such a way that the space allotted to each rivet is

exactly right, thereby making the studs themselves an integral part of the composition as a whole. Depending on which way you look at it, this ironwork manifests itself either as an organic plant-like growth or as a systematic composite whole made up of a large number of parts, each of which is delicately shaped and subtly attached.

CASTEL BÉRANGER, PARIS 1896 / H. GUIMARD (678)
Hector Guimard, who is especially famous for elegant plant-like metal sculptures framing Metro entrances in Paris, was also quite capable of working with standard L-

678

679   680

and T-profiled metal rods. Instead of simply sawing them off at the required length as most people would do, he paid special attention to the extremities of each piece of profile-bar. Being standard mass-produced elements, the bars would of course all have the same thickness, but for

the finishing of the ends of the bars he turned to the smith: thus each section became a hand-crafted element in the end. But however much is done in the way of adaptation, the basic profile of the prefabricated components remains, and, paradoxically, the sinuous extremities actually emphasize that basic characteristic of the material.
The elegance of these studied flourishes at the ends makes each rod not only an element with its own distinct identity but also an element within the composition of the whole.

681 682
683

Apollo Schools (681,682)

We do not make balustrades with flowing lines made up of lengths of metal tubing welded together or of profile rods, but we do try to make them of separate components, in such a way that the emphasis is not only on the actual components but equally on the spaces in-between them. And in places where the different components meet and are attached, so that the proper space is allotted to each, the attention is drawn to the edges.

'A building, but also part of a building, explains itself by showing how it works and what it's for. We try to make each element clearly legible both independently and in its relation with the others and thus to make it not only part of a larger structure, but also a self-contained whole.
Thus details can claim complete priority where it matters: in this respect there is not that much difference from the approach to the building in its entirety.
The whole and the parts define each other mutually, and they require the same measure of attention; this is also true in urban planning, where the details obviously figure very prominently. While the criteria that apply in urban planning may be different, the thought-process is basically the same as in the urban

design of details, including the design of a balustrade, for instance.'[10]
By showing how things work, and letting each element speak for itself as far as its function in the larger whole is concerned, the architecture of a building can intensify our awareness of the phenomena that make up our environment.
If it is clear how a thing works, that is because it looks as if it can be taken apart. The expression of analyzability and the apparent possibility of being dismantled are not only characteristic features of Horta's Art Nouveau designs and of the architecture of Chareau, Bijvoet and Dalbet as exemplified in their wonderful Maison de Verre, but also of the contemporary constructivism (undoubtedly influenced by these celebrated artists) of people like Renzo Piano, Richard Rogers and Norman Foster - and of course of

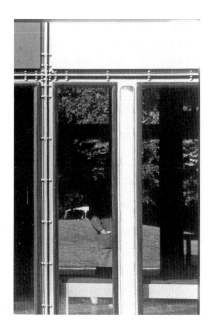

*IBM Travelling Pavilion,
Paris, 1982-84/
Atelier Piano*

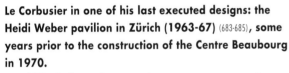
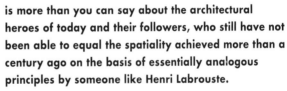

Le Corbusier in one of his last executed designs: the
Heidi Weber pavilion in Zürich (1963-67) (683-685), some
years prior to the construction of the Centre Beaubourg
in 1970.

By giving independence to the component parts these
do not only gain more identity thanks to the
expression of their specific function within the whole,
for in addition attention is drawn to the joins and
encounters between the parts. A shift of emphasis
occurs from the objects themselves to what connects
them, to their interrelationships.

Not only did Horta as well as Chareau et al. give each
component part its due within the whole, they also
ultimately concerned themselves with space, and each
of them succeeded in their own way in developing both
revolutionary and magnificent spatial mechanisms. This
is more than you can say about the architectural
heroes of today and their followers, who still have not
been able to equal the spatiality achieved more than a
century ago on the basis of essentially analogous
principles by someone like Henri Labrouste.

686 688 690
687 689 691

684 685

*Heidi Weber pavilion,
Zürich, 1963-67/
Le Corbusier*

Although enclosed by massive neo-Renaissance walls, the elongated reading room of the Sainte Geneviève Library (from 1843-50!) has a surprisingly fragile-looking span with two parallel barrel-vault-like shells forming the ceiling. The delicate ironwork is like a modern addition to the heavy remains of the past, and even though you can still find classicist motifs on the slender columns, they are no more than superficial decorations. The plant-like tracery decorating the curved spans does little to conceal the fact that iron framework serves a purely constructional purpose: the architect's solution, here, is in fact an

BIBLIOTHÈQUE STE GENEVIÈVE, PARIS 1843-50/ H. LABROUSTE
(692-699)

Henri Labrouste was the first architect-engeneer to design an iron span construction in which the actual framework is a deliberate architectonic expression. Metallic spans that had been applied previously, as in shopping arcades, greenhouses, conservatories and of course the Paris Exchange of 1808, had started out from the skylight principle, the technical aspects of the material being tolerated rather than serving as a means of arriving at a new sort of spatial design.

692
694
695
693 696

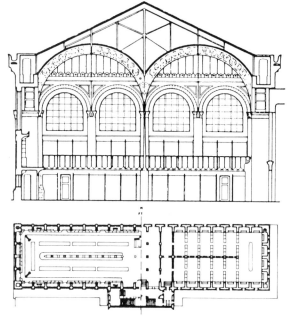

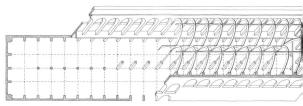

example of Art Nouveau avant la lettre. Although the ceiling consists of two parallel spans gracefully barrel-vaulted at each end, the space is not divided into two halves: it remains a unified whole. This is partly due to the fact that the row of columns in the centre does not extend all the way from one end to the other, leaving the areas at each end uncluttered.

The building is much longer than it is wide, but the treatment of the long and short façades is identical: the same articulation, the same fenestration and also the same book galleries going all the way round with staircases placed diagonally in each corner (so that no side can impose a hierarchical direction on the space).(Would you have placed the stairs in this way in the corners?) This equivalence of short and long walls is what makes the library so unique from the point of view of spatiality: the way the double-vaulted ceiling leaves the space undivided, intact, is truly amazing.

But let us take a look to find out how Labrouste achieved this: if the spans had really been semi-circular in shape (as they appear to be), this spatial *tour de force* would not have been possible, if only because there would simply be no way of turning a corner. However, Labrouste used *quarter-circle* spans, which enabled him to create a natural and flowing transition by extending them to make half a circle where necessary and by using right-angled connections to attach the quarter-circle segments to the complementary span elements in the corners. His application of just two basic types of elements in such ingenious combinations brought about a breakthrough, deliberately or not; with his liberating use of identical components he was in fact anticipating a development that was to come in the next century.

In the same way that Labrouste put together his elements to create an extraordinary, unified spatiality, so in his

case the art of making and the making of art are indistinguishable. His solution is not merely the result of what he was capable of, but, also and indeed more importantly, he was capable of attaining what he envisaged in terms of spatiality. [12]

697

698 699

6 EQUIVALENCE

When something that was a secondary feature in one situation can become the main feature in another, in other words that both features can adapt to specific conditions, then we have a system of values in which there is no hierarchy of importance among component parts. And when, for instance, something in any architectonic ordering, an element or an organization of elements, can perform different functions depending on its placement in different situations, then its value is no longer constant.

Each element can then, depending on the way it is introduced, perform a pivotal function, that is, it can become a centre of a system in its own right; in that case equivalence can be said to exist. Conversely, an architectonic ordering in which primary and secondary elements are recognizable as such cannot but refer to a hierarchy of constant and unalterable values: a system of values which is unequivocal and which consequently precludes interpretation on more than one level. In a strictly symmetrical composition you can for instance visually express no more than that the content of the right-hand side is the same as that of the left-hand side.

700 701

But if we start out from the principle that each element has its own specific value, not more nor less value than any of the other elements, i.e. that they are all equal, then our designs will have a fundamentally different organization: it will be a matter of creating the right balance between all the elements so that each can function optimally in its own right as well as in its relation to others.

OPEN AIR SCHOOL, AMSTERDAM 1930 / J. DUIKER (700-704)
There is a story that Duiker could only get permission to build his Open Air School on a site that was largely hidden from view by buildings, so that it would not clash too much with its surroundings in this well-to-do neighbourhood.
Whatever Duiker himself may have felt about the enclosed site on which he was to build the school, there is no doubt that the glass building would have been very vulnerable indeed in an entirely open setting (even though traffic noise was not yet a problem at that time). The protective enclosure of the fairly massive blocks surrounding the building emphasizes its openness   rather than vice-versa, while the proximity to the untidy backs of the dwellings with their small gardens and balconies, combined with the informal atmosphere of this little palace of glass, strengthens the feeling of living in a community. The adoption in urban planning of the perimeter block-siting principle with its differentiation of street side and enclosed courtyard obviously results in more formal house-fronts and more informal backs.
In this case a kind of reversal of inside and out has taken place, because the presence of the school with its playground and entrance, informal as they are, creates a front within the enclosed space. Due to this relativization of the enclosed space the situation in fact comes closer to the open site plan. What strikes one about the building is the at first sight somewhat illogical addition of the gymnasium on the right, which does not match the otherwise largely symmetrical main layout. This is all the more remarkable here in view of the exceptionally principled and lucid structure, with the concrete

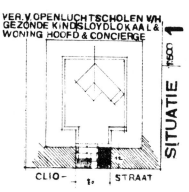

framework consistently defining the structure throughout. In the case of an architect like Duiker, it is especially interesting to examine the ideas underlying his meticulous and well-thought-out solutions. An attempt to analyse those thought processes yields the following results.

702 703

704

The plan evidently required the inclusion of seven classrooms - a number that, regardless of whether you arrange them in twos or in threes, means that one classroom takes up a separate position, which inevitably affects the symmetry of the overall design. The building consists of layers of two classrooms each which could thus share one outside classroom, grouped around the stairwell. The remaining classroom could thus occupy the ground floor, positioned in the same way as the other classrooms above, while the space on the other side could be used as a gymnasium.

There were several reasons to raise the ground floor classroom somewhat: in the first place no doubt to make up for the extra height that was needed for the gymnasium so that its roof would not be higher than the first floor. Another reason was that the children in the ground floor classroom would easily be distracted from their work when children from other classes were in the directly adjoining playground. This situation was greatly improved by the difference in level, so that the children sitting inside are higher than those playing outside. But when you look at the entrance there is more to it than that.

The actual, formal entrance is situated under the small gate-house in which the nursery school is located. Once the children are on the playground, in the courtyard, they are in a sense already inside, and there is no need therefore (inasmuch as Duiker ever felt such a need) to emphasize the entrance to the building itself - for the entrance cannot be missed. Nonetheless you could call the

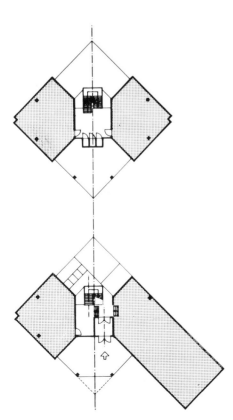

'approach' - under the loggia-like porch flanked by the two symmetrical columns of the wholly symmetrical framework - classical, in a sense. This solution is really so 'normal' and at the same time almost monumental that it is all the more striking that the front door itself is placed - informally - to the right of the axis of the building.

On closer inspection it becomes clear that some steps were necessary to reach the main staircase leading up from the landing in front of this classroom. A functional reason, then, to move the entrance with draught-door to the right; indeed it seems quite logical, especially because once you are in the 'loggia' (i.e. between the two 'entrance columns') it really doesn't make any difference whether the door is exactly in front of you or slightly to one side. But for everyone other than Duiker this solution would have been the least obvious. Indeed one must have a very specific and highly exceptional attitude to be able

to deviate from one's carefully balanced symmetry for the sake of a convenient entrance, instead of trying to cram it into the preconceived design.

The point is that Duiker did not simply make do with the circumstances as they presented themselves but took precisely those measures that resulted in an organization that created the best possible conditions for usage, view and routing. Over the formal order of a consistent symmetry he gave priority to an arrangement in which each part functions optimally both in its own right and as part of the whole. This example of Duiker's school provided the key, if not directly then at any rate indirectly, to the solutions presented in the following examples.

705
706
707 708

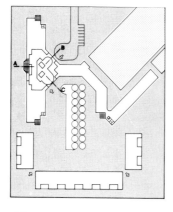

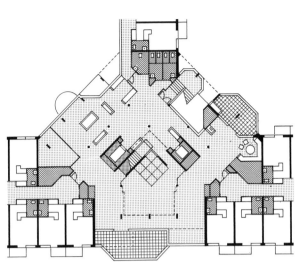

DE OVERLOOP, HOME FOR THE ELDERLY (705-711)
This home for the elderly in Almere is situated on a residual site in this new town; on one side it adjoins a parking garage, on the other it branches out freely, without any point of support in the urban surroundings. All the façades facing outwards thus take on the role of frontages. In other words, there are no backs to the buildings with rear entrances for delivery etc. (the kitchen delivery entrance is located at the end of one of the wings). Nor is there one single main entrance, because the pedestrian entrance to the enclosed inner court, where the less mobile residents can venture out into the world, is no more and no less important than the entrance on the other side, which can be reached by cars.
From whatever direction the building is approached, its main shape is seen to be a symmetrical composition, grouped around a central area which is higher than the rest and where the different wings come together. The symmetrical aspect of the design is not due so much to a preconceived plan as to the fact that there was simply no valid reason here to depart from the obvious principle of symmetry. However, this was not a strict rule: wherever deviation from the symmetrical would benefit the functional organization the principle was abandoned, in other words no concessions were made at the expense of requirements from within which did not automatically fit in with 'the system'. As a consequence a whole range of incidental deviations have risen, which together determine the overall aspect just as much as the main outline. One of the innumerable examples of this is the middle section of the west façade: to allow the central hall area to benefit fully from the view it was reasonable to incorporate both a bay and a balcony in that section. There were, in theory, two ways of retaining a strict symmetry: either two bays on either side of a balcony, or two balconies on either side of a bay. But both solutions would have clashed with the spatial requirements of the two elements regarding their optimal functioning, and besides, the asymmetrical placement made the space of the bay link up much better with the spatial organization of the centre as a whole. Instead of designing two balconies that are too small or two bays that are too small simply for the sake of the overall composition, each element is given its due. The dimensions of the balcony, moreover, made it possible to include a glass awning over part of the balcony space, so that there is a choice between more and less sheltered places to sit.

■ When you start out from a formal order it is important to avoid to having to force all the elements into that order, because then you will inevitably make them subservient to the whole, that is, the value that is given to the parts will be dictated by the order governing the whole. Only by starting out from each individual element and by making it contribute *in its own right* to the whole can an ordering be achieved in which each component, large or small, heavy or light, has its rightful place in accordance with the specific part it plays within the whole.

709

710 711

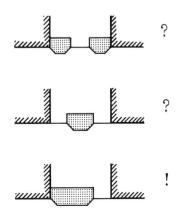

712

713 714

VILLA ROTONDA, VICENZA, ITALY 1570 / A. PALLADIO (712-722)
Palladio's Villa Rotonda is universally admired by architects. The simple, lucid floor plan and the purity of the
elevation make the building an unparalleled example of
absolute architecture, and of the architectural world as a

'reflection of divine perfection'. You can as easily imagine
it being used as a church, as a school or as a home, and
in its essential suitability for many purposes this elementary floor plan represents a kind of archetype. Especially
unique is the way in which the entirely symmetrical layout

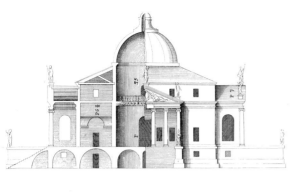

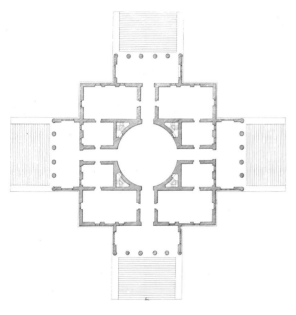

715 716
717 718
719 720
721 722

accommodates the four identical loggias along the four façades. There is indeed no front, no back, no side; the building is the same on all sides - at least as long as you look at it from the outside. Inside the building the situation is different. You can well imagine choosing which loggia to sit on depending on the time of day and the season, for - and this is quite remarkable - although all four are identical, each offers a completely different experience. Not only does the sunlight have a different effect on each side, also the views are completely different - of the avenue leading up to the house, of the garden, of the farmland belonging to the villa and of the hills beyond. Thus it is in the urban context that this free-standing villa manifests its most characteristic qualities. From the outside you can survey the house in its entirety, but it is inside the building that the diversity of spatial sensations can be experienced to the full. Countless architecture historians have devoted studies to this particular villa, but what Palladio himself had to say about it is far more interesting. Palladio's own main concern was, apparently, the magnificent views on all sides. So you see that it is not enough to look at a building from the outside alone, but that its true quality can be appreciated only when you also look out at the surroundings from the inside. Unfortunately the building is not open to the public, so if you want to get the feel of it you will have to go and see Joseph Losey's film 'Don Giovanni', which was shot for the most part in and around this villa.

'Amongst many honourable Vicentine gentlemen, there is Monsignor Paolo Americo, an ecclesiastik, and who was referendary to two supreme Popes, Pio the fourth and fifth, and who for his merit, deserved to be made a Roman citizen with all his family. This gentleman after having travelled many years out of a desire of honour, all his relations being dead, came to his native country, and for his recreation retired to one of his country-houses upon a hill, less than a quarter of a mile distant from the city, where he has built according to the following invention: which I have not thought proper to place amongst the fabrics of villas, because of the proximity it has with the city, whence it may be said to be in the very city. The site is as pleasant and as delightful as can be found, because it is upon a small hill, of very easy access, and is watered on one side by the Bacchiglione, a navigable river; and on the other it is encompassed with most pleasant risings, which look like a very great theatre, and are all cultivated, and abound with most excellent fruits, and most exquisite vines: and therefore, as it enjoys from every part most beautiful views, some of which are limited, some more extended, and others that terminate with the horizon; there are loggias made in all the four fronts; under the floor of which, and of the hall, are the rooms for the conveniency and use of the family. The hall

is in the middle, is round, and receiveds its light from above. The small rooms are divided off. Over the great rooms (the vaults of which are according to the first method) there is a place to walk round the hall, fifteen foot and a half wide. In the extremity of the pedestals, that form a support to the stairs of the loggias, there are statues made by the hands of Messer Lorenzo Vicentino, a very excellent sculptor.'

(Andrea Palladio, *I Quattro Libri Dell' Architettura,*Venice 1570)

Hierarchy

Persons or things can be different and yet equal. Whether you value the one more than the other depends on the situation you are in and on the value it represents for you at that moment. Just as the importance depends on the situation you are in, so the situation depends on a variety of external factors (think of the difference in the importance of water in the desert and in a country like Holland, for instance). When people or things are unequal, they tend to be treated unequally, too. And when that inequality is embodied in a system of valuation in which classification in degrees of importance takes place, you have hierarchy. By equivalence I mean different people or things which you value equally and which you can classify according to a value system without that resulting in inequality.

The following example from J.Hardy makes this clear:

If you want to classify a number of books according to value and you start by making a pile with the most valuable book on top and the least valuable one at the bottom, then this pile will, essentiallly, represent a hierarchy. Now if you place the books vertically in the same order then their position will be seen to be equivalent even though the classification is the same. The differences are still there, but the order is one of difference and not of priority. Of course the books could have been ordered according to other criteria, such as accor-ding to author, size, or date of publication, but as soon as the books have been stacked to form a pile there will inevitably be a top one and a bottom one. Once hierarchical arrangements have been introduced, they tend to be self-perpetuating. At first sight one might wonder whether hierarchy in architecture - as far as objects and the demands inherent in them are concerned - is such a bad thing, but unequal demands very soon give rise to unequal situations, which can in turn easily contribute to inequality among people. That is especially inclined to happen when you can only think in terms of your own personal standards, and are

decision-making powers than others are not automatically permitted to dominate the workplace on the level of spatial organization, too. In an office building the managers and department heads soon claim the most attractive rooms for themselves, regardless of whether those rooms are the most appropriate ones for them on the functional level. In the Centraal Beheer office the senior staff deliberately occupied the more inward-looking 'work-islands', which are less favourably placed as far as the view outside is concerned. Thus the general criterion of 'quality' with respect to the workplace was relativized: in no way did the spatial organization reaffirm the hierarchy within the company, in fact it had a mitigating effect. In the years since the office Centraal Beheer was built there has been a general tendency to reinstate the traditional hierarchic relationships, but the managing directors still occupy the same offices, and the areas occupied by the lower echelons are still unaffected by this trend.

Analogous examples can be found in the scale of urban planning. Thus there is a strong tendency to make the location of the more expensive dwellings more attractive and thus to distinguish between cheap and expensive housing. There is not so much wrong with that, provided the greater attraction of the more expensive housing is not achieved at the expense of cheaper housing, thereby unnecessarily widening the gap between the two. This is the case when the more expensive type of dwellings are all situated on the edge of a housing estate, thus obstructing the view of the cheaper type of dwellings crowded together in the middle. The more favourable the location of a residential neighbourhood, with a view, say, of a pleasing landscape, the more the architect will feel motivated to 'do something with it' ... and more often than not that means making a grand gesture in the form of an elongated, multi-storeyed apartment building, for instance - but where does that leave the houses and streets further back? The greater the number of dwellings in a beautiful location, the greater the number of dwellings in the area whose view is obstructed, and the greater the difference between privileged and under-privileged local residents.

723

therefore unable to relativize them vis à vis different situations. When designing we make ample use of classifications of the order of importance of component parts, as in a structure composed of main beams and subsidiary supports, or in a road network with main traffic arteries and minor roads. So long as such an order merely reflects a differentiation of qualities, there is no problem. However, when such an order implies placing one thing above the other rather than side by side, extra caution is needed.

An elementary example of spatial conditions confirming inequality or even contributing to it is the location of a foreman in a factory, in a small office on a raised level so that he can keep an eye on everything that is going on. But he would be in a better position to judge how the work is proceeding if he had more contact, i.e. if he stayed on the same level as those who are answerable to him. We must try to avoid putting the person in charge, who therefore has a higher position at the workplace, in a spatially more elevated position than the others, in other words to avoid placing undue emphasis on the superiority of his position within the organization. People in a physically higher position than others are always at an advantage over those down below. Even people who are simply taller than average are at an advantage, and if there is a choice between top and bottom bunk-beds the top ones are always taken first. In everyday language, too, people 'look up' to others or 'look down' on them, and the hierarchical implications of these expressions refer directly to the same kind of spatial preconditions in architecture. It is necessary to consider always whether a raised position is really functional, as in the case of the wheelhouse on a ship or the stage director's box in the theatre, and to take care that those people with more

With each solution we come up with we must ask ourselves whether the spatial conditions are equally distributed and whether, deliberately or accidentally, our solutions risk reconfirming, on the spatial level, that which was already dubious on the social level. Even if architecture as such can perhaps exert only a minor influence on the hierarchical relations within society, then at least we can try to avoid underscoring that hierarchy and instead propose spatial conditions to counter it. To what extent can architecture have a political implication? Is there such a thing as totalitarian architecture, or democratic architecture, or are these

terms merely fanciful interpretations based on a personal feeling and thus without any general validity? Everyone is inclinded to experience excessively large-scale buildings which dwarf human beings as oppressive, and indeed all totaliterian regimes demonstrate a remarkable fondness for awe-inspiring dimensions. This is especially obvious when the buildings that are erected by such a regime are in fact blown-up versions of an old, even familiar world and style of architecture. But not every building that is huge necessarily exudes an oppressive atmosphere. Indeed, the very lack of accessibility, or even a forbidding structure like that of many medieval castles, need not necessarily be experienced as oppressive either - the inhabitants may well be friendly people whose forbears had to defend themselves against a hostile outside world. By reversal of a situation of context architecture can also take on a different meaning - like a formal, impressive flight of steps can turn into an informal, friendly grandstand. Furthermore our sense of what one can and cannot do in architecture often arises from the association that a certain form or architectural idiom evoke in us. Classicism, for instance, tends to be associated with authoritarian regimes, because we know that it was favoured by those regimes, and so evidently held certain special attractions for them and presumably suited their purposes. Still, it is not quite as simple as that: for there are certain classicist buildings that have a friendly and by no means authoritarian appearance. To name just a few of them: the Palais Royal in Paris, the Crescents in Bath, and Klein Glienecke Castle in Berlin. And a clas-sicist design can even be the expression of undisputed democratic intentions, such as the Place Stanislas and the Place de la Carrière in Nancy. The one

724 727
725 728
726 729

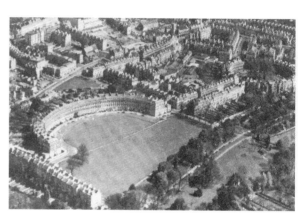

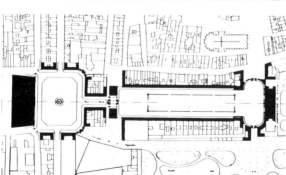

Place Stanislas and Place de la Carrière, Nancy 1751-55/ H.E. Heré

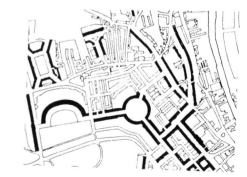

Royal Crescent, Bath 1767-74/J. Wood, J. Nash

aspect that show unequivocally whether an environment is authoritarian or tolerant is the degree of freedom offered by the organization of the architectural space (or indeed lack of it) to choose one's visual focus of attention: is one's attention forcibly drawn to a single point or is one free to ignore that focus and concentrate on other aspects, other features of one's own choosing. The most elementary example is perhaps the difference between a round table and a rectangular one. The round table offers identical conditions to all who sit at it: there is no spatial suggestion whatsoever as to who might be more important than the others. With a rectangular table the situation is obviously different. Such differentiation of places need not, of course, cause problems, and usually doesn't but in certain situations it could encourage a tendency towards 'bossiness' - which is not sufficient reason to get rid of all rectangular

Schloss Klein Glienicke, Berlin 1826/ K. Schinkel

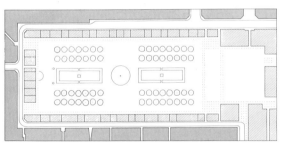

Palais Royal, Paris 1780/ J.V.Louis

733
730
731
732

tables and make only round ones from now on, but still these kinds of small details are often only the beginning. In office buildings, for instance, the size of the room indicates how 'high up' the occupant is in the hierarchy, thereby ignoring functional criteria - the managers are the only ones who are allowed to place their desk diagonally. Even if architecture in itself cannot be blamed for abuse of power, and certainly cannot prevent it, it is surely better to guard against creating spatial conditions in which 'bossiness' thrives.

The most extreme example of abuse of spatial conditions is Hitler's insistence on sitting at a desk on a raised platform at the end of a very long, high room so that visitors would have to cover a considerable distance while he looked down at them: a calculated effort to make the visitor feel small and unsure of himself. There are many other less extreme examples of misuse of space, not always intentional, perhaps, but due to lack of foresight. Functional solutions that appear quite innocent can turn out to reiterate the exertion of power. Think of the star-shaped arrangement of the bookcases in many libraries, with the supervisor in the middle so that he or she can oversee everything at one glance - like in a prison. And the persistence of those ridiculous little balconies on the fronts of 'important' public buildings which, however pleasing the sculptural effect on the front façade, are really only suitable for 'talking down' to an assembled group of people.

MOSQUE, CORDOBA, SPAIN 786-1009 (734-740)

This mosque, founded in the eighth century, consists of several architectural components together forming a large hall of about 135 x 135m. Unlike Christian churches, a mosque is basically a piece of holy land, rectangular in shape enclosed by walls and filled with columns: a sort of forest of petrified trees with vaults and cupolas overhead. Although the orientation to Mecca is all-important in the Mohammedan religion, it does not play a part in this building. Here there is no axis expressing a specific orientation apart from the obvious practical constructional dictates. Communal prayers are held in mosques, and there are 'sermons', but mostly people pray individually. The vast space of the hall in the Cordoba mosque can accommodate a huge crowd of worshippers, whose sole points of reference in the space are the numerous columns, if only because people can lean against them: there are no seats, everyone sits on the floor. But the mosque also serves as a large roofed public square, where people come for peace and coolness besides prayer. The forest of columns articulates and defines the space in such a way that there is no single explicitly

Before sixteenth century & after sixteenth century

734 735
736 737

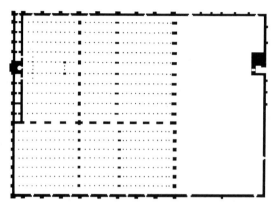

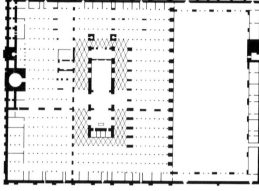

256 LESSONS FOR STUDENTS IN ARCHITECTURE

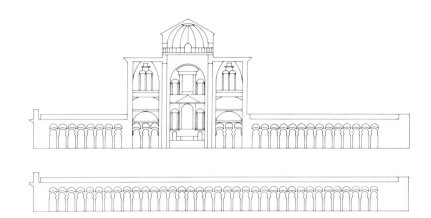

central focus - the focus can shift anywhere in the space. However strong the religious impositions of Islam may have been, the space of the Cordoba mosque itself does not impose anything on its visitors: it welcomes any group of people, regardless of their purpose. At any rate that was the situation until, in the sixteenth century, a huge hole was cut into the heart of the mosque to make room for a Christian church. The church was duly erected, in spite of vehement opposition from those who realized how much irreparable damage this would do to a building that is unique in the world.

This disastrous undertaking resulted in the creation of a centre which, due to the sheer size of the new structure and its position in the middle of the space, inevitably became a mercilessly dominating feature. It is quite remarkable how the church with its tall windows letting in the bright sunlight clamours for attention, overwhelming

the old environment with its finer articulation and subdued light. Regardless of where you stand in the building, you can never get away from the influence of what has undeniably become the main area; a spatial hierarchy has been inescapably and irreversibly established, while absolute equivalence ruled the space as a whole originally.

Because the original space had no explicit centre of attention, the centre could be anywhere and of any size, depending on the situation and the number of people. Without imposing any particular order or type of use the space (more like a covered market than a place of worship) presented itself as open and responsive to every form of attention. And thus this space, unlike the large 'columnless' mosques in Istanbul, represented the archetypal covered public square.

738 739

740

Plan St. Peter's / B. Peruzzi

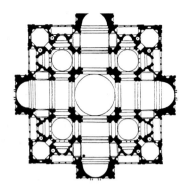

Plan St. Peter's / Bramante

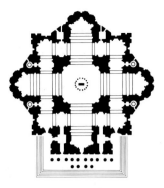

Plan St. Peter's / Michelangelo

ST. PETER'S, ROME (741-752)

The comparison of a few moments from the history of St. Peter's helps to clarify much about the attitude and ideas of the architects involved, precisely because the building is such a powerful symbol of hierarchy. Even when history is obscure on the subject the plans themselves, if regarded as projections of the architects' consciences, are still able to tell their own story about the standpoints and feelings of the people who designed them.

It seems to me that the Peruzzi plan, which prompted these considerations, would be difficult to surpass in richness. As a schematic plan is actually not much more than a diagram, but as an archetype it could also serve as a basis for many other things, maybe very different from a church. Take a school, for instance, where the classrooms could have their own separate domain in the towers, while the space in its entirety offers groups the greatest

741 742 743

744

opportunity imaginable for finding a place with the proportions, intimacy and connection with the others needed at that particular time. The closer you get to the centre the more open it becomes, which gives more scope for communal activity.

The plan is organized as a succession of places, each of which forms a centre in relation to those around it but no space dominates any other, so that the space in the middle does not necessarily have to be the principal space as well, but could also be regarded as the hallway to centres situated around it. So this plan is a perfect example of the principle of equality expressed in spatial organization. Its exceptional spatial qualities, moreover, enable each part to be interpreted separately even though this interpretation will have an influence on the surrounding parts, and vice versa, because of the open organization.

This polyvalence is thus anti-hierarchical in principle; you could go even further and say that it is a spatial model of freedom of opinion and choice, whereby various opinions are able to influence each other without dominating because of the 'transparency' of the whole.

Just imagine what it would be like if this plan had been worked out further and built instead of what is there now, with its one-sided relationships that actually could already have been detected at the planning stage.

The proportions, the articulation, the relationship of enclosure to the penetration of spaces, both as such and with respect to each other, the concavity and convexity of walls, the directions, the entrances and their positions, all combine to form the spatial organization which determines whether a plan lends itself to the promotion of domination or equality. Thus spatial relationships exert an influence on the relationships between people.

Another equally vital difference between the plans of both Bramante and Peruzzi and that of Michelangelo is to be found in the principle of accessibility. The consistent symmetry as well as the composition of the plans of Peruzzi and Bramante suggest several entrances on all sides, and the Bramante plan even proposes twelve entrances and exits all together: Michelangelo has only

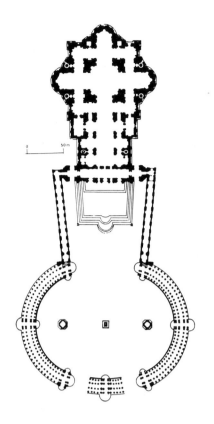

St. Peter's Square,
situation before 1935

unmistakably become the façade and that implies a back
and sides, and the main axis which Maderno was later to
extend with his addition to the church is already indicated
in Michelangelo's plan. So the spatial interpretation of the
centralized, hierarchical way of thinking which has
always characterized the Church was irrevocably
introduced into the organization of the building.
While a certain resistance to this hierarchy can be
detected in Michelangelo's rather forced attempt to give
at least the four interior sides the same value, Maderno
seems to have had no problem with it at all. His addition

745 747
746
748

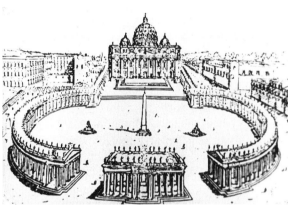

St. Peter's Square,
situation after 1935

one entrance which is further accentuated, moreover, by a
colonnade and steps. So, although his interior is still
symmetrical the accent on the exterior definitely falls on
the side with the only entrance. The fact that you can only
go in and out on one side would undoubtedly imposes
one direction on the interior, and causes its centre of
gravity to shift in such a way that the symmetrical form
would be belied by use. Bramante's many entrances help
to establish the independence and equality of the various
spaces, and they also seem to be saying that people are
welcome from all sides and directions.

Michelangelo altered the proportions of the spatial units
so that the whole church virtually became one central
space. If there should still be any doubts that his aim in
doing this was to create conditions which would shift the
focus of attention to the centre, then this single main
entrance is enough to dispel them. One side has

of a nave definitely formed a spatial main axis, which focuses the attention on the centre of Michelangelo's plan no matter where one is in the building. It thus becomes both the centre and the final point of attention. Everyone knows his place now, so clarity and order have been inexorably established in the architecture, thus demonstrating its subservience to power.

'The square or piazza which Bernini later placed opposite the church, already completed by Maderno, is not only a lesson in urban planning but also in counterpoint. The space enclosed by the circular, curved colonnades forms, as it were, an independent counterpoint to the church. The independence of the oval part is further increased by the fact that it is not directly connected to the church, nor does the oval serve, literally speaking, as a sort of gateway to it. After all, the trapezoidal forecourt resulting from the receding connecting arms is situated in-between. This recession certainly does not make the façade of the church more imposing, as is sometimes claimed in an attempt to interpret Bernini's plan in terms of the perspective power of these arms. However, since the perspective is reversed it actually increases the distance and, seen from the church, it promotes independence, if anything. It seems to me that the connecting arms were not made to recede for the sake of perspective, but because of Maderno's facade which was extremely wide in the limited space available, and because of the need to connect with the oval. Thanks to Bernini, whatever his objectives with regard to the Church may have been, the church has been relegated to the distance, in spite of its place of honour.

The colonnades enclose a separate space with a form of its own. It is the accommodating potential of this colossal space which theoretically enables the crowd of people there to assemble either in front of or opposite the church, or even to turn their backs on it.

Although the square is situated on the main axis of the church it does not really enhance it. Only the geographic centre marked by the existing obelisk, which Bernini had to take into account, is actually situated on the church

axis. However, each half of the oval has its own geometric centre and, moreover, the two fountains also serve as centres of gravity, as it were, despite their positions on the edge of each circle segment of the oval enclosed by the colonnades.

The centres of both halves of the oval are situated outside the axis and it is there, on either side within these two halves - between the fountains and colonnades - that the feeling of being inside is strongest. However, we must also realize that Bernini's plan is torn from its context in the present situation, with a yawning space in front of it, instead of the intimate Rusticcuci square, with its informal atmosphere, facing the oval. Otherwise, according to Bernini's plans, the square would have had a final, enclosing architecture which would not only have increased its seclusion but would also have resulted in the official entrances being situated to either side of the axis instead of upon it.

Bernini's truly original counterpoint teaches how approaching violence could be checked. In the working-out of this ingenious architectural concept he also showed that he had the right attitude and the right feeling to be able to carry through what must have been his aims so

749

750

consistently that they are also easy to discern in the parts. The fourfold colonnade, no mere partition but a substantial building itself, forms a visual boundary which is enough to give both halves of the oval the effect of being walled. Looking through this enclosure you can see the neighbouring houses which thus remain ever-present so that the two worlds, both shaped according to a logic of their own, the one informally and unpaved, the other entirely sculpturally formed, complement each other in their contrast. This, moreover, results in beautiful spaces in-between. Only when viewed from the centres of the oval segments, where the four rows of columns are, as it were, in conjunction, does the 'wall' lose its enclosing capacity and become transparent. Did Bernini do all this deliberately, and if so what does it matter? After all, his surprisingly original solution works and that's all that counts!

For nearly three centuries a sort of architectural balance continued to exist between the church and Bernini's square, even without the final arm which would have consolidated its counterpoint to the church, and would have made it more difficult to break open. Of course those who wanted to give even greater expression to the power

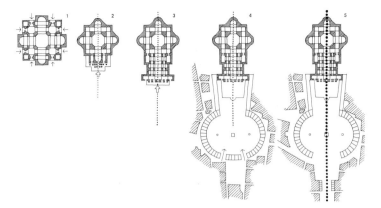

of the Church have always aimed to break it open and the street grid also helped to promote it. However, it was Mussolini who personally gave the orders in 1934 to demolish the 'Spina'! So this celebrated neighbourhood was duly replaced by the architects Pacentini and Spaccarelli with the cheerless setting of the Via della Consolazione. Fascism and the Church came to terms with each other in the field of urban planning, and it is difficult to imagine a more literal expression of their social intentions. The axis which originated from Michelangelo's single main entrance was thus extrapolated and blown up to the scale of the city. This placed the church in the visual field, thus expressing its domination in the context of urban planning.' ([6])

751

752

Bernini's square is not only a magnificent counterpoint to the church, it is also and especially the first public square in the world not to have been shaped by the buildings surrounding it. It is in fact an edifice in its own right, with the colonnades forming two transparent yet sturdy façades. Instead of being leftover space, the square itself is the focus of attention thanks to the shift in emphasis from the actual buildings to the urban space between them.

It looks as if the architect deliberately designed the oval area between the random irregular edges of the surrounding neighbourhoods with a view to creating a new urban space in its own right, thereby giving the residual fragments of space a certain form and stature, too.

The contrast between this large elliptical form with its graceful geometrical design and the historically evolved urban fabric of the surrounding area into which it was inserted must have been especially spectacular when the square with its obelisk and fountain were built, since it was the only consistently paved and properly drained place in the city at the time.

Fronts and backs

The example of the different stages of development of St. Peter's and Bernini's square show how architects can abuse space in order to impress, or conversely how they can use it to help create equality between men and things. It also confirms how problematical the position of the architect has always been, dependent as he always was on the large sums of money that were necessary for him to actually realize his ideas and all too often he allowed himself to make concessions in the end. So he always had a subservient role, and he was nearly always in the service of the reigning powers, and consequently allowed himself to be used time and again as a tool in the hands of a few rather than of the community at large.

Throughout history architects have been involved mainly in building pyramids, temples, churches and palaces, and hardly or not at all in providing dwellings for ordinary people. Architects as a rule concerned themselves only with the out-of-the-ordinary, and on the rare occasions that they did have to consider the facts of everyday life it was always in relation to the outward appearance of a building, and very often quite specifically with the front, the façade of a house that had to look grand.

The history of architecture is a history of façades - the buildings seem to have had no backs at all! Architects always searched for a formal order - they preferred to ignore the other side of the coin, the bustle of everyday life. And this is still largely true today, even though the design of public housing has in the course of this century become a full-fledged branch of architecture. There is still that invisible and subconscious dividing line between architecture with a capital A and without.

Dutch Painters

Dutch painting is especially remarkable for the fact that the subjects are mostly quite ordinary, run-of-the-mill situations with quite ordinary people. Even when the subject has a significance that transcends the ordinary - and what better medium than painting to make it do so - there is a tendency to interpret the lofty subject in terms of an everyday situation. Dutch painters did not pay much attention to the problem of the gods, nor for the ways in which they manipulate men; and their patrons, too, had little power to dictate the way they wanted themselves and their possessions portrayed.

All the more numerous, then, are the domestic scenes, such as Van Gogh's 'Potato Eaters' and of course Jan Steen's interiors, which offer us a glimpse of life behind the scenes. Such paintings show people in informal situations. Even though there were masters and servants,

The Happy Family/ Jan Steen (1625-79)

753

754 755

The Country House/ Pieter de Hoogh (1629-84)

Behind the Schenkweg/ Vincent van Gogh (1853-90)

*The Little Street/
Johannes Vermeer
(1632-75)*

the way in which the men and women, tramps and musicians, children and pets appear to coexist does not give one the impression that differences in social status, such as they were, were actually cultivated. In any case the great artists did not display particular interest in such matters, while their keen sense of proportion surely made them interested in showing what was really going on. Another artist, Pieter de Hoogh, shifts his attention - as soon as he steps outside the house - to the back yard, to the informal side of things (like Van Gogh, in fact). Even in Holland's most famous painting, 'The Nightwatch', the emphasis is not really on the fortitude and bravery of the soldiers of the civic guard, because of the liveliness of the scene with children and dogs running around. Sure enough, all sorts of symbolic meanings are attributed to these secondary figures, but that does not detract from the informality of their presence in the company. And our next most famous painting, Vermeer's 'Street in Delft', shows both back and front. The location itself is, almost as a matter of course, the back yard, as usual facing the street and as usual peopled by diligent women, cleaning, sewing or indeed pouring milk like the woman undeniably dominating the scene.

The Dutch Old Masters that are treasured as great masterpieces by the world's leading museums and to which Holland owes its reputation as a nation of painters contain an absolute denial of the distinction between formal and informal.

The Dutch painters of the seventeenth century demonstrate how the principle of equality has always been rooted in our tradition as a matter of course, and it is undoubtedly thanks to this tradition that an architecture that was neither intended to impress nor to oppress could develop, with a non-hierarchical spatial organization and a fairly down-to-earth attention to both people and the utilitarian aspects of things. It was not until the twentieth century that the world of architecture started concerning itself with public housing construction, and it is not so surprising that the Dutch were among the first - for once - to transfer the focus of attention from the formal exterior to the essence of a dwelling: the organization of the floor plan, of the

accessibility, and the integration into the urban context. From a formal order in which primary and secondary functions are disposed in a fixed hierarchy the attention shifted to an interrelated whole in which primary and secondary functions became interchangeable, depending on their role within the organization as a whole and on how that role is appreciated - in other words, depending on one's viewpoint and vantage point.

756 757

758

Nightwatch/Rembrandt van Rijn (1606-69)

LE CORBUSIER, FORMAL AND INFORMAL

No one has been more successful at bridging the gap between formal order and daily life than Le Corbusier, the twentieth century architect par excellence. Without ever actually quoting forms from the past, he derived his formal language not only from the classical monuments that he visited on his many travels, but also from primitive farmhouses and especially from what the new technologies had to offer. He transformed a mixture of ocean liners, aeroplanes, trains, Greek and Roman columns, vaults, massive stone walls, and modest adobe dwellings into an architecture in which all these ingredients can be tasted without them being individually recognizable.

His kitchen is suffused with a rich bouquet of aromas from diverse places and historical periods, rich and poor, city and countryside indiscrimately. His inspiration came from all over the world, but especially from his direct surroundings - and he was receptive to many things that are usually shunned by architects. You need only look carefully at one of his many perspective drawings (often outlined 'architectonically' by a draughtsman and then

filled in by himself) to see a variety of everyday features which would be rejected by most architects as bourgeois but which, as he realized full well, would shape the reality of everyday existence once the building was completed. When Le Corbusier used the term 'a machine for living' he was referring not so much to perfection and automation but rather to a special attention for how a dwelling actually functions and how it should therefore be designed with that in mind.

In Le Corbusier's later works (after the Second World War) and especially in the buildings he designed in India it seems, at first, as if the people occupy a rather subsidiary position as a result of a shift in emphasis to an unprecedented sculptural form. He decided to focus his attention on the seat of government in Chandigarh, the new capital of the Punjab for which he supplied the urban plan; the design of the dwellings was left to others. This new administrative complex was to give expression to the hope and optimism with which the tragically impoverished subcontinent sought to develop into a new, modern state - a dream in which architecture offers people a way out of their dismal situation.

The monumental sculptural power of the form Le Corbusier conjures up before our eyes is awe-inspiring and fantastic. But isn't it all rather more for architects than for the people in that city? More for those in power than for the electorate? Yes and no. At first sight it would seem so, but the extraordinary thing is that he succeeded in avoiding this pitfall, too. Architects who had never seen anything like it before regarded this new world of forms as an exclusive novelty, but in spite of their originality, the great rough blocks of concrete resembling artificial rocks are so integrated in the surroundings as to blend into the landscape, and in that sense they have a certain familiarity for the local inhabitants. For the rough unfinished concrete structures, so unlike the lightness and smoothness of stereotyped modern buildings, are not really so far removed from the traditional homes the local population built for themselves. It is because of their vast proportions and massiveness that Le Corbusier's buildings dominate the surroundings, certainly not because of any authoritarian echoes in the architecture! And there is no trace of references to classicist forms, nor indeed to any other forms that might evoke associations with the exertion of power.

Thus these buildings can be approached just as well riding a donkey as riding in a limousine, and people look the same inside and outside regardless of whether they are wearing expensive clothes or are shabbily dressed. It evidently makes little difference, here, who you are and what you represent.

PARLIAMENT BUILDING, CHANDIGARH, INDIA 1962/
LE CORBUSIER (761,762)

Especially the main hall around the assembly room is uniquely spacious. As big as a cathedral, filled with the tallest columns you ever saw, this space gives you the feeling that it has been there for thousands of years.

762

It could as easily have been used as a market, or as a place of worship, or for great festivities: you can imagine this space as the setting for a very wide range of events, over a very long period of time.

These later designs by Le Corbusier could quite easily change, you could even fill them up with whatever you like - not that that was Le Corbusier's intention - without this ever affecting the identity of the buildings. This might even be to their advantage, one day, just as they will retain their beauty, when they grow old and decay, as a sort of essentially, habitable landscape.

WATER RESERVOIR, SURKEJ, INDIA 1446 - 51 (763)
This large reservoir, of which type there are many in the environs of Ahmedabad, India, was conceived as an entourage for royal relaxation, but also as a water reservoir for periods of drought. Like everywhere in India, people flock to the waterside every day to wash and dry the lengths of brightly coloured cloth in which they dress themselves. The vast stepped surround ensures that the water is always easily accessible regardless of the level, while the horizontal articulation provides everyone with their own 'section' and hence with a temporary territory.

If ever an architectural environment demonstrate how a generous gesture of royal form can offer space to accommodate the daily life of countless people, it must be these steps in India. They show clearly that there need not be an unbridgeable gap between a formal architectonic order (which architects are so keen on) on the one hand and meeting the requirements of informal everyday occupations (which architects treat with disdain) on the other. We believe that this gap is only unbridgeable if the architects concerned are themselves lacking in quality and competence.

The royal or grand gesture need not therefore automatically exclude everyday life, on the contrary, if can lend it a touch of royalty and grandeur: the ordinary becomes extraordinary. It is a widespread misconception among architects that they should concern themselves with the extraordinary, i.e. that they bring the exceptional down to the level of the ordinary instead of rendering the ordinary extraordinary.

In our work we must always aim at quality on so many levels as are needed to create an environment which does not exclusively serve a particular group of people but which serves all people. Architecture must be both generous and inviting to all alike. Architecture can be described as inviting if its design is as forthcoming to the outsiders of society as to members of the establishment, and if one could imagine it existing in any other conceivable cultural context.

The architect is like the physician - there is no room for discrimination between values in his thinking; he must devote his attention equally to all values, and he must simply see to it that what he does makes everyone feel better.

763

BIOGRAPHY
PROJECTS
REFERENCES

BIOGRAPHY

1932	Born in Amsterdam
1958	Graduates from Delft Technical University
1958	Sets up his own office
1959-1969	On editorial board of the Dutch architectural magazine Forum (with Aldo van Eyck, Jaap Bakema and others)
1965-1969	Lectures at Academy of Architecture in Amsterdam
Since 1970	'Extraordinary professor' at Delft Technical University (now Delft University)
1979	Member of advisory committee for award of the Merkelbach Prize 1979
Since 1986	'Extraordinary professor' at Université de Genève
Since 1990	Chairman of the Berlage Institute, Amsterdam

Guest Professorships

1966-1967, 1970, 1977, 1980	M.I.T., Cambridge (U.S.A.)
1968	Columbia University, New York (U.S.A.)
1969-1971, 1974	Toronto University (Canada)
1978	Tulane University, New Orleans (U.S.A.)
1979	Harvard University, Massachusetts (U.S.A.)
1981	University of Pennsylvania (U.S.A.)
1982-1986	Université de Genève (Switzerland)
1987	Various universities in the U.S.A.

Awards

1968	City of Amsterdam Prize for Architecture for the students' house in Weesperstraat
1974	Eternit Prize for Centraal Beheer office building at Apeldoorn
	Fritz-Schumacher Prize for his complete oeuvre
1980	A.J. van Eck Prize for Vredenburg Music Centre, Utrecht
	Eternit Prize (honorary mention) for Vredenburg Music Centre
1985	Merkelbach Prize, architectural award by the City of Amsterdam; for the Apollo Schools
	First prize in competition for Filmhaus Esplanade project in West Berlin
1988	Merkelbach Prize for De Evenaar school in Amsterdam
1989	Richard Neutra Award for Professional Excellence
	Berliner Architekturpreis awarded by West Berlin; for the LiMa housing project on Lindenstrasse/Marktgrafenstrasse in Berlin
1991	Premio Europa Architettura for his complete oeuvre

PROJECTS

Executed Projects

1962-1964	Extension Linmij laundry, Amsterdam; 128
1959-1966	Weesperstraat Student Accommodation, Amsterdam; 55, 152, 178, 203
1960-1966	Montessori School, Delft; 25, 28, 33, 62, 153, 193, 203
1967	House conversion, Laren
1968-1970	Extension Montessori School, Delft
1969-1970	Diagoon Dwellings (experimental houses), Delft; 41, 157
1968-1972	Centraal Beheer, Office Building, Apeldoorn; 17, 23, 25, 80, 114, 133, 194
1964-1974	De Drie Hoven, Home for the Elderly, Amsterdam-Slotervaart; 35, 40, 46, 61, 130, 192
1972-1974	De Schalm, Neighbourhood Centre, Deventer-Borgele; 112
1973-1978	Vredenburg Music Centre, Utrecht; 26, 81, 136, 180, 198, 210, 227
1978-1980	Housing, Westbroek; 115
1977-1981	Second extension Montessori school, Delft; 33
1980-1982	Design of parts of the Vredenburg Square, Utrecht; 156
1978-1982	Haarlemmer Houttuinen Housing, Amsterdam; 50, 190
1979-1982	Documata Urbana Dwellings, Kassel-Dönche (Germany); 35, 206
1980-1983	Apollo Schools: Amsterdamse Montessori School and Willemspark School, Amsterdam; 31, 142, 183, 186, 213, 242
1980-1984	De Overloop, Home for the Elderly, Almere-Haven; 34, 210, 220, 249
1982-1986	LiMa Housing, Berlin-Kreuzberg (Germany); 41, 207
1984-1986	De Evenaar, Kindergarten and Elementary School, Amsterdam; 182, 186, 224
1986-1989	Het Gein, Housing, Amersfoort; 58
1988-1989	Schoolvereniging Aerdenhout Bentveld, extension of 8 classes for Kindergarten and Elementary School, Aerdenhout
1989-1990	Housing, Almere
1979-1990	Ministry of Social Affairs, Office Building, The Hague; 138

Projects in preparation/under construction

Esplanade Film Centre, Berlin (Germany)
Floating 'water houses', experimental housing project
Zuiderpolder, Haarlem
Theatercentrum Spui, The Hague
Koningscarré, housing project, Haarlem
Amsterdamse Buurt, housing project, Haarlem
Maagjesbolwerk, urban design, Zwolle
Jegerkwartier, urban design, Maastricht
Merwestein Noord, urban design, Dordrecht
Extension for the office building Centraal Beheer, Apeldoorn
Study of extension for the Music Centre Vredenburg, Utrecht
Office building, Benelux Merkenbureau, The Hague
Elementary school, Almere

Parkwijk, housing project, Almere
Media Park Köln, housing projects, Cologne (Germany)
Office Block, Media Park Köln, urban design, Cologne (Germany)
St. Jansstraat, Library and Cultural Centre, Breda

Not Executed Projects

1968	Houses type Monogoon
1969	Town planning for an extension of Deventer, Steenbrugge; 122
1971	Memorandum of objectives and criteria for renewal of the old city centre of Groningen, in co-operation with De Boer, Lambooij, Goudappel and others
1974	City centre plan for Eindhoven, with Van den Broek and Bakema
1975	Houses/shops/parking near Musis Sacrum (Theatre) as well as renewal of Musis Sacrum, Arnhem
	Town planning consultant for the University of Groningen
	Proposal for a university library, involving a 19th century church, Groningen
1976	Institute for Ecological Research, Heteren
1977	Town planning Schouwburgplein (Theatre square), Rotterdam
1978	Library, Loenen a/d Vecht
1979	Extension 'NV Linmij', Amsterdam-Sloterdijk
1980	Building upon Forum area, The Hague
	Housing project, Berlin-Spandau (Germany)
1984	Extension Academy for the Arts 'Sint Joost', Breda

Competitions

1964	Church, Driebergen
1966	Town-hall, Valkenswaard
1967	Town-hall, Amsterdam
1970	Town planning Nieuwmarkt, Amsterdam
1980	Town planning Römerberg, Frankfurt a.M. (Germany)
1982	Crèche, West-Berlin (Germany)
1983	Town planning Cologne/Mülheim-Nord (Germany)
	Office building Friedrich Ebert Stiftung, Bonn (Germany)
	Office building Grüner & Jahr, Hamburg (Germany)
1985	Office building Stadtwerke, Frankfurt a.M. (Germany)
	Film centre (academy/museum/library, etc), West-Berlin (Germany)
	Extension town-hall, Saint-Denis (France)
1986	Town planning Bicocca-Pirelli, Milan (Italy) Museum for paintings (Gemäldegalerie), West-Berlin (Germany)
1988	Housing project, Maastricht
	Office building for Schering, West-Berlin (Germany)
1989	Building for national library 'Bibliothèque de France', Paris (France)
	Cultural centre with concert building 'Kulturzentrum am See' Luzern (Switzerland)
1990	Agency for the Nederlandse Bank, Wassenaar
	Office building for the Benelux Merkenbureau, The Hague
	Urban design competition for a suburb of Grenoble (France)
	Housing and kindergarten, project for the Media Park Köln, Cologne (Germany)
1991	Office Block for the Media Park Köln, Cologne (Germany)
	Office Block Richti Areal Wallisellen, Zürich (Switzerland)

REFERENCES

Publications by Herman Hertzberger

'Weten en geweten', *Forum* 1960/61 n°. 2, 46-49
'Verschraalde helderheid', *Forum* 1960/61 n°. 4, 143-144
'Naar een verticale woonbuurt', *Forum* 1960/61 n°. 8, 264-273
'Flexibility and polivalency' *Ekistics* 1963 april, 238-239 [1]
Bouwkundig Weekblad 1965 n°. 20 [2]
'Some notes on two works by Schindler', *Domus* 1967 n°. 9, 2
'Form and program are reciprocally evocative' *Forum* 1967 n°. 7
(article originally written in 1963) [3]
'Identity', *Forum* 1967 n°. 7 (article originally written in 1966)
[3a]
'Form und Programm rufen sich gegenseitig auf', *Werk* 1968 n°. 3,
200-201
'Looking for the beach under the pavement', *RIBA Journal* 1971
n°. 2
'Huiswerk voor meer herbergzame vorm', *Forum* 1973 n°. 3,
12-13 [4]
'De te hoog gegrepen doelstelling', *Wonen-TABK* 1974 n°. 14, 7-9
'Strukturalismus-Ideologie', *Bauen + Wohnen* 1976 n°. 1, 21-24
'El deber para hoy: hacer formas más hospitalarias', *Summarios*
1978 n°. 18, 322
Wonen -TABK 1979, n°. 24 [5]
'Un insegnamento da San Pietro', *Spazio e Società* 1981 n°. 11,
76-83 [6]
'De traditie van het nieuwe bouwen en de nieuwe mooiigheid' in:
Haagsma, I., H. de Haan, *Wie is er bang voor nieuwbouw?*,
Amsterdam 1980, 149-154 [7]
'Ruimte maken, ruimte laten', *Studium Generale Vrije Universiteit
Amsterdam. Wonen tussen utopie en werkelijkheid*, Nijkerk 1980,
28-37
'Shaping the Environment', in: Mikellides, B. (ed), *Architecture for
People*, London 1980, 38-40
'Motivering van het minderheidsstandpunt', *Wonen-TABK* 1980 n°.
4, 2-3
'La tradizione domestica dell'architettura "eroica" olandese',
Spazio e Società 1981 n°. 13, 78-85
Het openbare rijk , Technical University Delft 1982
'Het twintigste-eeuwse mechanisme en de architectuur van Aldo van
Eyck', *Wonen-TABK* 1982 n°. 2, 10-19 [8]
'Einladende Architektur', *Stadt* 1982 n°. 6, 40-43
'De schetsboeken van Le Corbusier', *Wonen-TABK* 1982 n°. 21,
24-27
Stairs, Technical University Delft 1987 (first year seminar notes) [9]
'Montessori en Ruimte', *Montessori Mededelingen* 1983 n°. 2, 16-
21
Forum 1983 n°. 3 [10]
'Une ruehabitation à Amsterdam', *L'Architecture d'Aujourd'hui*
1983 n°. 225, 56-63
'Le Royaume Public' and "Montagnes dehors montagnes dedans'
in: *Johan van der Keuken*, Brussels 1983, 88-118
'Una strada da vivere. Houses and streets make each other',
Spazio e Società 1983 n°. 23, 20-33
'Ruimte maken, ruimte laten , Technical University Delft 1984
'Over bouwkunde, als uitdrukking van denkbeelden'. *De Gids*
1984 8/9/10, 810-814.
'L'espace de la Maison de Verre', *L'Architecture d'Aujourd'hui*
1984 n°. 236, 86-90
'Building Order', *Via 7* 1984, Cambridge [11]
Indesem 85, Right Size or Right Size, Technical University Delft
1985, 46-57
'Stadtverwandlungen', *Materialien* 1985 n°. 2 (Reader of the
Hochschule der Künst-Berlin),
40-51
Biennale de Paris, Architecture 1985, Luik/Brussels 1985, 30-35
(exhibition catalogue)
'Architectuur en constructieve vrijheid', *Architectuur/Bouwen* 1985
n°. 9, 33-37 [12]
'Schelp en kristal' in: Strauven, F., *Het Burgerweeshuis van Aldo
van Eyck*, Amsterdam 1987, 3
'Henry Labrouste. La réalisation de l'art', *Techniques & Architecture*
1987/88 n°. 375, 33
'The space mechanism of the twentieth century of formal order and
daily life; front sides and backsides', in: *Modernity and Popular
Culture* (Alvar Aalto Symposium), Helsinki 1988, 37-46
Lecture in: *Indesem 87*, Technical University Delft 1988, 186-201
Uitnodigende Vorm , Delft Technical University1988
'Das Schröder-Haus in Utrecht', *Archithese* 1988 n°. 5, 76-78
'Het St. -Pietersplein in Rome. Het plein als bouwwerk', *Bouw* 1989
n°. 12, 20-21
Lecture in: *Indesem 1990*, Technical University Delft 1990
Hoe modern is de Nederlandse architectuur, Rotterdam 1990, 60-65

Architectural Citations

Baltard, V.
Les Halles, Paris 1854-66; 69
Bernini, G.S.H.
St. Peter's Square, Rome since 1656; 185, 261
Blom, P.
Kasbah, Hengelo 1973; 62
Bramante, D.
St. Peter's, Rome since 1452; 197, 258
Brinkman, M.
Spangen Housing, Rotterdam 1919; 49, 54
Brinkman, M. & L.C. van der Vlugt
Van Nelle Factory, Rotterdam 1927-29; 216
Broek, J.H. van den
Vroesenlaan Housing, Rotterdam 1931-34; 45
Candilis, Josic & Woods
Free University, Berlin 1963; 116
Cerdá, I.
Ensanche, Barcelona 1859; 122
Chareau, B., B. Bijvoet, L. Dalbet
Maison de Verre, Paris 1928-32; 238
Cheval
Le Palais Idéal, Haute Rives 1879-1912; 119
Descombes, G.
Pedestrian Underpass, Geneva 1981; 232
Duiker, J., B. Bijvoet, J.G. Wiebenga
Zonnestraal Sanatorium, Hilversum 1926-31; 225
Duiker, J., B. Bijvoet
Open Air School, Amsterdam 1930; 246
Duiker, J.
Cineac Cinema, Amsterdam 1933; 82, 226
Eiffel, G.
The Eiffel Tower, Paris 1889; 70
Eyck, A. van
Orphanage, Amsterdam 1955-60; 126
Gaudí, A., J.M. Jujol,
Parc Güell, Barcelona 1900-14; 211
Godin,J.B.A.
Familistère, Guise 1859-83; 44, 60

Illustrations

All photographs by Herman Hertzberger except:
R. Bolle-Reddat; 653
Hein de Bouter; 347
Burggraaff; 641
Richard Bryand; 525
Martin Charles; 587, 602, 616
Georges Descombes; 469, 648, 649, 650, 651, 652
Willem Diepraam; 30, 31, 75, 76, 95, 138, 139, 140, 423, 432, 434, 437, 445, 448, 453, 462, 478, 479, 527, 538, 539, 584, 596
Aldo van Eyck; 316, 319, 321
L. Feininger; 313, 541
Dolf Floors; 580
Reinhard Friednich; 297, 298
P.H. Goede; 315, 320
Werner Haas; 51
Jan Hammer; 145, 146
Akelei Hertzberger; 85, 86
Veroon Hertzberger; 719, 720, 721, 722
Johan van der Keuken; 15, 16, 17, 18, 19, 21, 22, 39, 44, 141, 207, 394, 395, 396, 397, 401, 404, 405, 406, 409, 414, 417, 449, 461, 465, 491, 535, 546, 594, 600, 623, 624
Klaus Kinold; 388, 483, 493, 499, 526
Michel Kort; 737
Bruno Krupp; 37
J. Kurtz; 203
Rudolf Menke; 429
Roberto Pane; 713
Louis van Paridon; 110
Marion Post Wolcott; 505
Uwe Rau; 84, 576
Renandeau; 389
Ronald Roozen; 599
Izak Salomons; 341
H. Stegeman; 430, 431
H. Tukker; 642
Jan Versnel; 323, 324, 325, 326, 329
Ger van der Vlugt; 61, 62, 66, 88, 89, 100, 102, 103, 371, 387, 496, 578, 579, 619, 626, 627, 705, 706, 707
Gordon Winter; 132
Cary Wolinsky; 467